Cyberterrorism

Thomas M. Chen • Lee Jarvis • Stuart Macdonald
Editors

Cyberterrorism

Understanding, Assessment, and Response

Springer

Editors
Thomas M. Chen
School of Engineering and Math Sciences
City University London
London, UK

Stuart Macdonald
College of Law
Swansea University
Swansea, UK

Lee Jarvis
School of Political, Social
 and International Studies
University of East Anglia
Norwich, UK

ISBN 978-1-4939-4483-5   ISBN 978-1-4939-0962-9 (eBook)
DOI 10.1007/978-1-4939-0962-9
Springer New York Heidelberg Dordrecht London

Printed on acid-free paper

Springer is part of Springer Science+Business Media (www.springer.com)

Introduction

This volume explores one of today's most widely discussed security challenges: cyberterrorism. The book has three primary objectives. First, it aims to engage with understandings of cyberterrorism and includes chapters exploring different definitions of this term within legal and academic debate. Second, it traces the threat posed by cyberterrorism today, with contributions discussing possible technological vulnerabilities, the motivation to engage in cyberterrorism, and the challenges of distinguishing this from other cyber threats. Third, it aims to explore the range of existing and potential responses to this threat. Here, contributors investigate policy and legislative frameworks as well as a diversity of techniques for deterring or countering terrorism in cyber environments. Case studies explored throughout the book are truly global in scope and include the United States, United Kingdom, Australia, New Zealand and Canada.

With contributions from distinguished experts with backgrounds including International Relations, Law, Engineering, Computer Science, Public Policy and Politics, this book offers a unique and cutting-edge overview of contemporary debate on, and issues around, cyberterrorism. This global scope and diversity of perspectives will ensure it is of interest to academics, students, practitioners, policy-makers and other stakeholders with an interest in cybersecurity today.

Preface

There is, at the risk of understatement, something of a disconnect between the amount of attention that cyberterrorism commands and the clarity with which it is understood. In common with many contemporary security issues—from piracy through to global climate change—the causes of, and scale of threat posed by, cyberterrorism are hotly debated. This is not in itself unusual. Estimations of threat require assessments about the future which are always open to contestation. Estimations of the threat posed by other people—in our case cyberterrorists—are doubly challenging because they require consideration of motives as well as capabilities and vulnerabilities. Thus, the threat posed by an anonymous intruder we encounter in our house is a combination of several factors including: the intruder's determination to cause us harm, her possession of the physical and other capabilities required to bring that harm about, our ability to defend ourselves against any attack and the potential scale of the damage she is capable of inflicting. Similarly, the threat posed by cyberterrorism—to us as citizens, to governments, to corporations and so on—encapsulates both the determination and capabilities of would-be 'cyberterrorists' as much as it does the vulnerability at any of these levels to such an attack.

So far, so straightforward. What is, however, a little more peculiar of cyberterrorism specifically is the absence of any real agreement on the still more fundamental question of what, exactly, cyberterrorism is. While the precise nature and parameters of potential challenges to the security of people or communities such as war, terrorism or poverty are, of course, contested, there is, it might be argued, some level of shared agreement around that to which these refer. We might debate the merits of including the allied firebombing of Dresden within a discussion of terrorism for any number of reasons—because conducted by states, conducted during wartime, and so on—without sacrificing some broad understanding of terrorism as involving violence and causing fear. So contested is the phenomenon of cyberterrorism, however, that a recent survey of researchers around the world found that 49 % believed that we had already witnessed a cyberterrorism attack, with another 49 % arguing that we were yet to do so (Macdonald et al. 2013)! Thus, where many of those attempting to define terrorism are willing to permit some ambiguity because—as with US Supreme Court Justice Potter Stewart's now-infamous ruling on pornography—'you know it when you see it', the same emphatically cannot be said for cyberterrorism.

The reasons for this contestability—or, less charitably, confusion—are manifold and explored in much greater detail in the chapters that follow. Part of the problem here is that many of the definitional problems associated with terrorism that will be familiar to readers have simply migrated alongside this term's application to the cyber realm. Terrorism is a word that is saturated with negative associations, rendering its neutral or objective application to 'real world' violences a less-than-straightforward task. Similarly, the meaning of terrorism has evolved throughout the 200 years since its first coinage: the term being now nearly entirely stripped of its original association with violences by the state or progressive political causes. On top of this, the sheer diversity of events and campaigns to which the term terrorism is applied—from Oklahoma to Omagh, the Earth Liberation Front to Aum Shinrikyo—means it is increasingly difficult to pinpoint precisely what is meant by those most discussed of contemporary security challenges.

As if this didn't make the task difficult of defining, understanding and analysing cyberterrorism sufficiently difficult, there are, in addition, a host of unrelated challenges that derive from the 'cyber' dimension of this concept. One aspect of this is the challenge of sourcing reliable information about what is happening—or what could happen—in a cyber domain which consists of multiple owners, technologies and actors. Many of these actors, moreover, have an interest in either exaggerating or camouflaging their activities online. This might be important, for instance, if we believe either that (cyber)terrorism involves a necessary communicative element such that its author desires identification, or if we believe that it can only be conducted by certain actors such as non-state groups. Second is the speed with which developments in cybersecurity occur, and the potential impact this has upon previously adequate security paradigms. Established ideas, doctrines and strategies such as deterrence here jostle with contemporary notions such as resilience in a world of new threats including bots, trojans, zombies and worms. While we need to beware of exaggerating cyberterrorism's novelty—let us not forget that more traditional security issues such as war continuously evolve—this pace of change certainly complicates consensus building in relation to cyberterrorism's reality and significance. A third set of challenges—linked to the second—is the seemingly relentless proliferation of new words and concepts by those seeking to capture these developments. Neologisms abound in academic and media discourse around cybersecurity—with cyberterrorism but one obvious example—many of which are characterised by hyperbole and more likely to generate heat than light. Cutting through this hyperbole, and penetrating the jargon associated with cyberterrorism, is a significant challenge for furthering understanding of this contemporary security concern.

The ten chapters that follow have all been contributed by authors with a global profile and recognised expertise in this area. Between them, the contributors have worked on a range of topics of direct relevance to cyberterrorism, stretching from the technicalities of cybersecurity, through to transformations in terrorist violences, the formulation and politics of counter-terrorism policy and the workings of criminal law. Importantly, the authors come to this topic from a range of disciplinary backgrounds. Where some approach cyberterrorism from a technical or scientific background in Engineering or Computer Science, others ground their analysis in subjects as diverse as Law, Political Science, Criminology, Politics, International Relations and Communications Studies. Although this makes consensus-building harder still, this multidisciplinarity is, we believe, vital for a thorough and balanced conversation around what cyberterrorism is, what threat it poses and how it could or should be addressed.

Background: The Cyberterrorism Project

The immediate background to this book is in an academic conference that was held in the city of Birmingham, UK, in April 2013. Nearly 50 researchers and policy-makers attended this event, arriving from a number of UK universities as well as from other countries including the Republic of Ireland, Israel, Italy, the Netherlands, Romania, Sweden, Greece, Australia and the United States. The focus of the conference was twofold. First, to share cutting-edge research relating to understandings of, and responses to, cyberterrorism. And second, to facilitate the multidisciplinary conversations that run through this book's chapters. The conference built on a smaller workshop on these themes that had taken place in Swansea University, UK, the previous autumn at which several of this book's contributors also participated.

Each of these events—and the book you are reading—was organised under the auspices of The Cyberterrorism Project. The Cyberterrorism Project was established in 2011 by academics who were then working in the School of Law, College of Engineering and Department of Political and Cultural Studies at Swansea University. The reasons for establishing the project were fourfold, each of which continues to underpin the activities of this research team. First, was a desire to improve understanding amongst scientific and academic communities by engaging in original research on the concept of, threat posed by, and possible responses to, cyberterrorism. The project's second rationale was to facilitate global networking activities around cyberterrorism and to bring together researchers from a range of backgrounds with something important to contribute to these discussions. Third was to engage with, and have impact upon, policymakers, opinion formers, citizens and other stakeholders at all stages of the research process, from data collection to dissemination. And, fourth, to try to do all of the above within a multidisciplinary and pluralist context that draws on expertise from the physical and social sciences alike. This multidisciplinary emphasis is one that underpins all of the work undertaken by this research team, and we hope to have captured it in the chapters that follow.

In our view, the multidisciplinary approach that characterises this book adds breadth to its coverage by allowing a discussion of a wider range of topics than would be possible in a more narrowly focused collection on cyberterrorism. Public policy and the criminal law are, arguably, as essential to the countering of cyberterrorism as more technical mechanisms such as air gaps, cryptography or digital forensics. Bringing together experts with a background in all of these areas therefore increases the comprehensiveness of the book's coverage. On top of this, our hope is that bringing authors from a range of specialisms into conversation with one another also offers an opportunity for new insights to emerge. Ideas and ways of thinking that are familiar in some academic disciplines may be far less recognisable in others. Similarly, knowledge seen as standard or common sense in some areas may be unheard of or even discredited elsewhere. Facilitating discussion between different subject areas, then, may help—amongst other things—to: identify blindspots in thinking on cyberterrorism; highlight factual or logical errors within established approaches to this topic; fill gaps in knowledge caused by disciplinary silos; and produce new questions and research areas from this cross-pollination of ideas.

Core Themes

Given the spread of contributors to this book there is—as one might expect (and perhaps even hope)—much disagreement in the pages that follow. This, in our view, is a good thing, as it enables our authors the opportunity to advance, clarify and defend different approaches to thinking about cyberterrorism and its importance. Because of this, the book has been written around a series of linked objectives rather than an effort to advance one overarching argument. These objectives are as follows:

- To trace and advance conceptual and definitional debates pertaining to cyberterrorism.
- To examine, from political and criminological perspectives, how the cyberterrorism threat has been presented or constructed within political language, legislation and other sites of discourse. Included within this is an effort to explore how these constructions vary across space and time and how they relate to other designations of threat and insecurity.
- To contextualise cyberterrorism in relation to other types of terrorism or unconventional violence. In other words, is cyberterrorism simply terrorism conducted with new types of technology? Or does the presence of cyber technologies fundamentally change the nature and rationalities of terrorism?
- To contextualise and explore the distinctiveness of cyberterrorism in relation to other cybersecurity threats. How, for example, can we separate cyberterrorism from cybercrime or cyber war, and should we attempt to do so?
- To evaluate the threat posed by cyberterrorist attacks to different referents including the state, national security architectures, corporations and individuals. And, in so doing, to explore different frameworks for assessing this threat.
- To chart and assess different attempts to counter cyberterrorism at various levels of analysis, from the local through to the national, regional and global.

- To evaluate the offences which might be used to prosecute cyberterrorists, exploring tensions between the reach of these offences and conventional principles of criminalisation. Important here are the implications of these offences for human rights concerns and other protections and safeguards for citizens.
- To understand how terrorists make use of the global communications network to advance their agendas.
- To evaluate the adequacy of practical approaches to deter, identify and respond to cyberterrorist attacks.

The book has been written in such a way that the following chapters do not have to be read in the order presented. There is a general movement from issues of definition and understanding in the earliest contributions through to matters of threat assessment and response as the book proceeds, although many explore several of these issues at once. Moreover, because contributors to this book come from a range of academic backgrounds and perspectives, the chapters have been written as accessibly as possible. While conscious of the need to avoid simplification, our authors have been assiduous in minimising the use of esoteric language that would be unfamiliar to students or researchers beyond their 'home' discipline. As such, we hope, and believe, that the interested reader with no specialist background will be able to engage with the debates in the pages that follow. To assist this further, each section of the book is followed by a collection of 'key points' summarising the preceding discussion, with each chapter specifying a list of further relevant reading.

Chapter Overview

The book begins with a chapter by Keiran Hardy and George Williams which explores the adequacy of different legal definitions of terrorism in relation to cyber attacks. Focusing on the United Kingdom, Australia, Canada and New Zealand, the chapter asks what uses of computer and Internet technology would qualify as terrorism in each of these jurisdictions. Tracing quite significant differences between them, Hardy and Williams conclude that each of these countries could do more to ensure that their laws appropriately capture the threat of cyberterrorism without criminalising less serious uses of computer and Internet technology.

Chapter 2, by Lee Jarvis, Lella Nouri and Andrew Whiting investigates the ways in which cyberterrorism has been produced—or socially constructed—as a security threat across political language, popular culture and academic debate. The chapter explores a number of very different understandings of cyberterrorism and brings into focus some of the major conceptual challenges that arise when we try to describe cyber activities of different sorts as 'terrorism'. Their response to these challenges is to argue that 'cyberterrorism' already exists as a social reality—in language, culture, academic debate and so on—and therefore avoiding the term offers an unsatisfactory response to its contested and contestable meaning.

As such, they appeal for a refocusing of attention away from the question of *what* cyberterrorism is, and toward the question of *how* cyberterrorism is constructed.

Panayotis Yannakogeorgos in Chap. 3 builds on the preceding discussion by exploring the very different types of activity that occur within the technical realities of cyberspace. The challenges of defining and understanding cyberterrorism, Yannakogeorgos argues, should be grounded in a clear understanding of the vulnerabilities, threat actors and nature of conflict within cyberspace. The chapter contributes a realistic look at the technical and operational facets of cyberterrorism focusing on how terrorists use the Internet to facilitate their operations, and how the Internet enables possible attacks ranging from denial of service (DoS) to sabotage of industrial control systems (ICS). The chapter concludes by arguing that cyberspace is an increasingly important environment for state and non-state actors, although the capacity of the latter to fully exploit its potential remains currently limited.

Chapter 4, by Michael McGuire bridges these definitional questions with issues of the level of threat posed by cyberterrorism. Focusing attention on what the 'cyber' prefix does in debates around the cyberterrorism threat, McGuire advances the notion of hyperconnection to describe the contemporary condition in which potential exists to connect with anyone, anywhere and at any time. This, he argues, poses potential for moving toward a more sophisticated understanding of technology and its social importance: one that presents opportunity for a more robust evaluation of the risks that cyberterrorism poses.

Michael Stohl, in Chap. 5, identifies parallels between contemporary discussions of cyberterrorism and cyber war on the one hand, and older discussions of terrorism and state terrorism on the other. As he argues, states condemn 'cyberterrorism' while building up their own cyber capabilities, just as they condemn the 'terrorism' of their enemies rather than theirselves and their allies. This inconsistency, however, is not merely a semantic one. For, the activity of states in the cyber domain means there is a real possibility that the norms required for international cooperation will be, or are being, undermined.

Chapter 6, by Maura Conway, considers four issues that each mitigates against the likelihood of cyberterrorism occurring. These issues relate to the cost factor of cyber attacks; their complexity; their capability for destruction; and their potential for media impact. Focusing on issues of motivation and interest such as these—rather than technological possibilities—is important, for Conway, as a way of correcting the dominance of the 'IT crowd' (Singer and Friedman 2014) within discussions of the cyberterrorism threat. Weighing each of them up leads Conway to conclude that traditional low-tech 'real world' terrorist attacks such as car bombings will continue to be more effective and therefore 'attractive' than their cyber equivalents for some time to come.

Chapter 7 by Clay Wilson continues Conway's engagement with the threat posed by cyberterrorism, although from a very different angle. Wilson not only focuses his attention more closely upon the technological risks posed for critical information infrastructures by cyberterrorism; he is also far less optimistic than is Conway about the likelihood of cyberterrorism's occurrence. For Wilson, cyber attacks on critical infrastructures are the main concern for governments at present. This is, not least, because critical infrastructures are increasingly dependent on electronically net-worked control. At the same time, Wilson points out that these infrastructures have numerous vulnerabilities that could be easily exploited by extremists or terrorists. His chapter therefore offers a far more sobering analysis of the potential for wide-spread cyberterrorism damage than Conway's which precedes it.

In Chap. 8, Tim Legrand brings a public policy perspective to this discussion that focuses specifically on the importance of governmental responses to cyberter-rorism. His chapter concentrates on the UK example, and illustrates the range of institutions and actors mandated with addressing cyberterrorism and related threats. His chapter argues, first, that the UK government's conception of cyberterrorism has been limited, not least in its eliding the differences between cybersecurity chal-lenges. And, second that the post-privatisation attempt to deal with cyberterrorism by combination of private and public sector institutions generates a tension between the profit-maximising instincts of the former, and the latter's role in protecting the public interest.

In Chap. 9 Lord Carlile QC and Stuart Macdonald continue the question of how to respond to cyberterrorism by focusing on the criminalisation of online activities which are preparatory to acts of terrorism. They examine the tension between, on the one hand, the imperative of prevention and early intervention when faced with the threat of severe harm on a large scale and, on the other hand, the impact on human rights and the rule of law of excessively broad and vague criminal offences. The chapter advocates the use of the principle of normative involvement to both justify the extension of the ordinary criminal law to encompass terrorists' prepara-tory activities and evaluate whether these offences overreach. It also urges the importance of extra-legal constraints on prosecutorial discretion as a means of limit-ing these offences' practical application.

In Chap. 10, Gil Ad Ariely brings our discussion to a close by outlining the spec-trum of responses available in relation to cyberterrorism, differentiating these according to two dimensions: type and time span. He argues that learning from the past is insufficient as a way of meeting this current threat. Instead, a holistic approach that focuses on the development of adaptive and agile responses to cyber-terrorism is needed. Ariely takes this further by arguing that—contra more tradi-tional forms of security framework—deterrence will not be effective in the cyber domain. These evaluations lead Ariely to a proposal for an ecosystem supporting adaptive responses spanning intelligence sharing and education.

The conclusions attempt to bring together all the "lessons" learned from the experts. At this point, definitive answers are few and not really the goal. An ongoing dialogue to share different viewpoints and insights is healthy but it will take time to bridge the differences. A few observations are offered to continue the dialogue.

London, UK   Thomas M. Chen
Norwich, UK   Lee Jarvis
Swansea, UK   Stuart Macdonald

References

Macdonald S, Jarvis L, Chen T, Lavis S (2013) Cyberterrorism: a survey of researchers. Cyberterrorism Project Research Report (No. 1). Swansea University. www.cyberterrorism-project.org

Singer P, Friedman A (2014) Cybersecurity and cyberwar: what everybody needs to know. Oxford University Press, Oxford

Acknowledgements

This book, and the research project from which it derives, would not exist without the hard work of a number of people who have been more than generous with their time, expertise and material assistance for the project. As such, we gratefully acknowledge the following for their support at various stages of the writing of this book: the NATO Public Diplomacy Programme, Brussels; the United States Office of Naval Research Global Collaborative Science Programme; the Swansea Academy of Learning and Teaching at Swansea University; and the EPSRC Bridging the Gaps Escalator Fund at Swansea University.

As a comparatively young research initiative, the cyberterrorism project has benefited tremendously from an enthusiastic and very talented pool of interns, associates and research students. Simon Lavis and Joanna Halbert provided excellent research assistance in surveying the academic profession on cyberterrorism and in compiling a database of different understandings of this phenomenon. Simon was also vital in producing this project's earliest research reports. David Mair has been unstinting in disseminating this project's research, and in building new connections and partners within and outside of academia. Lella Nouri and Andrew Whiting—both of whom have contributed to this book—have been involved in the project since its formation and have provided invaluable research assistance at various stages as well as maintaining its website. Our most recent interns—Alicia Payne and Jordan McErlean—were extremely helpful in cataloguing media representations of cyberterrorism. Deepa Madhu has been an enthusiastic driver of a number of our research activities, including pushing forward our 'Research as Art' work; and we all also have benefited greatly from Wynne Jones' knowledge and experience of counter-terrorism policing in the UK context and beyond.

Beyond the above, we would also like to express our gratitude to Andrea Buck and Rhian Morris in the Bridging the Gaps programme at Swansea University which provided financial assistance in the early stages of this project. We are grateful, too, to Michael Harper and Michael A. Schwartz for their interest in our research and the support for the conference held at Birmingham from which this book derives. We express our thanks for the time, help and encouragement given to this project at different stages by academic colleagues including Jonathan Bradbury, Kevin Haines,

John Horgan, Matt Jones, John Linarelli and Harold Thimbleby: all of whom were generous in offering their own time and experience to us for no personal gain. Susan Lagerstrom-Fife at Springer has been a great support and we are grateful for her initial enthusiasm for the project.

Finally—and most importantly—as always, we would like to thank our friends and families for all of their support (and patience!) in the writing of this book. It would not have been possible without them.

Contents

1   **What is 'Cyberterrorism'? Computer and Internet Technology in Legal Definitions of Terrorism** 1
Keiran Hardy and George Williams

2   **Understanding, Locating and Constructing Cyberterrorism** 25
Lee Jarvis, Lella Nouri, and Andrew Whiting

3   **Rethinking the Threat of Cyberterrorism** 43
Panayotis A. Yannakogeorgos

4   **Putting the 'Cyber' into Cyberterrorism: Re-reading Technological Risk in a Hyperconnected World** 63
M.R. McGuire

5   **Dr. Strangeweb: Or How They Stopped Worrying and Learned to Love Cyber War** 85
Michael Stohl

6   **Reality Check: Assessing the (Un)Likelihood of Cyberterrorism** 103
Maura Conway

7   **Cyber Threats to Critical Information Infrastructure** 123
Clay Wilson

8   **The Citadel and Its Sentinels: State Strategies for Contesting Cyberterrorism in the UK** 137
Tim Legrand

9   **The Criminalisation of Terrorists' Online Preparatory Acts** 155
Lord Carlile QC and Stuart Macdonald

10 Adaptive Responses to Cyberterrorism 175
    Gil Ad Ariely

Conclusions... 197

Acronyms.. 205

Glossary.. 207

Index... 209

Contributors

Gil Ad Ariely teaches at the Lauder School of Government Diplomacy and Strategy in The Interdisciplinary Center (IDC) Herzliya, as well as consulting in the government sector. He previously taught courses on Cyberspace and Security, International relations, and innovation and entrepreneurship at California State University (CSU). As CKO (Chief Knowledge Officer) and senior researcher at the International Policy Institute for Counter-Terrorism (ICT), he researches learning patterns and innovation in asymmetric conflicts. Dr. Ariely is a Lt. Colonel (ret.) and earned his Ph.D. at the University of Westminster, London. He serves on the editorial boards of several academic journals, and is a founding member of ICTAC (International Counter-Terrorism Academic Community), a member of the Proteus USA futures group, and an associate fellow of ICSR (International Centre for the Study of Radicalisation and Political Violence) at King's College, London.

Lord Carlile QC is a serving Life Peer of the House of Lords, a former MP of the House of Commons representing Montgomeryshire (1983–1997), a Bencher at Gray's Inn, and a practising QC with Barristers' Chambers 9–12 Bell Yard. He sits as a Recorder of the Crown Court, as a Deputy High Court Judge, and as a Chairman of the Competition Appeal Tribunal. Between 2001 and 2011, he was the Independent Reviewer of Terrorism Legislation, the Independent Reviewer of the Government's new PREVENT policy and remains the independent reviewer of National Security policy in Northern Ireland. He plays a senior role in the formulation of policy on mental health and youth justice issues. He was appointed a Life Peer in 1999 and awarded the CBE in 2012 for services to national security.

Thomas M. Chen is Professor in Cyber Security at City University, London, and an expert in computer and network security. His previous research projects have explored Internet security, intrusion detection, attack modelling, malicious software and cybercrime, with support from various US agencies and companies. He is co-editor of *Broadband Mobile Multimedia: Techniques and Applications* (2008) and *Mathematical Foundations for Signal Processing, Communications, and Networking* (2011), co-author of *ATM Switching Systems* (1995) and has published papers in a number of IEEE journals including *IEEE Computer*, IEEE *Security and Privacy*, *IEEE Internet Computing* and *IEEE Transactions on Smart Grid*.

Maura Conway is a Senior Lecturer in International Security in the School of Law and Government at Dublin City University (DCU) in Dublin, Ireland, and Principal Investigator on VOX-Pol, a major EU-funded project on violent online political extremism. Her principal research interests are in the area of terrorism and the Internet, including academic and media discourses on cyberterrorism, the functioning and effectiveness of violent political extremist online content, and violent online radicalisation. She has presented upon these issues before the United Nations in New York, the Commission of the European Union in Brussels, the Royal United Services Institute (RUSI) in London, and elsewhere. Her articles have appeared in, amongst others, *Current History, First Monday, Media, War & Conflict* and *Parliamentary Affairs*.

Keiran Hardy is a Ph.D. Candidate at the University of New South Wales on Professor George Williams' Laureate Fellowship: Anti-Terror Laws and the Democratic Challenge. He has published in Australian and international journals on cyberterrorism, definitions of terrorism, control orders and the security assessments of refugees. He has lectured at the University of New South Wales in public law, national security law and advanced criminal law.

Lee Jarvis is a Senior Lecturer in International Security at the University of East Anglia. His books include *Times of Terror: Discourse, Temporality and the War on Terror* (Palgrave 2009) and *Terrorism: A Critical Introduction* (Palgrave 2011, with Richard Jackson, Jeroen Gunning and Marie Breen Smyth). He has published his research in a range of international journals including *Security Dialogue, Political Studies, International Relations, Millennium: Journal of International Studies, Terrorism and Political Violence, Studies in Conflict and Terrorism* and *Critical Studies on Terrorism*. His most recent funded research project (with Michael Lister) was the ESRC-sponsored 'Anti-terrorism, Citizenship and Security in the UK'.

Timothy Legrand is a lecturer at the National Security College at the Australian National University and adjunct research fellow at the ARC Centre of Excellence in Policing and Security at Griffith University. He is the co-editor, with Allan McConnell, of Emergency Policy (Ashgate, 2013), and the author of articles published in Policy Studies on policy transfer and evidence-based policy. His interdisciplinary research traverses political science, public administration and criminology and investigates policy learning, emergency policy-making, critical infrastructure protection and the application of counter-terrorism laws.

Stuart Macdonald is Associate Professor at the College of Law, Swansea University. He has written a number of articles on counter-terrorism laws and policy which have been published in leading international journals, including *Criminal Law & Philosophy, Sydney Law Review* and the *Cornell Journal of Law and Public Policy*. He has held visiting scholarships at Columbia University Law School, New York, and the Institute of Criminology at the University of Sydney. His recent project on security and liberty was funded by the British Academy.

Michael McGuire is a Senior Lecturer in Criminology in the University of Surrey and has a particular interest in the study of technology and its impacts upon the justice system. His first book *Hypercrime: The New Geometry of Harm* (Glasshouse 2008), critiqued the notion of cybercrime as a way of modelling computer-enabled offending and was awarded the 2008 British Society of Criminology runners up Book Prize. His most recent publication—*Technology, Crime & Justice: The Question Concerning Technomia* (Routledge 2012)—provides one of the first overviews of the fundamental shifts in crime and the justice system arising from new technologies. His theoretical research is complemented by a range of applied studies, including recent work on the impacts of e-crime upon the UK retail for the British Retail Consortium, a study of Organised Digital Crime Groups for BAE/Detica, and a comprehensive evidence review of cybercrime for the Home Office.

Lella Nouri is a Ph.D. student at Swansea University conducting research into the presentation of the cyberterrorism threat within the UK and the US political discourse. Drawing on post-Marxist and post-structuralist theories of discourse, Lella's research is primarily concerned with the implications of speculative security politics. Lella has a Masters in International Relations from Swansea University, graduating with a distinction. Her research to date involves an exploration of the relationship between traditional forms of terrorism and cyberterrorism; exploring the conceptual, normative and political implications of thinking about cyber activities as terrorist. Her work has been published in *Studies in Conflict & Terrorism* and is forthcoming in several edited books on (counter-)terrorism.

Michael Stohl is Professor of Communication, and affiliate Professor of Political Science and Global and International Studies at the University of California, Santa Barbara (UCSB). Dr. Stohl's research focuses on political communication and international relations with special reference to political violence, terrorism, and human rights. He is the author or co-author of more than 100 scholarly journal articles and book chapters and the author, editor or co-editor of 15 books. His most recent publications include *Fragile States: Violence and the Failure of Intervention* (with Lothar Brock, Georg Sorensen and Hans Henrik Holm), Polity: 2012; and *Crime and Terrorism* with Peter Grabosky (SAGE 2010). His 2007 article with Cynthia Stohl, 'Networks of Terror: Theoretical Assumptions and Pragmatic Consequences' *Communication Theory* 47,2:93–124 was awarded both the International Communication Association's best published article of the year award and the National Communication Association's best published article in Organizational Communication award. Dr. Stohl has been the recipient of numerous fellowships and awards, including the International Communication Association Applied/Public Policy Research Award for career work on State Terrorism and Human Rights in 2011.

Andrew Whiting is a Ph.D. student at Swansea University whose research seeks to understand how contemporary understandings of cyberterrorism have emerged through the use of Foucauldian genealogical methods. Before undertaking his Ph.D., Andrew obtained a B.A. in Politics and an M.A. in Global Security from the University of Sheffield, graduating with distinction. During his time at Swansea,

Andrew has explored the definition and threat of cyberterrorism, as well as response, from a multidisciplinary perspective. He has also spent time looking into the relationship between power, knowledge and discourse. His work is in print or forthcoming in several edited volumes on terrorism and counter-terrorism.

George Williams is the Anthony Mason Professor, a Scientia Professor and the Foundation Director of the Gilbert+Tobin Centre of Public Law at the Faculty of Law, University of New South Wales. As an Australian Research Council Laureate Fellow, he is engaged in a 5-year international project on anti-terror laws and democracy. He has appeared as a barrister in the High Court of Australia in a number of leading cases on constitutional law.

Clay Wilson is the Program Director for Cybersecurity Studies at the American Public University. The program emphasises a multidisciplinary approach to cybersecurity which examines the interconnectedness and complexity of cybersecurity management for both macro- and micro-critical infrastructures. Dr. Wilson is past Program Director for Cybersecurity Policy at the University of Maryland University College (UMUC), where he oversaw development of graduate-level courses. Prior to that, Dr. Wilson researched national defence policy at the Congressional Research Service where he analysed cyber intelligence reports for the US Congress and NATO committees on net-centric warfare, cybersecurity, nanotechnology and other vulnerabilities of high-technology military systems and critical infrastructures.

Dr. Wilson is a member of the Landau Network Centro Volta, International Working Group, an organisation that studies non-proliferation of CBRN and Cyber Weapons. He has moderated panels for the National Nuclear Security Administration on non-proliferation for Cyber Weapons in Como, Italy, and has presented at the China Arms Control and Disarmament Association in Beijing. He has also presented at the US Defense Cyber Investigations Training Academy, at the US National Defense University on the topic of cybercrime and at the Cyber Conflict Studies Association on the cyber capabilities of terrorist groups. Other projects involved research for Abu Dhabi government officials on computer security and network technology for defence and crisis management while living in the United Arab Emirates. His Ph.D. from George Mason University concentrated on Protection of Intellectual Property.

Panayotis A. Yannakogeorgos is a Research Professor of Cyber Policy and Global Affairs at the Air Force Research Institute. His expertise includes the intersection of cyber power, national security and military operations; international cyber policy; cyber arms control; global cyber norms; and Eastern Mediterranean studies. He is co-editor of the recent book *Conflict and Cooperation in Cyberspace* and has authored articles or chapters including: 'Keep Cyber War Narrow' (*National Interest*), 'Chinese Hacking Only Part of the Story' (*CNN Online*), 'Internet Governance and National Security' (*Strategic Studies Quarterly*), 'Challenges in Monitoring Cyber Arms Control' (*Journal of Information Warfare and Terrorism*), 'Pitfalls of the Private-Public Partnership Model' in *Crime and Terrorism Risk: Studies in*

Criminology and Criminal Justice (Routledge) and 'Cyberspace: The New Frontier and the Same Old Multilateralism' in *Global Norms: American Sponsorship and the Emerging Pattern of World Politics* (Palgrave). Dr. Yannakogeorgos has participated in the work of global cybersecurity bodies including the High Level Experts Group of the Global Cybersecurity Agenda of the International Telecommunications Union. In 2006 he served as an Adviser within the United Nations Security Council on nuclear non-proliferation, the Middle East (including Iran), Al-Qaida and Internet misuse. He holds a Ph.D. and an M.S. in Global Affairs from Rutgers University, and an A.L.B in Philosophy from Harvard University.

Chapter 1
What is 'Cyberterrorism'? Computer and Internet Technology in Legal Definitions of Terrorism

Keiran Hardy and George Williams

1.1 Introduction

The idea that terrorists could cause massive loss of life, worldwide economic chaos and devastating environmental damage by hacking into critical infrastructure systems has captured the public imagination. Air traffic control systems, nuclear power stations, hospitals and stock markets are all viable targets for cyber-terrorists wanting to wreak havoc and destruction (see Weimann 2005a; Yannakogeorgos 2014). The implication here is not so much that a new breed of cyber-terrorists will emerge, but that existing terrorist organisations in the al-Qaeda mould might use advanced computer and Internet technology instead of planes and bombs for their next major attack. As President Obama explained when outlining the United States' cyber-security plan:

> Al Qaeda and other terrorist groups have spoken of their desire to unleash a cyber attack on our country—attacks that are harder to detect and harder to defend against. Indeed, in today's world, acts of terror could come not only from a few extremists in suicide vests but from a few key strokes on the computer—a weapon of mass disruption ... [I]t's now clear this cyber threat is one of the most serious economic and national security challenges we face as a nation (White House 2009).

The United Kingdom's national security strategy lists cyber-attacks by terrorists as one of four 'highest priority risks' (Cabinet Office 2010:11). The strategy explains that cyber-attacks on government, military, industrial and economic targets could have a 'potentially devastating real-world effect' (Cabinet Office 2010:30). Academic debates continue about whether terrorists are likely to use computer and Internet technology to launch such attacks, or whether they would find it cheaper and easier to stick to 'analogue' means, such as crude explosive devices (see Conway 2003,

K. Hardy (✉) • G. Williams
University of New South Wales, Law Building, UNSW Kensington Campus,
Sydney, NSW 2052, Australia
e-mail: k.a.hardy@unsw.edu.au

T.M. Chen et al. (eds.), *Cyberterrorism: Understanding, Assessment, and Response*,   1
DOI 10.1007/978-1-4939-0962-9_1, © Springer Science+Business Media New York 2014

2014; Stohl 2006). Nonetheless, even the possibility that terrorists will use computer and Internet technology to devastating effect means that the issue deserves serious attention from national security legislators and policymakers. In any case, it is clear that terrorists also use the Internet for means other than attack, such as funding, recruitment, propaganda and communication (Home Office 2011:73–76; Carlile and Macdonald 2014; Walker 2005/2006; Weimann 2005b).

At the less serious end of the spectrum, cyber-attacks against websites and other non-essential infrastructure by political **hacktivists** are becoming more numerous by the day. The infamous 'Anonymous' group has protested a range of political issues by launching **distributed denial-of-service (DDoS) attacks** against the web- sites of government bodies and prominent organisations, including the Australian Parliament, PayPal, MasterCard, Visa, the US Federal Bureau of Investigation (FBI) and the US Department of Justice. These cyber-attacks have not, so far, led to any- thing resembling the physical and emotional impact of terrorist attacks in New York and Washington, Bali, Madrid, London or Mumbai. Conway has therefore under- standably argued that these hacktivists should be conceived not as terrorists, but as the mischievous 'heirs to those who employ the tactics of trespass and blockade in the realm of real-world protest' (Conway 2003: 13). Most would likely agree that disrupting the website of a government department or private organisation, even for political motives, is not an act of terrorism as traditionally understood. And yet, there may be some overlap between hacktivism and terrorism. Recently, a group claiming affiliation with Anonymous posted a bomb threat on its Twitter account, warning that 200 kg of military-grade explosive was waiting in a government build- ing to be detonated remotely by computer technology (Huff 2012).

It seems, therefore, that there are two key problems relating to the threat of cyberterrorism. The first is the possibility that a terrorist organisation like al-Qaeda will use computer and Internet technology to devastating effect against critical national infrastructure. The second is the likelihood that hacktivists will continue attacking websites and other non-essential infrastructure for political motives, com- bined with the possibility that such online protests could become increasingly seri- ous to the point where they should be classified as cyberterrorism. Other cyber-attack scenarios could be thrown into this mix. Inter-state cyber-attacks used alongside conventional military offensives—such as those launched by Russia against Georgia in the 2008 crisis—might be described as 'cyber-warfare' rather than cyberterror- ism (see Stohl 2014). The stealing of sensitive national security or economic infor- mation via computer technology—as in the ongoing WikiLeaks saga, or the recent use of Chinese malware to infiltrate the networks of the Reserve Bank of Australia (see Kerin and Joyce 2013)—might be described as 'cyber-espionage'. A cyber- attack by an individual or organisation for financial gain, such as a common phish- ing scam to gather bank account details and computer passwords, might be described as 'cyber-crime'. Defining the boundaries of cyberterrorism is therefore an incred- ibly difficult task, and one that can be approached from a variety of angles (see Jarvis et al. 2014; Carlile and Macdonald 2014; Yannakogeorgos 2014). In this chapter, we address this definitional question by examining which cyber-attack sce- narios might qualify as acts of terrorism under domestic law.

Our primary aim in this chapter is to answer the question: what uses of computer and Internet technology does domestic law regard as acts of terrorism? Since the 9/11 attacks, Western governments have enacted a wide range of laws directed specifically towards the threat of terrorism, but there has been little analysis of how these laws apply to the use of computer and Internet technology. In this chapter we fill this gap by investigating the uses of computer and Internet technology that would fall under **statutory definitions of terrorism** in a range of jurisdictions. This analysis is extremely important because the definitions discussed below trigger a range of criminal offences and other statutory powers that can have serious consequences for individuals. By investigating the question from this legal perspective we can also provide a clear starting point for discussing cyberterrorism in other fields—throughout the remaining chapters of this book, and beyond.

Below we examine legal definitions of terrorism in four Commonwealth nations: the United Kingdom, Australia, Canada, and New Zealand. These countries are all comparable in this context because each has enacted a definition of terrorism with a similar wording and structure. This is because Australia, Canada and New Zealand have each followed the United Kingdom's approach to defining terrorism. Each jurisdiction is also a liberal democracy with a similar legal system and an expressed commitment to protecting human rights. And yet, despite these similarities, there are a number of significant differences in how these four countries have defined terrorism. Exploring these differences provides a useful way of opening up broader questions about how cyberterrorism should be defined, both in legislation and political discourse.

The United States, while broadly comparable to these other four jurisdictions, is not included in the following discussion because it has taken a different approach to defining terrorism in its domestic legislation. The purpose of this chapter is to closely analyse and compare the words and phrases that determine the scope of each legal definition of terrorism, and to draw conclusions from this analysis as to how cyberterrorism should be defined. The different structure of the United States' definition makes it difficult to compare on these grounds. To compare the United States' approach would also raise larger and more difficult legal questions, such as how to devise structured penalty schemes for terrorism offences. For readers interested in how the United States has defined cyberterrorism in legislation, one of the authors has addressed this question in another article (see Hardy 2011:159–161).

While other criminal offences involving the use of computer technology exist in the United Kingdom, Australia, Canada and New Zealand, we focus on definitions of terrorism because these are the only provisions determining what qualifies as an *act of terrorism* under each nation's domestic law. There is no offence of 'cyberterrorism' in any of these jurisdictions, but we can answer the question by speculating as to what uses of computer and Internet technology would fall under each nation's legal definition of terrorism. By investigating definitions of terrorism in this way, we arrive at an understanding of which cyber-attack scenarios would qualify as acts of terrorism under domestic law.

To experts on domestic anti-terror laws, much of the information covered below will be familiar. Our aim, however, is to extend this basic understanding of anti-terror laws to academics in the other fields gathered together in this collection—which span the physical and social sciences—and to a more general audience. For this reason, we provide some background and context on each nation's legal responses to terrorism, and we try to avoid complicated legal issues and jargon where possible.

In investigating the measures that exist for countering cyberterrorism in domestic law, our aim is not only to address the question 'what is cyberterrorism?' In canvassing this material, our secondary aim is to address the following question: 'are existing legal responses to terrorism sufficient to cover the possibility of a serious act of cyberterrorism?' In the conclusion we return to and suggest some answers to these important questions.

Key Points

- The possibility of an act of cyberterrorism against critical national infrastructure requires serious attention from legislators.
- The UK, Australian, Canadian and New Zealand governments have legal powers to prevent and prosecute terrorism. The scope of these laws is determined by statutory definitions of terrorism.
- A wide range of possible cyber-attack scenarios exist (including acts of hacktivism against websites) and it is not clear which of these scenarios would fall within definitions of terrorism under domestic law.

1.2 Cyberterrorism in Legal Definitions of Terrorism

1.2.1 United Kingdom

The UK definition of terrorism is found in section 1 of the Terrorism Act 2000 (TA2000). The TA2000 was enacted some 14 months before 9/11 when the Blair government decided to introduce laws that could apply generally to any kind of terrorism. Previously, the UK had enacted temporary and emergency powers that applied specifically to the threat of terrorism in Northern Ireland, but it did not have permanent terrorism laws of general application. When introducing the TA2000 into Parliament, Home Secretary Jack Straw explained that the UK needed laws to address the possibility of terrorist attacks on UK soil by groups operating outside Northern Ireland. He gave the example of Aum Shinrikyo, the millenarian cult which had released sarin gas into the Tokyo subway in 1999 (House of Commons 1999).

The TA2000 was therefore enacted for a broad, general purpose, although the specific threat of cyberterrorism was contemplated at the time. In the House of Lords, Lord Cope of Berkeley explained that sub-section (2)(e) in section 1, which refers to the disruption of electronic systems, 'extends the definition to cover what is known in the jargon as cyberterrorism' (House of Lords 2000). He explained that this was very important because 'great damage can be caused to public life and the public can be held to ransom by computer hacking of one kind or another' (House of Lords 2000). Since 9/11, the UK has enacted several other anti-terror laws, although these have only made minor changes to the definition as enacted in 2000.[1]

Section 1 of the TA2000 sets out three requirements for an act to qualify as 'terrorism'. The first, in sub-section (1)(b), is an **intention requirement**. It requires that an act of terrorism be 'designed to influence the government or an international governmental organisation, or to intimidate the public or a section of the public'. The second, in sub-section (1)(c), is commonly referred to as a **motive requirement**. It requires that an act of terrorism be committed 'for the purpose of advancing a political, religious, racial or ideological cause'. The third, in sub-section (2), is a **harm requirement**. Sub-section (2) lists a range of alternative harms that an act needs to cause in order to qualify as terrorism, including 'serious violence against a person' and 'serious damage to property'. Most importantly in this context, sub-section (2)(e) provides that an act will qualify as terrorism if it is 'designed seriously to interfere with or seriously to disrupt an electronic system'. Another important factor to take into account is that sub-section (1) begins by defining terrorism as the 'use *or threat* of action where...'. This means that a person who *threatens* to commit a terrorist act would fall under the definition in the same way as if he or she actually followed through with the threatened action. These elements are combined in section 1 of the TA2000 as follows:

1. Terrorism: interpretation

   (1) In this Act 'terrorism' means the use or threat of action where –

       (a) the action falls within subsection (2);
       (b) the use or threat is designed to influence the government or an international governmental organisation or to intimidate the public or a section of the public; and
       (c) the use or threat is made for the purpose of advancing a political, religious, racial or ideological cause.

   (2) Action falls within this subsection if it –

       (a) involves serious violence against a person;
       (b) involves serious damage to property;
       (c) endangers a person's life, other than that of the person committing the action;
       (d) creates a serious risk to the health or safety of the public or a section of the public; or
       (e) is designed seriously to interfere with or seriously to disrupt an electronic system.

---

[1] The first change, made by section 34 of the Terrorism Act 2006, was to extend the definition to attacks against 'international governmental organisations'. The second change, made by section 75 of the Counter-Terrorism Act 2008, was to extend the definition to acts committed for the purpose of 'racial' causes. We have included these amendments when setting out the TA2000 definition.

Another important consideration is sub-section (3), which provides that an act will qualify as terrorism under UK law even if it is committed outside the UK:

(3) In this section –

(a) 'action' includes action outside the United Kingdom;
(b) a reference to any person or to property is a reference to any person, or to property, wherever situated;
(c) a reference to the public includes a reference to the public of a country other than the United Kingdom; and
(d) 'the government' means the government of the United Kingdom, of a Part of the United Kingdom or of a country other than the United Kingdom.

In *R v F*,[2] the England and Wales Court of Appeal made clear that sub-section (3) extends the UK definition of terrorism to acts designed to influence oppressive foreign regimes. In that case, a Libyan national had fled to the UK and was subsequently charged under the TA2000 with two counts of possessing or recording a document likely to be useful for preparing an act of terrorism (section 58). Those documents were part of an alleged plan to remove Colonel Gaddafi and his military forces from power. On appeal, F contended that the phrase 'the government' in sub-section (1)(1)(b) should only apply to democratic governments like the UK, because an act designed to influence an oppressive foreign regime would be morally justifiable. The court rejected this argument by citing the phrase 'a country other than the United Kingdom' in sub-section (3)(d). Because this phrase does not specify any particular *type* of government, the court held that an act designed to influence a tyrannical government would qualify as an act of terrorism in the same way that an act designed to influence the UK government would qualify as an act of terrorism. Unlike some of the other definitions examined below, the UK definition does not include a specific exemption for acts of political protest or self-determination, so there was no possibility of mounting a legal argument on this ground.

With these factors in mind, it is possible to describe the scope of the UK definition of terrorism with regard to cyber-attacks. Firstly, it is clear that the definition would apply to the *threat* of a cyber-attack in the same way that it would apply to an *actual* cyber-attack. Secondly, the definition would apply to cyber-attacks that are designed merely to 'influence' a government. No higher standard of intention—such as 'coercing' or 'intimidating' a government—is required. Thirdly, the definition would apply to cyber-attacks against 'international governmental organisations' such as the United Nations or NATO. Fourthly, to qualify as an act of terrorism, a cyber-attack need not seriously interfere with critical infrastructure such as a power-grid or nuclear power station; the attack could seriously interfere with anything that the courts consider to be an 'electronic system'. This could plausibly include website servers affected by a flood of emails under a DDoS attack launched by a hacktivist group. Indeed, the fact that sub-section (2)(e) uses the phrase '*designed to*' suggests

---

[2] [2007] EWCA Crim 243.

that a cyber-attack would not need to actually *cause* any interference; the mere intention of causing interference would be enough for an individual to be prosecuted for terrorism. Fifthly, the definition would apply to cyber-attacks designed to influence oppressive foreign regimes. Lastly, there is no specific exemption for cyber-attacks that could be classified as political protest or self-determination.

This means that the UK definition of terrorism could be used to prosecute an individual who aimed to influence an oppressive foreign leader for political or religious reasons by threatening to seriously interfere with non-essential infrastructure, such as a website server. One could imagine, for example, the Anonymous group threatening to seriously interfere with the Zimbabwean government's website servers to protest Robert Mugabe's presidency. Most would likely agree that such an act should not be classified as terrorism, and yet the UK definition of terrorism could extend this far.

The striking breadth of this definition becomes even more apparent when one considers how it operates through various criminal offences. The TA2000 does not explicitly criminalise *acts* of terrorism per se, but the section 1 definition determines the scope of various offences for prior and related conduct. The preventive rationale underlying these offences is examined in more detail by Carlile and Macdonald (2014). The TA2000 includes, for example, an offence for funding terrorism that attracts a maximum penalty of 14 years imprisonment (section 15). This means that one person (A) could be prosecuted for using computer technology to provide money to a second person (B) where A has 'reasonable cause to suspect' that B will use those funds to launch a cyber-attack against an electronic system. The TA2000 also includes an offence of collecting information that is 'likely to be useful' to a person preparing an act of terrorism (section 58). The offence carries a maximum penalty of 10 years imprisonment. This means that an individual could, for example, be prosecuted for using the Internet to research how to seriously interfere with an electronic system.

The TA2000 definition also determines the scope of **preparatory offences** contained in the Terrorism Act 2006 (TA2006). The broadest of these is the offence of preparing acts of terrorism (section 5), which provides a maximum penalty of life imprisonment for 'any conduct' done in preparation for a terrorist act. Other examples are the offences for encouraging terrorism (section 1), disseminating terrorist publications (section 2), and providing or receiving training for terrorism (section 6). A key related provision is section 3, which provides that an individual will be deemed to have endorsed material he or she has posted online if the government has issued a notice to take down that material and the individual refuses. The case of *R v Gul*[3] demonstrates the potential breadth of these provisions. In that case, a law student in the UK had uploaded videos onto YouTube of insurgents attacking Coalition forces in Iraq and Afghanistan. The videos were accompanied by statements praising the bravery of the insurgents and encouraging further attacks. The student received 5 years imprisonment for disseminating terrorist publications with intent to encourage terrorism.

---

[3] [2012] EWCA Crim 280.

R v Gul is a prime example of how far the UK's anti-terror laws regulate the use of computer and Internet technology with respect to terrorism. The offences that stem from the definition of terrorism mean that individuals could receive serious prison terms for using technology in ways that do not cause any direct harm to others, such as uploading videos onto a website. Taken at their broadest, the definition of terrorism in combination with these offences means that somebody could be prosecuted for uploading a video onto YouTube that encouraged further threats of cyber-attacks against the website servers of the Mugabe government, as described above. Such an act could not be described as an *act* of cyberterrorism in the same way that the 9/11 and 7/7 attacks were acts of terrorism—but it could be described under the broader heading of 'cyberterrorism' insofar as it involves the use of Internet technology and is a punishable terrorism offence under UK law (see Walker 2005/2006:633–634).

The TA2000 definition also determines the availability of statutory powers for preventing terrorism. These powers could be used to prevent cyber-attacks that fall under the definition of terrorism in the same way that they can be used to prevent 'real world' terrorist attacks. Under the Terrorist Asset-Freezing etc. Act 2010, for example, the Treasury is able to freeze an individual's assets and property if it reasonably believes that the individual is involved in terrorism (section 2). Under the Terrorism Prevention and Investigation Measures Act 2011, which replaced the Blair government's 'control order' regime, the state can impose various restrictions on an individual's liberty (much like parole requirements). The Act provides that a 'TPIM Notice' setting out these restrictions can be imposed if the Home Secretary (1) reasonably believes that the individual is involved in terrorism, and (2) reasonably considers that imposing those restrictions would be necessary to protect the public from a risk of terrorism (section 2(1)). This means that an individual involved in any of the conduct described above could be subjected to a range of serious restrictions on their finances and liberty without proof that they have engaged in any criminal act.

Taken together, these three aspects—the definition of terrorism, the criminal offences in the TA2000 and TA2006, and the statutory powers for preventing terrorism—demonstrate that the UK is certainly well equipped to address the possibility of a serious act of cyberterrorism. Indeed, the issue is that the UK may be *over-equipped*, to the point where legitimate online protests and forms of illegal hacking other than terrorism could also be targeted under the legislation. Of course this does not mean that every action that falls under the legislation will be prosecuted and attract the maximum available penalty, but it does have serious implications for the rule of law given the level of discretion available to the government. It also has implications for the right to freedom of speech if online protestors refrain from criticising government policy out of fear they will be targeted with serious terrorism offences and special statutory powers.

On a report on the UK definition of terrorism, Lord Carlile (then Independent Reviewer of Britain's anti-terror legislation) supported the inclusion of sub-section (2)(e) because acts of cyberterrorism could cause serious physical and economic harm. He stated:

Section 1(2)(e) deals with the design seriously to interfere with or seriously to disrupt an electronic system. This has the potential to include internet service providers, financial exchanges, computer systems, controls of national power and water, etc. The huge damage to the economy of the nation, and the potential for injury as a result, are self-evident. This category too should be included in the definition. I have concluded that the provision remains justified (Carlile 2007:40)

The UK definition of terrorism certainly covers such threats; the important question is whether it goes too far in targeting less serious uses of computer and Internet technology, and if so, how its scope could appropriately be reduced. In the other jurisdictions below, we see some examples of how the scope of the UK's anti-terror laws with respect to cyber-attacks could be improved.

Key Points

- The UK definition of terrorism is set out in section 1 of the Terrorism Act 2000. It encompasses politically motivated acts that are designed to seriously interfere with or disrupt electronic systems.
- The UK definition of terrorism is drafted so broadly that it could apply to the threat of a cyber-attack against non-essential infrastructure owned by an oppressive foreign government.
- The section 1 definition determines the scope of a range of serious offences and statutory powers. This means that individuals can receive serious penalties for using computer and Internet technology in ways that do not cause direct harm to others, such as posting videos onto YouTube that glorify terrorist acts.

1.2.2   Australia

On 9/11, Australia did not have any national laws in place to address the threat of terrorism. It therefore looked directly to the UK's TA2000 when drafting its own legal responses. This was partly because of the UK's much longer history of dealing with terrorism, partly because of obvious legal and cultural ties between the two nations, and partly because Australia was on a short timetable to comply with United Nations Security Council Resolution 1373. Resolution 1373 was adopted by the UN Security Council shortly after 9/11 and it required Member States to enact terrorism offences and other preventive measures, such as restrictions on terrorist financing. Resolution 1373 did not, however, provide any guidance on how states should define terrorism in their own legislation. After 9/11, states were therefore largely '[l]eft to their own devices' in drafting their legal definitions of terrorism (Roach 2008:111).

Australia's main legislative response to 9/11 was a package of five Bills enacted in March 2002. The main piece of legislation in this package was the Security Legislation Amendment (Terrorism) Act 2002. That Act inserted a definition of terrorism into Part 5.3 of the Criminal Code Act 1995. This definition, found in s 100.1

of the Criminal Code, was modelled closely on the UK definition. It therefore displays a number of similarities, although it is not identical to the UK definition.

Like the UK definition of terrorism, the Australian definition of terrorism includes three requirements for an act to qualify as terrorism. These also encompass threats in addition to actions. Firstly, in sub-section (1)(b), the Australian definition includes a motive requirement which provides that the action or threat must be made 'with the intention of advancing a political, religious or ideological cause'. This is equivalent to the UK sub-section (1)(c), except that it does not extend to 'racial' causes. Secondly, in sub-section (1)(c), the Australian definition includes an intention requirement. This is equivalent to the UK sub-section (1)(b), but it does not encompass acts which intend merely to 'influence' a government. It sets a higher standard by requiring that the person must intend to 'coerce' a government or influence a government 'by intimidation'. In addition, sub-section (1)(c) does not encompass terrorism directed at 'international governmental organisations'.

Thirdly, in sub-section (2), the Australian definition includes a list of possible harms. This is equivalent to the UK sub-section (2), although there are some important differences. Most importantly in this context, sub-section (2)(f) refers to acts that seriously interfere with or disrupt electronic systems—but it includes a list of electronic systems with which an act of terrorism may seriously interfere, such as financial systems and essential public utilities. Sub-section (2)(f) also refers to acts that 'destroy' electronic systems. It also restricts the Australian definition to acts which actually *cause* interference with or destroy electronic systems (as opposed to acts which are merely '*designed to*' cause interference). Combined together, these elements are set out in section 100.1 of the Australian Criminal Code as follows:

(1) *terrorist act* means an action or threat of action where:

  (a) the action falls within subsection (2) and does not fall within subsection (3); and
  (b) the action is done or the threat is made with the intention of advancing a political, religious or ideological cause; and
  (c) the action is done or the threat is made with the intention of:

    (i) coercing, or influencing by intimidation, the government of the Commonwealth or a State, Territory or foreign country, or of part of a State, Territory or foreign country; or
    (ii) intimidating the public or a section of the public.

(2) Action falls within this subsection if it:

  (a) causes serious harm that is physical harm to a person; or
  (b) causes serious damage to property; or
  (c) causes a person's death; or
  (d) endangers a person's life, other than the life of the person taking the action; or

(e) creates a serious risk to the health or safety of the public or a section of the public; or

(f) seriously interferes with, seriously disrupts, or destroys, an electronic system including, but not limited to:

    (i)   an information system; or

    (ii) a telecommunications system; or

    (iii) a financial system; or

    (iv) a system used for the delivery of essential government services; or

    (v) a system used for, or by, an essential public utility; or

    (vi) a system used for, or by, a transport system.

A significant improvement on the UK definition is sub-section (3), which sets out a **political protest exemption**. Sub-section (3) provides that protest, dissent or industrial action will only fall under the definition of terrorism if it intends to cause death or serious physical harm, endanger a person's life, or create a serious risk to health or safety. Political protest that only intends to cause property damage is excluded from the scope of the definition:

(3) Action falls within this subsection if it:

    (a) is advocacy, protest, dissent or industrial action; and

    (b) is not intended:

        (i)   to cause serious harm that is physical harm to a person; or

        (ii) to cause a person's death; or

        (iii) to endanger the life of a person, other than the person taking the action; or

        (iv) to create a serious risk to the health or safety of the public or a section of the public.

Like the UK definition, the Australian section 100.1 includes a sub-section (4) which extends the definition to acts outside Australia. There have been no court decisions deciding whether this would extend the definition to acts committed against oppressive foreign regimes, as in the *R v F* decision in the UK, but there is no reason to suspect that an Australian court would interpret the provision any differently:

(4) In this Division:

    (a) a reference to any person or property is a reference to any person or property wherever situated, within or outside Australia; and

    (b) a reference to the public includes a reference to the public of a country other than Australia.

With these factors in mind, it is possible to describe the scope of the Australian definition with regard to cyber-attacks and compare this to the UK situation. Firstly, like the UK definition, the Australian definition of terrorism would apply to the threat of a cyber-attack in the same way that it would apply to an actual cyber-attack. Secondly, the Australian definition would not apply to cyber-attacks that are intended merely to 'influence' a government. A cyber-attack would need to be coercive or intimidatory to fall under the Australian definition. Thirdly, the Australian definition would not likely encompass cyber-attacks against the UN, NATO or similar bodies because sub-section (1)(c) does not include a specific reference to 'international governmental organisations' (as in the UK definition). Fourthly, to fall under the Australian definition a cyber-attack would need to cause serious interference with or destroy an electronic system; it could not simply be intended to do so. Fifthly, it seems the Australian definition would apply to cyber-attacks against oppressive foreign governments, although the political protest exemption in sub-section (3) would limit the scope of the definition in this scenario. Lastly, if a cyber-attack could be classified as protest, dissent or industrial action, it would fall under the Australian definition only if the protestors intended to cause one of the harms listed in sub-section (3)(b).

Generally, then, the Australian definition of terrorism criminalises a narrower range of conduct relating to cyber-attacks than its UK counterpart. The exemption for acts of political protest is a notable inclusion when one considers the growing number of cyber-attacks on websites by hacktivist groups protesting political causes. These improvements on the UK definition, however, should not be overstated. Sub-section (2)(f) may appear as if it is restricted to cyber-attacks affecting critical national infrastructure, such as essential public utilities, but the list is non-exhaustive because it is prefaced with the phrase 'including, but not limited to'. Effectively, this means that the Australian definition of terrorism could apply to a cyber-attack against any electronic system in the same way as the UK legislation. In addition, sub-section (2)(f) does not refer to any intention on behalf of the individual. This leaves open the possibility that someone could be prosecuted for being 'reckless' as to whether their actions were likely to seriously disrupt or destroy an electronic system. While the Australian definition sets a higher harm threshold than the UK definition by requiring *actual* interference with an electronic system, it therefore sets a lower intent threshold by allowing the possibility that someone may be reckless as to the outcome of their actions (as opposed to the UK definition, which explicitly requires that the act be 'designed' to seriously interfere with an electronic system).

The political protest exemption in sub-section (3) may also have more apparent than actual value as its usefulness is yet to be tested by the courts. All that the government would need to prove in order for a protest to fall outside the exemption is that the protestors intended to cause one of the harms listed in sub-section (3)(b). In this list, the lowest threshold would appear to be sub-section (3)(b)(iv): that the protestors intended to 'create a serious risk to the health or safety of a section of the public'. This could be said of many legitimate political protests, such as nurses striking or environmental activists protesting in treetops. Nonetheless, the exemption in sub-section (3) is a positive inclusion. It could discourage the Australian government from targeting legitimate acts of hacktivism with counter-terrorism offences and powers, even if these acts could technically fall under the definition.

Like the UK definition of terrorism, the Australian definition also operates through a range of broadly drafted criminal offences. The offence of committing a terrorist act is found in section 101.1 of the Criminal Code and attracts a maximum penalty of life imprisonment. Other offences exist for providing or receiving training connected with terrorist acts (section 101.2), possessing 'things' connected with terrorist acts' (section 101.4), collecting documents likely to facilitate terrorist acts (section 101.5) and a catch-all offence that criminalises any 'other acts done in preparation for … terrorist acts' (section 101.6).

The case of *R v Lodhi*[4] illustrates how broadly these offences regulate the use of technology with respect to terrorism. In that case, an associate of French terrorist Willie Brigitte received 20 years in prison for using the Internet to research bomb-making information and collect plans of an electricity grid. Brigitte and Lodhi had planned to damage the power grid with explosives, but one could imagine the Internet being used to research how to hack into a power grid and disrupt it remotely by computer. The act of researching how to interfere with a power grid might not be described as an *act* of cyberterrorism, but it could nonetheless constitute a serious offence under Australia's anti-terror laws.

The section 100.1 definition also determines the scope of wide-ranging statutory powers for preventing terrorism. As in the UK, these could apply to cyber-attacks that fall under the definition of terrorism in the same way that they could apply to 'real world' terrorist attacks. Under Division 104 of the Australian Criminal Code an individual can be subjected to a 'control order'. This is much like a TPIM notice in the UK although the scope of possible restrictions is wider. A control order can involve a range of serious restrictions on liberty amounting to virtual house arrest. The restrictions can be imposed if 'making the order would substantially assist in preventing a terrorist act' and a court is satisfied on the balance of probabilities that the restrictions are 'reasonably necessary, and reasonably appropriate and adapted, for the purpose of protecting the public from a terrorist act' (section 104.4). Another striking example is the questioning and detention powers given to Australia's domestic intelligence agency, the Australian Security Intelligence Organisation (ASIO). The Australian Security Intelligence Organisation Act 1979 allows ASIO to detain citizens not suspected of any involvement in terrorism for up to a week if doing so would 'substantially assist in the collection of intelligence that is important in relation to a terrorism offence' (section 34F).

As in the UK, it is clear that Australia is well equipped with laws that address the possibility of a serious act of cyberterrorism. The Australian definition of terrorism is narrower than its UK counterpart, although it is nonetheless wide-ranging, and could equally apply to cyber-attacks against non-essential infrastructure that do not cause any wider physical or economic harm. The definition also determines the scope of a wide range of criminal offences and statutory powers, such that any Australian citizen could be detained for up to a week by ASIO if doing so would substantially assist in the collection of intelligence relating to an act of cyberterror-ism. As in the UK, the question seems to be not whether Australia is sufficiently equipped to deal with the possibility of a serious act of cyberterrorism, but how Australia could reduce the risk that online activity and illegal forms of hacking other than cyberterrorism will be targeted under the same provisions.

---

[4] [2006] NSWSC 691.

Key Points

- Australia's definition of terrorism is set out in section 100.1 of the Australian Criminal Code. It is similar to the UK's definition, but it includes a statutory exemption for acts of political protest.
- The political protest exemption is a useful mechanism that is likely to prevent the Australian government from prosecuting legitimate acts of hacktivism as terrorist acts.
- Australia's counter-terrorism laws also include a range of special offences and statutory powers, such that individuals could receive serious penalties for downloading schematics of power grids and other utilities.

1.2.3 Canada

Like Australia, Canada also looked to the UK when drafting its legal responses to 9/11. The major piece of legislation passed by the Canadian government in response to 9/11 was the Anti-Terrorism Act 2001 (ATA). The ATA was enacted on 18 December 2001, just over 2 months after 9/11. It inserted a definition of terrorism into section 83.01 of the Canadian Criminal Code. The section 83.01 definition defines 'terrorist activity' in two alternative ways. The first, in sub-section (a), defines 'terrorist activity' according to a number of international conventions on specific types of terrorism (for example, acts of hijacking and hostage-taking). The second, in sub-section (b), is Canada's equivalent to the UK and Australian definitions set out above. Sub-section (b) in section 83.01 defines terrorist activity as follows:

'terrorist activity' means

...

(b) an act or omission, in or outside Canada,

  (i) that is committed

    (A) in whole or in part for a political, religious or ideological purpose, objective or cause; and

    (B) in whole or in part with the intention of intimidating the public, or a segment of the public, with regard to its security, including its economic security, or compelling a person, a government or a domestic or an international organization to do or to refrain from doing any act, whether the public or the person, government or organization is inside or outside Canada, and

  (ii) that intentionally

    (A) causes death or serious bodily harm to a person by the use of violence;

    (B) endangers a person's life;

(C) causes a serious risk to the health or safety of the public or any segment of the public;

(D) causes substantial property damage, whether to public or private property, if causing such damage is likely to result in the conduct or harm referred to in any of clauses (A) to (C); or

(E) causes serious interference with or serious disruption of an essential service, facility or system, whether public or private, other than as a result of advocacy, protest, dissent or stoppage of work that is not intended to result in the conduct or harm referred to in any of clauses (A) to (C), and includes a conspiracy, attempt or threat to commit any such act or omission, or being an accessory after the fact or counselling in relation to any such act or omission, but, for greater certainty, does not include an act or omission that is committed during an armed conflict and that, at the time and in the place of its commission, is in accordance with customary international law or conventional international law applicable to the conflict, or the activities undertaken by military forces of a state in the exercise of their official duties, to the extent that those activities are governed by other rules of international law.

There are a number of obvious similarities between this definition and the UK and Australian definitions. All three apply equally to conduct and the *threat* of such conduct. All three definitions require that an act of terrorism be committed for a political, religious or ideological motive. All three require that an act of terrorism be intended to influence a government to some degree or to intimidate a section of the public. All three include a list of alternative harms that a terrorist act must cause. All three definitions apply to acts of terrorism within the country and beyond its borders. Like the Australian definition, though unlike the UK definition, the Canadian definition requires that an act of political protest will only fall under the definition if it is intended to cause death or serious bodily injury, endanger a person's life, or create a serious risk to the health or safety of a section of the public.

More notable, however, are a number of important differences between the Canadian definition and the two definitions discussed above. Firstly, the Canadian definition requires that an act of terrorism 'compel' a government to act or refrain from acting in a particular way. This appears to set a higher standard than its equivalents in the UK ('influence') and Australia ('influence by intimidation'). Secondly, the Canadian definition encompasses attacks against domestic and international organisations. This is broader than the phrase 'international governmental organisations' in the UK definition; it could plausibly apply to non-governmental organisations such as Greenpeace and domestic service providers such as gas companies and Internet service providers (ISPs). Thirdly, the Canadian definition encompasses attacks against individual persons, such as an attack on a single Member of Parliament. Fourthly, and most importantly in the context of cyberterrorism, sub-section (ii)(E) in the Canadian definition requires that an attack against infrastructure be directed at an 'essential service, facility or system'. This sets the highest standard of all three definitions by requiring that the system being attacked is 'essential' and not simply *any* electronic system. Lastly, sub-section (ii)(E) in the Canadian definition requires that an act of terrorism both be *intended to* and *actually cause* interference with the essential service, facility or system. This is a higher standard than both the UK definition (which requires only intent to seriously interfere) and the Australian definition (which requires only that serious interference be caused).

With these factors in mind, it is possible to describe the scope of the Canadian definition with respect to cyber-attacks and compare this to the UK and Australian situations above. The Canadian definition is broader in some respects than the other definitions, and narrower in others. The Canadian definition is broader than the UK definition in that it could apply to cyber-attacks against Greenpeace, a domestic gas company or an ISP. The Canadian definition could also plausibly apply to a cyber-attack that compelled an individual Member of Parliament to act in a particular way. The higher standard set in sub-section (ii)(E), however, significantly restricts these possibilities because any cyber-attack would need to seriously interfere with an 'essential' service, facility or system. It is not clear whether the service, facility or system would need to be essential *to the organisation or person* or to *Canada as a nation*. Nonetheless, the wording suggests a much higher standard than the UK and Australian definitions, which clearly extends to non-essential electronic systems. In addition, the Canadian sub-section (ii)(E) would require that the person or group launching the cyber-attack both *intended to* and *actually caused* serious interference with the essential facility, service or system.

The Canadian Criminal Code also contains broad criminal offences and statutory powers related to terrorism that could apply to the use of computer and Internet technology, although these are generally less severe than in the UK and Australia. For example, the Canadian Criminal Code includes an offence for financing terrorism (section 83.02) which could apply to the electronic funding of terrorist activity. Section 83.02 provides a maximum penalty of 10 years imprisonment where a person provides funds to another person and intends or knows that the funds will be used to carry out a terrorist act. This resembles the UK offence of funding terrorism in section 15 of the TA2000, although it sets a higher standard by requiring that the person actually *intends* or *knows* that the funds will be used to commit a terrorist act (as opposed to the UK offence, which only requires 'reasonable cause to suspect' that the funds will be used for terrorism). Recently, the Canadian government has re-enacted two controversial counter-terrorism powers that lapsed in 2007—preventive arrests and investigative hearings—although the possible scope of these powers with respect to cyber-attacks will be restricted according to the definition set out above.[5]

Generally, then, the scope of the Canadian anti-terror laws with respect to cyber-attacks is more restrained than the scope of similar laws in the UK and Australia. Canada is still adequately equipped to address the possibility of a serious act of cyberterrorism, but the limits imposed on the definition of terrorism and its related offences and powers mean that there is less risk of other online activity and illegal hacking also being targeted under the legislation.

---

[5] See Combating Terrorism Act (SC 2013, c 9), which came into force 24 May 2013.

The Canadian definition suggests two important amendments that the UK and Australian governments could make to their definitions of terrorism. The first would be for the definitions to specify that an attack against an electronic system *intentionally cause* serious interference' with that system. Currently the UK definition only requires intent, and the Australian definition only requires that the system be seriously interfered with. The second amendment, which would have greater effect, would be to limit the UK and Australian definitions to attacks against an *essential facility, service or system*'. This wording captures the need to target serious attacks of cyberterrorism against critical national infrastructure, whereas the UK and Australian definitions go far beyond this by extending to cyber-attacks against any electronic system.

Key Points

- The Canadian definition of terrorism is set out in section 83.01(b) of the Canadian Criminal Code. It generally sets higher standards of harm and intent than the UK and Australian definitions, and like the Australian definition it includes an exemption for legitimate acts of political protest.
- The Canadian definition of terrorism would be limited to cyber-attacks that interfere with 'essential' infrastructure. This wording appropriately captures the threat of cyberterrorism against critical national infrastructure.
- Canada has sufficient legal powers to address the possibility of a serious act of cyberterrorism, but the narrower scope of its definition reduces the risk that less serious uses of computer and Internet technology will be targeted under the legislation.

1.2.4 New Zealand

Of all the definitions of terrorism discussed in this chapter, the New Zealand definition is the most restrained. The New Zealand definition of terrorism is found in section 5 of the Terrorism Suppression Act 2002 (TSA). The TSA was originally introduced into the New Zealand Parliament before 9/11 as the Terrorism (Bombings and Financing) Bill. After 9/11, the Bill was re-labelled and later enacted in October 2002. While New Zealand does not have a significant threat of terrorism, the New Zealand government like many smaller Commonwealth nations recognised the importance of joining the international community in denouncing and criminalising terrorism. When introducing amendments made to the Bill after 9/11, the New Zealand Minister for Foreign Affairs and Trade, Phil Goff, emphasised the importance of New Zealand 'play[ing] its part as a member of the international community by taking every step it can to deal with terrorism' (NZPD 2002).

Like the Australian and Canadian definitions, the New Zealand definition of terrorism follows the same basic structure as the UK definition. Sub-section (1)(b) in the New Zealand definition, however, resembles section 83.01(a) in the Canadian definition by defining terrorism according to a range of specified international conventions. The definition is set out in section 5 of the TSA as follows:

5 Terrorist Act defined

    (1) An act is a terrorist act for the purposes of this Act if—

        (a) the act falls within subsection (2); or

        (b) the act is an act against a specified terrorism convention (as defined in section 4(1)); or

        (c) the act is a terrorist act in armed conflict (as defined in section 4(1).

    (2) An act falls within this subsection if it is intended to cause, in any 1 or more countries, 1 or more of the outcomes specified in subsection (3), and is carried out for the purpose of advancing an ideological, political, or religious cause, and with the following intention:

        (a) to induce terror in a civilian population; or

        (b) to unduly compel or to force a government or an international organisation to do or abstain from doing any act.

    (3) The outcomes referred to in subsection (2) are—

        (a) the death of, or other serious bodily injury to, 1 or more persons (other than a person carrying out the act):

        (b) a serious risk to the health or safety of a population:

        (c) destruction of, or serious damage to, property of great value or importance, or major economic loss, or major environmental damage, if likely to result in 1 or more outcomes specified in paragraphs (a), (b), and (d):

        (d) serious interference with, or serious disruption to, an infrastructure facility, if likely to endanger human life:

        (e) introduction or release of a disease-bearing organism, if likely to devastate the national economy of a country.

    (4) However, an act does not fall within subsection (2) if it occurs in a situation of armed conflict and is, at the time and in the place that it occurs, in accordance with rules of international law applicable to the conflict.

    (5) To avoid doubt, the fact that a person engages in any protest, advocacy, or dissent, or engages in any strike, lockout, or other industrial action, is not, by itself, a sufficient basis for inferring that the person—

        (a) is carrying out an act for a purpose, or with an intention, specified in subsection (2); or

        (b) intends to cause an outcome specified in subsection (3).

There are several ways in which this definition is more restrained than the UK, Australian and Canadian definitions. Firstly, the definition does not extend to the *threat* of conduct. Secondly, instead of requiring that an act of terrorism be intended to 'intimidate' a section of the population (as in the UK, Australian and

Canadian definitions) sub-section (2)(a) requires that an act of terrorism be intended to 'induce terror' in the population. This wording indicates that the act must be intended to generate a feeling of intense fear or dread in the population. Thirdly, sub-section (2)(a) alternatively requires that an act be intended to 'unduly compel or force' a government to do or refrain from doing some act. This sets a higher standard than its equivalents in the UK ('influence'), Australia ('influence by intimidation') and Canada ('compel'). Lastly, and most importantly, sub-section (3)(d) requires that an act of terrorism against an infrastructure facility be 'likely to endanger life'. This sets a much higher standard than its equivalents in the other three definitions, which do not include any such additional requirements.

With these factors in mind, it is possible to describe the scope of the New Zealand definition of terrorism with respect to cyber-attacks. Firstly, the New Zealand definition would not apply to the threat of a cyber-attack. Secondly, the New Zealand definition would only apply to cyber-attacks that are intended to unduly compel a government or induce terror in a population. Thirdly, the New Zealand definition would apply to cyber-attacks against international organisations. This could include cyber-attacks against international governmental organisations like the UN or non-governmental organisations like Greenpeace. However, it would not include cyber-attacks against domestic organisations or individual persons (as in the Canadian definition). Fourthly, the New Zealand definition would be restricted to cyber-attacks against 'infrastructure facilities'. This would not likely include cyber-attacks that disrupt essential services (such as gas or electricity) or those that disrupt individual systems, such as a collection of website servers. Fifthly, the New Zealand definition would require that any cyber-attack against an infrastructure facility be 'likely to endanger life'. This would certainly exclude less serious acts of hacktivism from the scope of the legislation. Lastly, as with the Australian and Canadian definitions, the New Zealand definition would not ordinarily encompass cyber-attacks that could be classified as protest, dissent or industrial action.

The TSA also includes various offences and special statutory powers for preventing terrorism, such as financing terrorism (section 8), recruiting members of terrorist groups (section 12), and participating in terrorist groups (section 13). As in Canada, however, these are generally less severe than comparable offences and powers in the UK and Australia. The TSA does not include broad preparatory offences for 'any act' done in preparation for terrorist acts (as in section 5 of the TA2006 and section 101.6 of the Australian Criminal Code); nor does it include expansive powers like control orders or the detention of non-suspect citizens.

The three jurisdictions above could learn much from the New Zealand definition of terrorism, which excludes the threat of action and is restricted to attacks against infrastructure facilities that are likely to endanger life. This excludes the possibility that an individual or group could be targeted under terrorism legislation for threatening to seriously interfere with infrastructure where no human life is in danger.

One downside of this New Zealand definition, however, is that it may be too narrow to cover the scenario where a cyber-attack interferes with an essential public service and causes significant economic or environmental damage without endangering life. One could imagine, for example, a cyber-attack against a financial system that sent a national economy into chaos, or a cyber-attack against a sewage system that caused major environmental damage. Neither of these would be included under the New Zealand definition because sub-section (3)(d) requires that attacks against infrastructure facilities be likely to endanger life. This suggests two possible amendments that would improve the current New Zealand approach. The first would be to 'significant economic or environmental damage' to sub-section (3)(d) as an alternative to endangering life. The second would be to draw on the Canadian approach by replacing the phrase 'infrastructure facility' with 'essential service, facility or system'. In combination, these two amendments would ensure that the New Zealand definition of terrorism adequately covers the possibility of a serious act of cyberterrorism.

Key Points

- The New Zealand definition of terrorism is set out in section 5 of the Terrorism Suppression Act 2002. Of the four definitions discussed in this chapter, the New Zealand definition is the narrowest in scope.
- The New Zealand definition of terrorism would only apply to a cyber-attack against an infrastructure facility that was 'likely to endanger life'.
- However, the New Zealand definition of terrorism is perhaps too narrow in that it would not encompass cyber-attacks that cause significant environmental or economic damage without endangering life.

1.3 Conclusions

The dangers posed by cyberterrorism require serious attention from national security legislators and policymakers. In this chapter we have canvassed domestic responses to terrorism in four Commonwealth countries: the UK, Australia, Canada and New Zealand. We have done this for two purposes: to determine what would qualify as an act of cyberterrorism in each jurisdiction, and to determine whether each jurisdiction is adequately equipped to address the possibility of a serious act of cyberterrorism.

As detailed above, each nation has a unique definition of terrorism. This itself can be an issue given the global nature of acts of cyberterrorism, but the general thrust of these definitions is the same: cyberterrorism means conduct involving computer or Internet technology that (1) is motivated by a political, religious or ideological cause, (2) is intended to intimidate a government or a section of the public to varying degrees, and (3) seriously interferes with infrastructure. Only Canada requires that the infrastructure is 'essential', and only New Zealand requires that the attack be 'likely to endanger life'. To qualify as an act of terrorism under these nations' anti-terror laws, a cyber-attack would not need to cause massive loss of life, economic chaos or major environmental damage. It seems that legal definitions of cyberterrorism are therefore much wider than concepts of cyberterrorism in political discourse, in which cyber-attacks by terrorists are said to have 'potentially devastating real-world effect' (Cabinet 2010:30).

Each of these four nations, with the possible exception of New Zealand, has sufficient laws in place to target serious acts of cyberterrorism against national infrastructure. It is not sufficient, however, to say that these laws cover the possibility of a serious cyber-attack without asking what additional forms of conduct might also be included within their scope. The UK and Australian definitions of terrorism clearly go beyond the threat of serious cyber-attacks by encompassing attacks against non-essential electronic systems. In addition, these definitions operate through broad offences and statutory powers that expose individuals to serious restrictions on liberty. This creates a risk that individuals will be targeted under the UK and Australian anti-terror laws for using computer and Internet technology in ways that do not cause any direct harm to others. In the UK this risk is particularly serious because the TA2000 definition does not include an exemption for legitimate acts of political protest.

The Canadian and New Zealand definitions of terrorism are more restrained, and they provide useful insights into how an appropriate legal definition of cyberterrorism might be drafted. The Canadian reference to 'essential services, facilities or systems' appropriately captures the threat of a serious cyber-attack against critical national infrastructure. The New Zealand requirement that an attack against an infrastructure facility be 'likely to endanger life' captures the idea that an act of cyberterrorism would have some substantive additional effect beyond interfering with infrastructure. However, the New Zealand wording is perhaps too narrow because it fails to address the threat of cyberterrorism against essential services and systems, and because it fails to address the possibility that an act of cyberterrorism might cause significant economic or environmental harm without endangering life. The New Zealand definition could be improved in these respects by adopting the Canadian reference to 'essential services, facilities and systems' and by including significant economic and environmental damage as alternative harms to endangering life.

By examining legal definitions of terrorism in this way, it becomes clear that these four nations could still do much to ensure that their laws appropriately capture the threat of cyberterrorism without criminalising less serious uses of computer and Internet technology. We therefore conclude by offering a legal definition that combines the elements we believe best capture this threat:

> 'Cyberterrorism' means conduct involving computer or Internet technology that (1) is carried out for the purpose of advancing a political, religious or ideological cause; (2) is intended to intimidate a section of the public, or compel a government to do or abstain from doing any act; and (3) intentionally causes serious interference with an essential service, facility or system, if such interference is likely to endanger life or cause significant economic or environmental damage.

Key Points

- The UK, Australia, Canada and New Zealand all have different legal definitions of terrorism, but the general thrust of these definitions is the same: cyberterrorism means conduct that (1) is motivated by a political, religious or ideological cause; (2) is intended to intimidate a government or a section of the public; and (3) interferes with infrastructure.
- Only Canada requires that the infrastructure be 'essential', and only New Zealand requires that an act of cyberterrorism be 'likely to endanger life'.
- An appropriate legal definition of cyberterrorism would be limited to acts that intentionally cause serious interference with essential infrastructure or are likely to cause significant environmental or economic damage.

Further Reading and Resources

Bronitt S, Gani M (2003) Shifting boundaries of cybercrime: from computer hacking to cyber-terrorism. Crim Law J 27:303–321

Conte A (2007) Counter-terrorism and human rights in New Zealand. New Zealand Law Foundation, Wellington

Hardy K (2010) Operation titstorm: hacktivism or cyber-terrorism? Univ New S Wales Law J 33(2):474–502

Hardy K, Williams G (2011) What is 'terrorism'? Assessing domestic legal definitions. UCLA J Int Law Foreign Aff 16(1):77–162

Lynch A, Williams G (2006) What price security? Taking stock of Australia's anti-terror laws. Federation Press, Sydney

Lynch A, Macdonald E, Williams G (2007) Law and liberty in the war on terror. Federation Press, Sydney

Ramraj VV et al (2011) Global anti-terrorism law and policy. Cambridge University Press, Cambridge

Roach K (2011) The 9/11 effect. Cambridge University Press, Cambridge

Roach K (2003) September 11: consequences for Canada. McGill-Queen's University Press, Montreal

Walker C (2009) Blackstone's guide to the anti-terrorism legislation. Oxford University Press, Oxford

References

Cabinet Office (2010) The national security strategy: a strong Britain in an age of uncertainty. Cm 7953

Carlile A (2007) The definition of terrorism: a report by Lord Carlile of Berriew QC, Independent Reviewer of Terrorism Legislation. Cm 7052

Carlile L, Macdonald S (2014) The criminalisation of terrorists' online preparatory acts. In: Chen T, Jarvis L, Macdonald S (eds) Cyberterrorism: understanding, assessment, and response. Springer, New York

Conway M (2003) Hackers as terrorists? Why it doesn't compute. Comput Fraud Secur 12:10–13

Conway M (2014) Reality check: assessing the (un)likelihood of cyberterrorism. In: Chen T, Jarvis L, Macdonald S (eds) Cyberterrorism: understanding, assessment, and response. Springer, New York

Hardy K (2011) WWWMDs: cyber-attacks against infrastructure in domestic anti-terror laws. Comput Law Secur Rev 27:152–161

Home Office (2011) Prevent strategy. Cm 8092

House of Commons (1999) Hansard 341:Column 159

House of Lords (2000) Hansard 352:Column 161

Huff S (2012) Anonymous group poses bomb threat for Nov. 5, pisses off Anonymous. Betabeat (online)24October.http://betabeat.com/2012/10/anonymous-group-posts-bomb-threat-for-nov-5-pisses-off-anonymous/

Jarvis L, Nouri L, Whiting A (2014) Understanding, locating and constructing 'cyberterrorism'. In: Chen T, Jarvis L, Macdonald S (eds) Cyberterrorism: understanding, assessment, and response. Springer, New York

Kerin J, Joyce J (2013) RBA confirms cyber attacks. The Australian Financial Review. http://www.afr.com/p/national/rba_confirms_cyber_attacks_ZsVpeJas8JX6UXCLwOVJKP.

New Zealand Parliamentary Debates (NZPD) (2002) Hansard

Roach K (2008) Defining terrorism: the need for a restrained definition. In: LaViolette N, Forcese C (eds) The human rights of anti-terrorism. Irwin Law, Toronto, pp 97–127

Stohl M (2006) Cyber terrorism: a clear and present danger, the sum of all fears, breaking point or patriot games? Crime Law Soc Change 46:223–238

Stohl M (2014) Dr. Strangeweb: or how they stopped worrying and learned to love cyber war. In: Chen T, Jarvis L, Macdonald S (eds) Cyberterrorism: understanding, assessment, and response. Springer, New York

Walker C (2005/2006) Cyber-terrorism: legal principle and law in the United Kingdom. Penn State Law Rev 110:625–665

Weimann G (2005a) Cyberterrorism: the sum of all fears? Stud Confl Terrorism 28:129–149

Weimann G (2005b) How modern terrorism uses the Internet. J Int Secur Aff 8. http://www.securityaffairs.org/issues/2005/08/weimann.php.

White House (2009) Remarks by the president on securing our nation's cyber infrastructure. http://www.whitehouse.gov/the-press-office/remarks-president-securing-our-nations-cyber-infrastructure.

Yannakogeorgos P (2014) Rethinking the threat of cyberterrorism. In: Chen T, Jarvis L, Macdonald S (eds) Cyberterrorism: understanding, assessment, and response. Springer, New York

Chapter 2
Understanding, Locating and Constructing Cyberterrorism

Lee Jarvis, Lella Nouri, and Andrew Whiting

2.1 Introduction

As the Internet and associated digital technologies continue their expansion through-out social life, the 'cyber' prefix has become applied to a growing list of diverse activities and phenomena. This encroachment into new spheres of social and politi-cal existence has cemented the Internet's place as the poster child of globalisation: a lubricant facilitating the exchange of ideas, information and things. Yet, this capacity to shrink social space and accelerate social time has also generated anxieties around the emergence of seemingly new 'cyber-threats' made manifest by opportunities pre-sented by the Internet. Although much discussed, feared and predicted, such threats remain often poorly or variably understood (see McGuire 2014). None more so, perhaps, than cyberterrorism. Indeed, although this term has existed for over 30 years now, there remains very little consensus on many of the most fundamental questions surrounding this term (Jarvis and Macdonald forthcoming). Thus, what cyberterrorism is—and what it is not—remains enormously contested, as does its relation to other types of terrorism and cyber-activity.

As we demonstrate throughout this chapter, there exists a number of very different understandings of cyberterrorism within academic and other literature on this con-cept. Several authors, for instance, prefer a graduated approach, distinguishing between 'pure' and other types of cyberterrorism. In these cases, the former is often used most sparingly to refer only to attacks on digital targets via digital means, while the latter, in contrast, may incorporate activities such as propagandizing or fundrais-ing online (Malcolm 2004; also Anderson 2009). Desouza and Hensgen (2003:387),

L. Jarvis (✉)
School of Political, Social and International Studies,
University of East Anglia, Norwich, UK
e-mail: l.jarvis@uea.ac.uk

L. Nouri • A. Whiting
Department of Political and Cultural Studies, Swansea University,
Singleton Park, Swansea SA2 8PP, UK

T.M. Chen et al. (eds.), *Cyberterrorism: Understanding, Assessment, and Response*,
DOI 10.1007/978-1-4939-0962-9_2, © Springer Science+Business Media New York 2014

for example, employ the term 'unique' cyberterrorism to describe, "...the use of legitimate electronic outlets to facilitate communication among terrorist groups" (Desouza and Hensgen 2003:387). Other authors apply far stricter criteria, questioning whether even seemingly significant disruptions to computer networks might be considered terrorism at all. Here, Soo Hoo et al. (1997:147), for example, ask whether, '...network attacks like shutting down a long-distance telephone network or a company's internal network [might] be considered terrorism?' For, as they continue, 'No violence is used; no life-threatening terror is instilled' (Soo Hoo et al. 1997:147).

That such a familiar term can sustain such different meanings, we argue, raises a number of important questions. Are some understandings of cyberterrorism more accurate or more useful than others, for example (and, if so, why)? Or, are different conceptions of the term a product of the differing motivations and contexts in which it is used? Does the meaning of cyberterrorism change over time? And, do the geographical and jurisdictional differences identified by Hardy and Williams (2014) matter? Finally, are the consequences of using the term cyberterrorism as important as any meaning it might have?

To explore these questions, the chapter begins by identifying four reasons for the contestability of the term cyberterrorism. These concern: (i) Competing views of the significance of different stages of an attack's preparation, conduct, and consequences for its categorisation; (ii) A debate over whether or not physical—offline—damage is a necessary feature of cyberterrorism; (iii) A lack of clarity around cyber terminology more broadly; and (iv) Collective fears of that which is ill-understood or seemingly uncontrollable: fears that are stimulated, at times, by media hyperbole. The chapter's second section then locates cyberterrorism within a wider history of terrorist violence, asking whether and how cyber-activities might be located therein. While recognising terrorism's evolving character and notoriously contestable meaning, we argue that cyber-activities of any sort rarely meet the criteria that many would see as necessary for an act to be considered terrorism. The chapter's final section then considers three ways in which this tension might be addressed. These are, first, simply to abandon the concept of cyberterrorism as a misnomer or an inappropriate stretching of the language of terrorism. Second, to engage in further definitional work in order to better clarify the types of activity to which the label cyberterrorism might refer. And, third—our preferred route—to eschew the question of definition altogether and explore cyberterrorism as a social construction rather than a coherent and stable ontological phenomenon. In doing this, we reflect on the importance of debates around definition within this context and beyond, and sketch a diversity of potential research areas for future work in this field.

Key Points

- As the Internet's centrality to social life continues to grow, the 'cyber' prefix has been applied to a growing list of activities and entities.
- Despite its prominence, the term cyberterrorism remains a fundamentally contested one.
- This contestability is a product, in part, of different approaches to the concept's flexibility.

2.2 Defining Cyberterrorism

Although coined in the 1980s (Collin 1997), it was not until a decade later that the concept cyberterrorism really came to prominence. That it did so at this time, in particular, may be linked to two key dynamics. The first, as Bendrath et al. (2007:58) note, was the movement toward a post-Cold War world in which previously stable security imaginaries and assumptions were undergoing dramatic challenges, and rapid, radical, change. A host of seemingly known and predictable threats seemed to disappear with the collapse of the Soviet Union, resulting in the attention of security professionals turning to 'new' types of risk. This presented space for a greater consideration of cybersecurity threats such as cyber-warfare, cyber-espionage, cyber-crime, and, of course, cyberterrorism (Stohl 2014). Second, and just as importantly, this period also witnessed the spread of the Internet and the interconnectivity it made possible: national and international, public and private (Harknett 2003:18). This growing sense of interdependence established new fears amongst security experts and political elites, leading some famously to conclude that, "tomorrow's terrorist may be able to do more damage with a keyboard than with a bomb" (National Academy of Sciences 1991:7).

In the years that have now passed since this earliest interest, the term cyberterrorism has become ever more widely recognised and used. One study from November 2012, for example, estimated that 31,300 magazine and journal articles have now been written on the subject (Singer 2012). This prominence, however, has not translated into anything like consensus on what cyberterrorism means, or how it should be used (something it shares, of course, with the wider concept of terrorism, discussed further below). Thus, some authors, such as Dorothy Denning, are reluctant to identify specific examples of 'cyberterrorism' in their work, preferring to identify, 'damaging acts in support of terrorist objectives' (2010:201–205). Others, instead, argue that identifiable cases of cyberterrorism do indeed exist, and are even willing to include politically motivated website defacement under this term's remit (Olmstead and Siraj 2009:16–17). In the following, we sketch four important reasons for these disagreements. These, we argue, help explain how this term can be applied to activities as diverse as Critical Information Infrastructure disruption, on the one hand, and 'cyber graffiti', on the other (Kostopoulos 2008:165).

The first, and perhaps the most important, reason for the term's contestability is a temporal one. If we divide the perpetration of a terrorist attack into three broadly discrete stages—preparation, conduct, and consequences—it is possible to see how the digital world might be present in any of these. Preparation, for instance, might include target surveillance over the Internet through web mapping programmes such as Google Maps. The conduct of an attack might involve the release of a computer virus, or a Distributed Denial of Service (DDoS) attack that prevents certain websites from functioning. The consequences of an attack, finally, might include permanent damage to digital technologies or data, and so on. Given the myriad ways in which the digital world might be present in an attack, the question becomes which—and how many—of these engagements are necessary to designate such an event 'cyberterrorism'.

One response, and a common one in the academic literature, is to reserve the term for attacks conducted through—and perhaps targeted against—cyber-technologies. Dorothy Denning's (2000) much-cited testimony to the Special Oversight Panel on Terrorism of the US House of Representatives' Committee on Armed Services, for instance, pursued this approach. Here, she positioned cyberterrorism as a product of, 'the convergence of terrorism and cyberspace', arguing:

> It is generally understood to mean unlawful attacks and threats of attack *against* computers, networks, and the information stored therein when done to intimidate or coerce a government or its people in furtherance of political or social objectives (emphasis added).

Defining cyberterrorism in this way leads to a comparatively narrow understanding of this term in which the *target* (or consequences) of an attack differentiate this type of politically motivated activity from others. This approach contrasts markedly with Gordon and Ford's (2003:4) discussion of Denning's testimony in a Symantec White Paper, in which they argue:

> we believe that the true impact of her opening statement ("the convergence of terrorism and cyberspace") is realized not only when the attack is launched against computers, but when many of the other factors and abilities of the virtual world are leveraged by the terrorist in order to complete his mission, whatever that may be.

Although they identify some of the problems associated with excessively broad uses of this term, the understanding developed by Gordon and Ford clearly allows for a much wider spectrum of actions to be discussed as cyberterrorism than does Denning's original account. Indeed, pursuing this broader reading of Denning's formulation, Gordon and Ford (2003:4) are willing to consider understandings of this concept that are sufficiently expansive to incorporate even the online purchase of aircraft tickets for the execution of the September 11th attacks.

The differences between these comparatively narrow and broad approaches to cyberterrorism is reflective of current academic debate in this area. On the one hand, there are authors such as Maura Conway (2002) who wish to distinguish between "terrorist use of computers as a facilitator of their activities" and, "terrorism involving computer technology as a weapon or target" (also Conway 2014). On the other hand are those such as Devost et al. (1997:78) who posit a continuum between terrorism, information terrorism, and pure information terrorism. For these authors, if the target and tools of an attack are 'physical' entities, then the attack is an example of 'traditional terrorism' (Devost et al. 1997:78). However, if either the tools or the target of an attack can be considered 'digital'—London's square mile is offered as an example of a digital target; a hacker conducting a spoofing attack is presented as an example of a digital tool—then the attack is an example of 'information terrorism'. Furthermore, they argue that when target *and* tool are both digital (the example of a Trojan horse in a public switched network is provided) then an attack should be considered 'pure information terrorism' (Devost et al. 1997:78).

If the importance of different stages of an attack's life cycle offers one source of disagreement around the concept cyberterrorism, a second involves the issue of an attack's destructiveness. While many authors reserve the cyberterrorism label for behaviours leading to destruction or damage (physical or otherwise), others, such as Devost et al. (1997:78) are willing to soften this condition. As they argue:

> there are more subtle forms of information terrorism (e.g. electronic fund theft to support terrorist operations, rerouting of arms shipments, etc.) which would still be political crimes, but perhaps more dangerous because they are less dramatic than a 'cyber-Chernobyl', and thus more difficult to detect, and can even appear as 'common' crimes.

A similar flexibility is evident within Kostopoulos' (2008:165) differentiation between three 'basic types of cyberterrorists': the professionals who 'aim at inflicting physical or cyber damage onto victim's resources', the amateurs who 'find pleasure in applying cyber graffiti' and the thieves who 'have immediate personal illicit economic benefit from their actions'. Kostopoulos' emphasis here upon the perpetrator's type and motive thus broadens cyberterrorism to include an array of different behaviours spanning nuisances through to direct attacks. Thus, while a number of scholars argue that, 'violence against persons or severe economic damage' (Conway 2004:84) must occur for an event to be termed cyberterrorism, others believe any terrorist usage of the Internet to constitute a sufficient criterion (Desouza and Hensgen 2003:388).

If the first two areas of contestability are endogenous to the term cyberterrorism and reflect differing levels of importance attached to its constituent parts, the next two are exogenous and concern the way in which the term is used by different actors. So, third, is the regularity with which the term is used interchangeably with other—often also inconsistently used—cyber terminology. As Weimann (2006:132) points out, "…the mass media frequently fail to distinguish between hacking and cyberterrorism and exaggerate the threat of the latter". Conway (2002), similarly, identifies significant confusion between cybercrime and cyberterrorism. Once we recognise the sheer diversity of cyber-terms in contemporary usage—including, cyberterrorism, cybercrime, hacking, cracking, hacktivism, cyber-activism, cyberwarfare, information warfare, and cyberjihad—it becomes easier still to see how the boundaries of cyberterrorism may escape ready identification (see Macdonald et al. 2013:12–13; Jarvis and Macdonald 2014). This porosity has a real risk of introducing analytical confusion into the concept: muddying what is meant by cyberterrorism and any of its related terminology.

Fourth, and alluded to above, is the role of misleading hyperbole around cyberterrorism (Isenberg 2000), in which "[t]he mass media have added their voice to the fearful chorus with scary front page headlines" (Weimann 2006:151). Indicative here are stories such as that in the UK's Daily Mail, headlined, 'Attack of the Cyber Terrorists' which outlined a hypothetical nightmare scenario including thousands of government web pages suddenly disappearing, tens of millions of pounds being wiped off the share price of companies like Amazon and the entire Internet credit card payment system being put in disarray (Hanlon 2007). This hyperbole feeds off a sense of the uncontrollable and unknown integral to cybersecurity concerns. As Pollitt (1998:8) notes, 'The fear of random, violent victimisation segues well with the distrust and outright fear of computer technology'. Cyberterrorism offers a perfect example of this, incorporating the randomness, incomprehensibility and uncontrollability of terrorism with the complexity and seeming abstractness of technology (Cavelty 2007:29). One result, as Ayn Embar-Seddon (2002:1003), suggests, is the media's tendency to label "…any computer break-in by a 12 year-old script kiddie "cyberterrorism"".

The sense of fear that cyberterrorism produces, coupled with media hyperbole and a lack of understanding of modern digital technologies adds further confusion to this term. These factors are contributory, we argue, to the dualism between physical and cyberspace embraced by some writers and commentators as a way of recognising the latter's distinctiveness. Here, actions unlikely to be deemed 'terrorist' in physical space appear to be viewed differently when they occur in a cyber or digital environment. Others, in contrast, prefer a narrower conception of cyberterrorism, in part because this enables consistency with understandings of non-cyber forms of terrorist violence.

Key Points

- Although coined in the 1980s, the term cyberterrorism became increasingly prevalent at the end of the Cold War because of geopolitical and technological developments.
- There is currently little consensus on the meaning of cyberterrorism, with a major tension between narrow and broad understandings of this concept.
- Reasons for this disagreement include differing approaches to the term's elasticity, a broader confusion amongst 'cyber'-terms, and media hyperbole.

2.3   Locating Cyberterrorism

The previous section outlined four of the most significant factors that contribute to the continuing contestability around the term cyberterrorism. In this section, we build on that discussion by asking what value, if any, there is in even attempting to describe cyber-related activities as terrorism.

'Terrorism', as is well known, is a highly contested term with its own politics. How the term is applied, to whom, and in what contexts, should be thought of as a contingent, rather than an objective, decision. It is a decision, in other words that often reflects political interests and agendas as much as any analytical or 'scientific' considerations (Halkides 1995; Jackson et al. 2011; Gibbs 2012). On top of this, the terrorism label also suffers from considerable "'border' and 'membership' problems" of its own (Weinberg et al. 2004:778) in relation to the kinds of political violence to which commentators are willing to see it applied. Thus, although a number of themes do recur across many different understandings of this term—including (instrumental) violence, political motivation, randomness of targets, theatrical or spectacular violence, the creation of fear in a secondary audience, an effort at communication, non-state perpetratorship, and so on—there currently exists nothing approaching a consensual definition of terrorism amongst either academics or policymakers (Laqueur 1997; Silke 1996; Schmid and Jongman 1988; Fletcher 2006; Gibbs 2012). This lack of consensus is important for us because it helps to account for the quite dramatic changes within understandings of terrorism that have taken place over the 200 years that have now passed since the word was first coined. As Jackson et al. (2011:104–105) note, the term terrorism:

> was originally constructed not to describe the actions of non-state actors such as al-Qaeda, ETA or the Fuerzas Armadas Revolucionarias de Colombia (FARC) to whom we are instinctively drawn when we now hear it. Rather, it was created at the time of the French revolution to refer to the actions undertaken by the state against dissidents and dissenters in their own populations.... Moreover, in its original usage it lacked the negative, pejorative connotations that are now inherent to the term. Indeed, even in the aftermath of World War II, when the term became attached to anti-colonial struggles in Asia, Africa and elsewhere, it lacked, for many, the sense of illegitimacy we now frequently attach to it.

As this suggests, there has been considerable change over time in what the term terrorism both denotes—i.e. what it refers to—and what it connotes—i.e. what associations it calls forth when it is used and heard. That this evolution has taken place itself offers some measure of support for proponents of this lexicon's utility for describing cyber-attacks. For, if the meaning of terrorism has altered so dramatically historically, on what absolute grounds might its application to new types of activity might be denied or critiqued?

If the meaning of the term terrorism has altered so dramatically throughout its history, so too have the types of activities typically included under this label. One prominent account of these change is Rapoport's (2012) 'Four Waves of Modern Terrorism', which seeks to situate terrorism both historically and socially by highlighting transformations within terrorist motivations, weapons and strategies. Thus, Rapoport posits a movement through 'Anarchist', 'anticolonial', 'New Left' and 'Religious' types of terrorism from the late nineteenth century to the present day. Another high profile categorisation centres on the distinction between 'old' and 'new' terrorism (see for example, Burnett and Whyte 2005; Laqueur 1999; Neumann 2009; Schmid and Jongman 1988). 'Old' terrorism is frequently used to refer to groups such as the IRA which are viewed as politically motivated, hierarchically organised, and (often) engaged in the discriminate use of violence against targets they deem legitimate. 'New' terrorism, in contrast tends to refer to the emergence of networked, transnational, religiously-inspired organisations engaged in, "mass-casualty attacks against civilians" using "excessive violence" (Neumann 2009:29). And, where 'old terrorism' is often seen as a backlash to dynamics of empire or other forms of domination, 'new terrorism' is frequently interpreted as part of a response to US-led dynamics of globalisation (Cronin 2002:34).

Whilst there are differences between these two accounts of the history of terrorist violence, they share a view that the actual phenomenon of terrorism—aside from the term's meaning and nuances—has itself undergone considerable, qualitative, change over time. Understanding terrorism as a historically variable entity in this way is again important for thinking about cyberterrorism because it further supports the possibility that previously unheard of activities or violences might be legitimately brought under this label. In other words, because the tactics and targets of terrorism change so dramatically over time we might be wary of efforts to rule out any discussion of cyber- activities as terrorist on *a priori* grounds. Indeed, any number of relevant precedents might be readily identified to help advocates of the 'cyberterrorism' label defend its utility, including eco-terrorism, narco-terrorism, bio-terrorism and so on.

The two above points are, perhaps, the most promising general grounds for resisting attempts to deny any validity to the notion of cyberterrorism outright. Given that the meaning of the word terrorism, and the behaviour to which it is typically applied, have changed so dramatically in 200 years, it would seem difficult to argue that it is simply off limits to actions undertaken with a keyboard rather than a bomb or a gun, for example. Yet, the term obviously cannot refer to anything and everything. As the label terrorism becomes attached to an ever-wider range of behaviours, its meaning inevitably becomes further diluted (see Weinberg et al. 2004). Are there, then, any reasons to accept the application of the language of terrorism to new types of activity in principle, but, at the same time, to resist its use in the cyber domain in practice?

One possible challenge here is the widespread assumption that some kind of violence—often understood as a threat to human security—is necessary for an action to be designated terrorism (Schmid and Jongman 1988). Some acts undertaken in the digital realm—whether real at the moment or still only hypothetical—clearly have the capacity to meet this assumption. If a hacker was able to access air traffic control systems, for example, this would obviously meet this criterion, as would the initial examples given by Denning (2000:71), when she described as cyberterrorism "attacks that lead to death or bodily injury, explosions, plane crashes, water contamination, or severe economic loss." It is less clear, however, whether causing harm to property might be considered a form of violence rather than criminal damage, sabotage or vandalism, for instance. Moreover, while we might be willing to use the term violence to describe an individual destroying another's computer with a hammer, we might be more suspicious of its application to an individual's destruction of data, on the same computer, via a virus (see Gordon and Ford 2002:640). If we turn to some of the broadest, umbrella, uses of the term cyberterrorism considered in the opening section—those that allow for the use of the term in relation to any combination of cyber technologies and terrorism—then we might be more wary still.

This criterion of violence might be more manageable than first impressions suggest given that some legal accounts of terrorism—such as the UK Terrorism Act (2000)—expand this term to encompass attacks that bring about, "serious damage to property" in section 1(2)(b). Indeed, as Hardy and Williams (2014) note, section 1(2)(3) of this act, allows for the interpretation of the term to include, the use or threat of action "designed seriously to interfere with or seriously to disrupt an electronic system." On top of this, there are established, and important, traditions of thinking about violence away from direct, physical forms of harm within sociology, peace studies and beyond (for instance, Galtung 1969; Bourdieu et al. 1999). Thus, while removing mention of physical violence may work to dilute the concept's legal and academic value, for some (Post et al. 2000:100), it is at least possible to think through DDoS attacks and the spreading of computer viruses as violences—and therefore potentially as terrorisms—depending on how these terms are themselves approached. As Laqueur (1996:25) notes, "in its long history terrorism has appeared in many guises."

A further issue here is the importance placed upon theatre, performativity, fear and intimidation within many academic definitions of terrorism (Cowen 2006; Conway 2014). Scholars often cite the importance of media coverage and publicity as a primary way of separating this form of violence from others (Tsfati and Weimann 2002). Yet, in the context of 'cyberterrorism', it is possible to argue that, "attack scenarios put forward, from shutting down the electric power grid to contaminating the water supply ... are unlikely to have easily captured, spectacular (live, moving) images associated with them" (Conway 2011:28). These examples of 'cyberterrorism' would undoubtedly cause severe disruption for populations and governments. They might be unlikely, however, to have a traumatising effect on audiences in the way that events such as 9/11 or the 2005 Madrid bombings appear to have done, given the broadcasting and endless recycling of images of those attacks (Gillespie 2006; Shoshani and Slone 2008). For authors such as Conway (2011:28) this absence of obvious theatricality is one important impediment to cyberterrorism's likelihood. On the other hand, this emphasis on terrorism as theatre could simply be viewed as a corollary of the contemporary prominence of organisations such as al Qaeda and their preference for high profile, spectacular attacks (Hoffmann 2001): a preference that is not, by any means, representative of the history of terrorist violence.

Key Points

- Because terrorism has such a varied history, it is possible and legitimate to explore whether new types of activity can be described in this way.
- If violence is seen as a central aspect of terrorism, this poses a challenge for some of the widest understandings of cyberterrorism.
- The importance of theatre and performativity within 'terrorism proper' raises further questions about the plausibility of the cyberterrorism concept.

2.4   Constructing Cyberterrorism

This chapter thus far has argued two things. First, that there exists a considerable diversity of understandings of cyberterrorism. This diversity, we noted, has real implications for thinking about the range of activities that might be incorporated under this concept. Second, we have also argued that the definition or discussion of cyber-activities as examples or instances of *terrorism* is a far from straightforward task. This is not, of course, to say that to do so is impossible, worthless, or doomed to fail. Rather, to suggest that real attention needs to be given to the extent to which actions undertaken in the cyber-domain can be reconciled with the constituent parts or characteristics of terrorism as typically understood (violence, theatricality, and so forth).

Three distinct routes present themselves in response to this dilemma. In the first instance, one might conclude that the types of activity typically labelled cyberterrorism (whether actual or hypothetical) bear so little resemblance to 'terrorism proper' that the term cyberterrorism is itself a misnomer. Here, a parallel debate within contemporary discussion on 'state terrorism' might be instructive, given the recurrence of similar questions therein around the flexibility of terrorism as a concept (compare, for example, Stohl and Lopez 1988; Blakeley 2007, 2009; Jackson et al. 2010; Jackson et al. 2011; Stohl 2014). As Andrew Silke suggested of terrorism and state terrorism: "while there are similarities between the two, they are ultimately two different creatures" (cited in Stohl 2012:45). Cyberterrorism may be viewed in an equivalent way: as similar to, but ultimately different from, non-cyberterrorisms. An argument of this sort does not, of course, necessarily imply that cyber-attacks or their threat are neither serious nor real. Rather, it suggests that whatever such activities might be, they are not cyber*terrorism*. Or, perhaps better, that whatever such activities might be, there is little value in *thinking about* them as cyberterrorism.

A second, and different, response would be not to argue against the label cyberterrorism *per se*. Rather, to appeal instead for greater conceptual and definitional work in order further to clarify the relationship between terrorism and cyberterrorism. With greater interpretive labour and some form of sustained debate around cyberterrorism's meaning, parameters, types, and so forth, it is possible that its specific nature—and its connection to other types of violence—might become gradually clearer. Beyond any conceptual value, greater definitional work of this sort might have additional analytical benefit. Explaining the causes of cyberterrorism, for example, might be made easier by a more sophisticated account of what precisely the term means. Policy issues of response and responsibility might also be assisted by further clarity of denotation (see Legrand 2014; Carlile and Macdonald 2014). There may also be normative reasons for the undertaking of such an enterprise, where greater certainty over cyberterrorism's meaning might assist in our construction of ethical judgements about the (il)legitimacy of a spectrum of cyber-activities. As Meisels (2009:348) has argued on the concept of terrorism more broadly: "Terrorism ought to be strictly defined. It is too central a concept to the moral understanding of our contemporary world to remain obscure."

An alternative approach to each of the above, and the one explored in the remainder of this section, would be to pursue a different type of research agenda entirely. Rather than attempting to define what cyberterrorism is, this approach involves redirecting our gaze instead to *how* cyberterrorism is socially constructed or produced. In the following we outline what such an approach might entail, before discussing some of its strengths and limitations.

In recent years there has emerged a much-discussed burgeoning of academic literature on terrorism. One important, and controversial, dynamic within this has been the development of an explicitly and self-consciously 'critical' scholarship that set out to challenge the assumptions and conventions of Terrorism Studies as previously constituted. One key dimension—or 'face' (Jarvis 2009)—of this scholarship has been a collection of broadly constructivist studies exploring representations of terrorism in political language, popular culture, policy documents and so on (see Jackson et al. 2011:50–73). Because constructivist in tone, these studies tend to share three common ontological premises (see Guzzini 2005). First, that the world around us is constituted, in part, by our beliefs and ideas about it. Second, that our beliefs about the world—the knowledge we have of the world—are themselves socially constructed and maintained: there is no objective, direct correspondence between our ideas and the world of things. And, third, that there is an important dynamic of interaction between these two dimensions such that our ideas and social realities shape, reinforce and impact on one another.

In the context of terrorism, this type of approach leads to the pursuit of very different research projects to those typical of more established studies in this area. As Hülsse and Spencer (2008:572; also Jackson et al. 2011) argue, such a perspective changes the very nature of terrorism, such that this phenomenon is no longer seen as a brute material fact; but rather, as a, "...a social construction, hence a social fact produced in discourse". As they continue, this rethinking of what terrorism *is* has repercussions for how and what might be studied:

> Accordingly, research needs to focus on the discourse by which the terrorist actor and his or her actions are constituted. Terrorism can only be known through the terrorism discourse. This is why we suggest a shift of perspective in terrorism studies, from the terrorist to terrorism discourse. Instead of asking what terrorism is like (what structures, strategies and motivations it has), we need to ask how it is constituted in discourse (Hülsse and Spencer 2008:572).

And, although arguments of this sort may raise philosophical questions about the nature of terrorism's existence, they need not imply any outright denial thereof:

> Analyzing terrorism as a concept that is used in practice by various social actors is not to deny that terrorism exists but to say that what counts as terrorism has to be represented and communicated for it to exist. Hence, it is the use of the symbol terrorism and communities' orientations towards it that are central. Indeed, for a completely constructivist approach, whether or not terrorism exists is less important than *how* terrorism and terrorists are constructed in practice and the identities and policies that are authorized therein (Stump and Dixit 2012:212).

For the phenomenon of cyberterrorism with which this book engages there is obvious and significant scope for the application of social constructivist insights in future research. Building on the recent explorations of terrorism noted above, as well as on related studies within International Relations, Foreign Policy Analysis and Political Science, these works could engage with a range of important, and as yet under-researched, questions. Chief amongst these, we suggest, are the following.

First, there is scope for exploring precisely how cyberterrorism is constructed in political and other forms of discourse. What language is used to describe this phenomenon and its threat, for example? What are the key tropes, predicates, metaphors and other rhetorical building-blocks that structure contemporary discussion? Within this, it would be crucial to explore how cyberterrorism is positioned spatially and temporally. So, for the former, is it depicted as an internal or external security threat, for example? Is it seen as amorphous and everywhere, or a threat that is located only in particular spaces of socio-political life? In terms of the latter, to what extent do claims about cyberterrorism's novelty and uniqueness link to and help exaggerate this threat? How, moreover, is cyberterrorism presented as a threat today, and which referent objects are employed in these constructions: are corporations, national security architectures, ordinary citizens or others seen, typically, as its target? There is scope here also, finally, for exploring the consistency of constructions of cyberterrorism. Do these change over time and across space, or do similar themes emerge in separate discourses? And, crucially, are there deviant, counter-hegemonic, or oppositional discourses at work that challenge seemingly accepted knowledge in this area? Who, if anyone, resists dominant constructions of this threat?

Second, there is also considerable scope for explorations of intertextuality in constructions of cyberterrorism. To what extent, for example, do representations of cyberterrorism link to and build on constructions of terrorism more broadly? Do we encounter the same rhetoric (perhaps of evil, of religious inspiration, of sleeper cells, and so on) being employed to describe this phenomenon (see Jackson et al. 2011:50–73), or are there distinctive rubrics at work in this context? Likewise, are there overlaps with the way the Internet is imagined in other social and political contexts? Do constructions of cyberterrorism rely, for instance, on fears of the digital realm as unregulated and dangerous? If so, do these reproduce or change broader discourses on the cyberworld? And, does the cyber- prefix work to amplify or reduce the constructed threat of cyberterrorism? Finally, to what extent do different representations of cyberterrorism connect to one another? Do policymakers, for example, draw on discursive resources from media or fictional depictions of this threat, and if so which and in what contexts?

A third set of research questions would focus on performative or political questions regarding what discourses of cyberterrorism actually 'do'. For example, how do representations of this phenomenon make possible and/or foreclose particular policy responses? Do constructions of this threat apportion responsibility for mitigating or responding to it, and if so how? Are specific technologies, actors or strategies prioritised in discourses on how to counter cyberterrorism? And, from where does the responsibility of actors privileged in these discourses derive: is it their expertise, or their location in particular socio-political sites, for example? Finally, where do normative questions around issues of legitimacy, rights or justice emerge in discussions of cyberterrorism? If they do, how are these articulated, and what type of limits or exceptions to the range of potential counter-measures are posited?

Fourth, a constructivist approach of this sort would also explore in whose interests discourses on cyberterrorism work. Who, if anyone, benefits from constructions of this entity, and, indeed, from efforts to amplify or minimise the threat that it poses? Are there discernible economic, political or other motivations behind discourses in this area, for example? How one responds to these questions is likely to be impacted by one's epistemological commitments: by the knowledge claims, in other words, one is willing to make. Here, 'thinner' or more 'conventional' constructivist analyses would tend to view cyberterrorism discourses as the creation of particular actors and their interests; as instruments, put otherwise, to achieve certain things. 'Thicker' or more 'critical' constructivisms, in contrast, would tend to view the identities, interests and subject positions of those actors as themselves constituted by discourses on cyberterrorism. Viewed thus, the 'cyberterrorist', the 'security professional' and the interests of each might be deemed part of, not separate from, such discursive frameworks.

As the above suggests, there exists immense scope for constructivist research into cyberterrorism. Such research might, we suggest, offer a valuable route for circumventing some of the difficulties of definition outlined in this chapter's opening sessions. A major strength of a constructivist approach such as that sketched above is that it allows an engagement with the concept of cyberterrorism *in spite of* the definitional complexities and debates that surround it. Cyberterrorism undoubtedly has a social and political existence, even if we believe this to be a purely rhetorical one. Policymakers and experts employ this language, funding is dedicated to its prevention, film producers hypothesise attack scenarios, and academics speculate on its existence and threat in books such as this! However contested a concept it may be, there are good grounds, therefore, for resisting the temptation to abandon it completely. As Jackson (2010:12) argued in relation to the (no less contested) concept of terrorism:

> ...pragmatically, the term 'terrorism' is currently so dominant within existing political structures, the academy, and the broader culture, that critically-oriented and responsible scholars cannot really afford to abandon it without risking marginalisation. ...it must be engaged with, deconstructed, challenged and used in more rigorous ways.

The flipside of this is that an approach of this sort may have limited policy relevance or problem-solving utility for those tasked with preventing, responding to, or assessing the threat of cyberterrorism. Constructivist approaches may be able to contribute far less to the types of debate explored in the later chapters of this book, given their emphasis on *how* cyberterrorism and its threat are constructed. How serious a limitation one perceives this to be will likely depend, in part, on one's view of academic roles and responsibilities. Is it our task, as students or analysts of cyberterrorism to quantify its risk and seek to prevent it? Or is our role to engage with social and cultural productions of 'cyberterrorism' with an eye to deconstructing dominant knowledge claims or practicing other forms of critique? While there are no definitive answers to these questions, there is, undoubtedly, a debate to be had along these lines. And, as outlined in this book's introduction, each of the chapters contained in this edition contributes to this discussion in one way or another.

Key Points

- The difficulties of describing cyber-activities as examples of (cyber)terrorism might be met by abandoning the term altogether, or by working toward a more accurate or consensual definition of this term.
- An alternative approach to either of these is to pursue a constructivist line of enquiry, and ask not *what* cyberterrorism is, but *how* it is constructed.
- An advantage of a constructivist framework is that it helps scholars to engage with this concept in the absence of any settled understanding of its meaning.
- A potential disadvantage might be constructivism's limited problem-solving utility.

2.5 Conclusion

In this chapter we have explored the value as well as some of the challenges associated with the concept of cyberterrorism. In so doing, we argued that there exists a general lack of consensus around fundamental questions relating to this term. The chapter's second section explored the possibility of locating cyberterrorism within the broader historical context of terrorism as itself a fluid and changing phenomenon. Historical variations in the meaning and methods of terrorism, we argued, potentially open space for incorporating cyber-activities under this heading. At the same time, doing so may not be entirely straightforward given the lack of similarity between current understandings of cyberterrorism and widespread assumptions around 'terrorism proper'. The chapter concluded by suggesting three competing ways to confront these challenges in an effort to add direction to an increasingly confused debate. Our view is that a constructivist framework offers the greatest potential for engaging with the concept of cyberterrorism in spite of its challenges, not least because it already exists as a category of discourse and hence social reality.

We finish our discussion, finally, by highlighting Collier and Mahon's useful reminder that, "when scholars take a category developed from one set of cases and extend it to additional cases, the new cases may be sufficiently different that the category is no longer appropriate in its additional form" (cited in Weinberg et al. 2004). This is important, because if we are to allow discussion of cyber-activities under the heading of terrorism, it is likely that this broader concept itself will be changed. This may be or may not be desirable, depending, in part, on one's view of terrorism's analytical, political or normative utility. Nonetheless, it requires consideration, not least given the term's resonance in current academic, political and media discourse.

Key Points

- Research into cyberterrorism needs to move beyond questions of definition, to recognise that cyberterrorism as a category of discourse is already a social reality. As such, it is one that requires serious analytical and critical engagement.
- If we are to allow discussion of cyber-activities under the heading of 'cyberterrorism', then it likely that our broader concept of 'terrorism' will change.

Further Reading and Resources

Conway M (2004) Cyberterrorism: media myth or clear and present danger? In: Irwin J (ed) War and virtual war: the challenges to communities. Rodopi, Amsterdam, pp 79–95

Denning D (2000) 'Cyberterrorism: testimony before the Special Oversight Panel on Terrorism Committee on Armed Service U.S. House of Representatives. http://www.stealth-iss.com/documents/pdf/CYBERTERRORISM.pdf. Accessed 31 Aug 2012

Denning D (2010) Terror's web: how the Internet is transforming terrorism. In: Jewkes Y, Yar M (eds) Handbook on internet crime. Wilan Publishing, Devon, pp 194–213

Gordon S, Ford R (2002) Cyberterrorism? Comput Secur 21(7):636–647

Weimann G (2006) Terror on the Internet: the new arena the new challenges. United Institute of Peace Press, Washington, DC

Weinberg L, Pedahzur A, Hirsch-Hoefler S (2004) The challenges of conceptualizing terrorism. Terrorism Polit Violence 16(4):777–794

References

Anderson K (2009) Hacktivism and politically motivated computer crime. Encurve. http://www.aracnet.com/~kea/Papers/Politically%20Motivated%20Computer%20Crime.pdf. Accessed 3 Aug 2012, pp 1–15.

Bendrath R, Eriksson J, Giacomello G (2007) From 'cyberterrorism' to 'cyberwar', back and forth: how the United States securitized cyberspace. In: Eriksson J, Giacomello G (eds) International relations and security in the digital age. Routledge, Abingdon

Blakeley R (2007) Bringing the state back into terrorism studies. Eur Polit Sci 6(3):228–235

Blakeley R (2009) State terrorism and neoliberalism: the north in the south. Routledge, London

Bourdieu P et al (1999) The weight of the world. Social suffering in contemporary society. Policy Press, Oxford

Burnett J, Whyte D (2005) Embedded expertise and the new terrorism. J Crime Conflict Media 1(4):1–18

Carlile L, Macdonald S (2014) The criminalisation of terrorists' online preparatory acts. In: Chen T, Jarvis L, Macdonald S (eds) Cyberterrorism: understanding, assessment, and response. Springer, New York

Cavelty M (2007) Cyber-terror—looming threat or phantom menace? The framing of the US Cyber-Threat Debate. J Inform Technol Pol 4(1):19–36

Collin BC (1997) The future of cyberterrorism. Crim Justice Int 13(2):15–18

Conway M (2002) Reality bytes: cyberterrorism and terrorist 'use' of the Internet. First Monday 7(11), (n.p.)

Conway M (2004) Cyberterrorism: media myth or clear and present danger? In: Irwin J (ed) War and virtual war: the challenges to communities. Rodopi, Amsterdam, pp 79–95

Conway M (2011) Against cyberterrorism: why cyber-based terrorist attacks are unlikely to occur. Viewpoints: Privacy Secur 54(2):26–28

Conway M (2014) Reality check: assessing the (un)likelihood of cyberterrorism. In: Chen T, Jarvis L, Macdonald S (eds) Cyberterrorism: understanding, assessment, and response. Springer, New York

Cowen T (2006) Terrorism as theater: analysis and policy implications. Publ Choice 128(1–2):233–244

Cronin A (2002/2003) Behind the curve globalisation and international terrorism. Int Secur 72(3):30–58

Denning D (2000) Cyberterrorism. Testimony before the Special Oversight Panel on Terrorism Committee on Armed Services U.S. House of Representatives. http://www.cs.georgetown.edu/~denning/infosec/cyberterror.html. Accessed 4 Feb 2012

Denning D (2010) Terror's web: how the Internet is transforming terrorism. In: Jewkes Y, Yar M (eds) Handbook on internet crime. Wilan Publishing, Devon, pp 194–213

Desouza KC, Hensgen T (2003) Semiotic emergent framework to address the reality of cyberterrorism. Technol Forecast Soc Change 70(4):385–396

Devost MG, Houghton BK, Pollard NA (1997) Information terrorism: political violence in the information age. Terrorism Polit Violence 9(1):72–83

Embar-Seddon A (2002) Cyberterrorism: are we under siege? Am Behav Sci 45(6):1033–1043

Fletcher G (2006) The Indefinable Concept of Terrorism. J Int Criminal Justice 4(5):894–911

Galtung J (1969) Violence, peace and peace research. J Peace Res 6(3):167–191

Gibbs J (2012) Conceptualization of terrorism. In: Horgan J, Braddock K (eds) Terrorism studies: a reader. Routledge, Abingdon, pp 41–62

Gillespie M (2006) Transnational television audiences after September 11. J Ethnic Migrat Stud 32(6):903–921

Gordon S, Ford R (2002) Cyberterrorism? Comput Secur 21(7):636–647

Gordon S, Ford R (2003) Cyberterrorism? Symantec security response. Symantec, Cupertino

Guzzini S (2005) The concept of power: a constructivist analysis. Millenn J Int Stud 33(3):495–521

Halkides M (1995) How not to study terrorism. Peace Rev 7(3/4):253–260

Hanlon M (2007) Attack of the cyber terrorists. The Daily Mail. http://www.dailymail.co.uk/sciencetech/article-457504/Attack-cyber-terrorists.html. Accessed 2 Aug 2012

Hardy K, Williams G (2014) What is 'cyberterrorism'? Computer and internet technology in legal definitions of terrorism. In: Chen T, Jarvis L, Macdonald S (eds) Cyberterrorism: understanding, assessment, and response. Springer, New York

Harknett R (2003) Integrated security: a strategic response to anonymity and the problem of the few. Contemp Secur Pol 24(1):13–45

Hoffmann B (2001) Change and continuity in terrorism. Stud Conflict Terrorism 24(5):417–428

Hülsse R, Spencer A (2008) The metaphor of terror: terrorism studies and the constructivist turn. Secur Dialog 39(6):571–592

Isenberg D (2000) Electronic pearl harbor? More hype than threat. CATO Institute. http://www.cato.org/publications/commentary/electronic-pearl-harbor-more-hype-threat Accessed 7 Sept 2012.

Jackson R (2010) In defence of 'terrorism': finding a way through a forest of misconceptions. Behav Sci Terr Pol Aggr 3(2):1–15

Jackson R et al (2010) Introduction: terrorism, the state and the study of political terror. In: Jackson R et al (eds) Contemporary state terrorism: theory and practice. Routledge, London, pp 1–11

Jackson R et al (2011) Terrorism: a critical introduction. Palgrave, Basingstoke

Jarvis L (2009) The spaces and faces of critical terrorism studies. Secur Dialog 40(1):5–29

Jarvis L, Macdonald M (Forthcoming) What is cyberterrorism? Findings from a survey of researchers. Terrorism Polit Violence

Jarvis L, Macdonald S (2014) 'Locating Cyberterrorism: how Terrorism researchers use and view the Cyber Lexicon', Perspectives on Terrorism 8(2):52–65

Kostopoulos G (2008) Cyberterrorism: the next arena of confrontation. Comm IBIMA 6(1): 165–169

Laqueur W (1977) Terrorism. Little Brown, Boston, MA

Laqueur W (1996) Postmodern Terrorism: New Rules for an Old Game. Foreign Affairs 75(5)

Legrand T (2014) The citadel and its sentinels: state strategies for contesting cyberterrorism in the UK. In: Chen T, Jarvis L, Macdonald S (eds) Cyberterrorism: understanding, assessment, and response. Springer, New York

Macdonald S, Jarvis L, Chen T, Lavis S (2013) Cyberterrorism: a survey of researchers. Cyberterrorism project research report (No. 1), Swansea University. Available via: www.cyberterrorism-project.org

Malcolm JG (2004) 'Testimony of Deputy Assistant Attorney General John G. Malcolm on Cyberterrorism', before the Senate Judiciary Committee Subcommittee on Terrorism. Technology, and Homeland Security, February 24, Washington, DC

McGuire M (2014) Putting the 'cyber' into cyberterrorism: re-reading technological risk in a hyperconnected world. In: Chen T, Jarvis L, Macdonald S (eds) Cyberterrorism: understanding, assessment, and response. Springer, New York

Meisels T (2009) Defining terrorism—a typology. Crit Rev Int Soc Polit Philos 12(3):331–351

National Academy of Sciences (1991) Computers at risk: safe computing in the information age. Computer Science and Tele-communications Board. National Academy Press, Washington, DC

Neumann P (2009) Old and new terrorism. Polity Press, Cambridge

Olmstead S, Siraj A (2009) Cyberterrorism: the threat of virtual warfare. CrossTalk: J Defense Software Eng 22(7):16–18

Pollitt M (1998) Cyberterrorism—fact or fancy. Comput Fraud Secur 3(2):8–10

Post J, Ruby K, Shaw E (2000) From car bombs to logic bombs: the growing threat from information terrorism. Terrorism Polit Violence 12(2):97–122

Rapoport D (2012) The four waves of modern terrorism. In: Horgan J, Braddock K (eds) Terrorism studies: a reader. Routledge, Abingdon, pp 41–62

Schmid A, Jongman A (1988) Political terrorism. Transaction, Piscataway

Shoshani A, Slone M (2008) The drama of media coverage of terrorism: emotional and attitudinal impact on the audience. Stud Conflict Terrorism 31(7):627–640

Silke A (1996) Terrorism and the blind men's elephant. Terrorism and Political Violence 8(3): 12–28

Singer PW (2012) The cyber terror bogeyman. Armed Forces J. http://www.brookings.edu/research/articles/2012/11/cyber-terror-singer. Accessed 16 Sept 2013

Soo Hoo K, Goodman S, Greenberg L (1997) Information technology and the terrorist threat. Survival 39(3):135–155

Stohl M (2012) State terror: the theoretical and practical utilities and implications of a contested concept. In: Jackson R, Sinclair J (eds) Contemporary debates on terrorism. Routledge, Abingdon, pp 43–49

Stohl M (2014) Dr. Strangeweb: or how they stopped worrying and learned to love cyber war. In: Chen T, Jarvis L, Macdonald S (eds) Cyberterrorism: understanding, assessment, and response. Springer, New York

Stohl M, Lopez G (eds) (1988) Terrible beyond endurance? The foreign policy of state terrorism. Greenwood Press, New York

Stump J, Dixit P (2012) Toward a completely constructivist critical terrorism studies. J Int Relat 26(2):199–217

Tsfati Y, Weimann G (2002) www.terrorism.com: terror on the Internet. Stud Conflict Terrorism 25(5):317–332

Weimann G (2006) Terror on the Internet: the new arena the new challenges. United Institute of Peace Press, Washington, DC

Weinberg L, Pedahzur A, Hirsch-Hoefler S (2004) The challenges of conceptualizing terrorism. Terrorism Polit Violence 16(4):777–794

Chapter 3
Rethinking the Threat of Cyberterrorism

Panayotis A. Yannakogeorgos

3.1 Introduction

To terrorize, people must feel an immediate danger. Human, physical and apprehensive emotional reaction to terrorist operations must occur for something to be cyberterrorism proper. Although the intent to do harm against physical processes exists in terrorist tracts, the capability is currently lacking according to Director of National Intelligence James Clapper statement that "We have seen indications that some terrorist organizations have heightened interest in developing offensive cyber capabilities, but they will probably be constrained by inherent resource and organizational limitations and competing priorities" (Clapper 2012). While low hanging fruit might exist that low skill actors could exploit, the targets that could cause events of national significance and terrorize a population are too complex for current capabilities. Furthermore, in the cops-and-robber game between cyber offenders/defenders, the defense does not remain static, and thus, the human capital of aspiring cyberterrorist organizations must remain on the cutting edge of the latest defensive posturing of critical infrastructure technology. Therefore, the emphasis of this chapter is to provide clarity on the operational realities of the misuse of cyber means by terrorist organizations to achieve operational objectives of recruitment, radicalizations, fundraising planning and execution of attacks. To do so, a clear distinction is drawn between cyber enabled terrorist operations, and operations in cyberspace creating physical effects equivalent to an armed-attack. Such categories include, but are not limited to:

- Misuse of the Internet for the logistics of a terrorist network (including radicalization, recruitment, financing).
- Cyber enabled terrorist attacks as observed in improvised explosive device to complex command and control and communications during an operation.

P.A. Yannakogeorgos (✉)
US Air Force Research Institute, 2047 Home Park Trail, #310, Prattville, AL 36066, USA
e-mail: yannakog@gmail.com

T.M. Chen et al. (eds.), *Cyberterrorism: Understanding, Assessment, and Response*,
DOI 10.1007/978-1-4939-0962-9_3, © Springer Science+Business Media New York 2014

- The threat of cyber terrorism to critical infrastructure and disruption of civilian networks.
- The emergence of psyber warfare to intimidate or mobilize populations without physical presence.

3.1.1   Definitions

To place these and other phenomena within their respective contexts, I introduce a spectrum of terrorist cyber operations. Drawing clear distinctions between the misuse of information technology for communications, reconnaissance, planning, recruiting, fundraising and cyber armed-attacks on critical infrastructure on the one hand and cyber-attacks on the other end of the spectrum is important (Kohlmann 2006). A broad definition of cyber attack risks treating crime and espionage as armed attack/threats to peace. Espionage, crime and armed attacks necessitate responses that fall under mutually exclusive sections of US Code, and relevant international laws. It is increasingly important that discussions of malicious cyber activities are accurately described. The operating paradigm required to address the terrorist misuse of the Internet to conduct espionage or criminal activities is not the same as that required for them to succeed in creating effects through a cyber operation that would rise to the level of an armed-attack.

As noted in preceding chapters, there is no concrete legal definition of cyberterrorism internationally (Hardy and Williams 2014). According to United States Code terrorism is defined as: "premeditated, politically motivated violence perpetrated against noncombatant targets by subnational groups or clandestine agents; "terrorist group" means any group practicing, or which has significant subgroups which practice, international terrorism". Cyber terrorism is more than just adding the cyber prefix to terrorist activity. I adopt the definition of cyberterrorism is "the use of computer network tools to shut down critical national infrastructures (such as energy, transportation, government operations) or to coerce or intimidate a government or civilian population" (Lewis 2002). As noted in the previous chapter: "The sense of fear that cyberterrorism produces, coupled with media hyperbole and a lack of understanding in relation to modern digital technologies adds further confusion to the term cyberterrorism" (Jarvis et al. 2014). This section aims to provide clarity to both the technological and operational aspects of how terrorists use cyberspace. To achieve their strategic objectives or missions across a spectrum of cyber conflict.

While the Internet is the term that is most often used synonymously with "cyberspace," cyberspace contains a lot more parts and portions that just the global network of networks. It includes both open multi-function, networks, such as the Internet, and closed, fixed-function networks, such as air traffic control systems. Both kinds of networks have different operating paradigms. Open networks have multiple functions, and have increasing utility as more people join. Closed networks typically have fixed functions, which includes operating critical infrastructure and key resources on which modern societies depend. For the purpose of this chapter, I therefore distinguish between the applications of open networks, and national security applications of closed networks.

> **Key Point**
>
> - There is no concrete legal definition of cyberterrorism internationally.
> - Cyberspace is more than the Internet.

3.2 A Spectrum of Cyber Enabled Terrorist Operations

It would seem from headlines that the amount of power that has come into non-state actors hands as a result of cyber space has qualitatively altered the amount of power violent non-state actors may wield. In a recent Senate Committee hearing, U.S. Cyber Commander and Director of the National Security Agency (NSA), General Keith Alexander, reported that:

"Cyber programs and capabilities are growing, evolving, and spreading; we believe it is only a matter of time before the sort of sophisticated tools developed by well-funded state actors find their way to groups or even individuals who in their zeal to make some political statement do not know or do not care about the collateral damage they inflict on bystanders and critical infrastructure. The United States is already a target. Networks and websites owned by Americans and located here have endured intentional, state-sponsored attacks, and some have incurred degradation and disruption because they happened to be along the route to another state's overseas targets. Our critical infrastructure is thus doubly at risk. On a scale of one to ten, with ten being strongly defended, our critical infrastructure's preparedness to withstand a destructive cyber attack is about a three based on my experience. There are variations in preparedness across sectors, but all are susceptible to the vulnerabilities of the weakest." (General Keith 2013).

Key in the statements above is that current observed activity by state and non-state actors amounts to degradation or disruption of service. This is a key distinction given that the effects of destruction require high-level knowledge of very specialized computer networking protocols, industrial equipment, cryptography, and computer programming. The disruption and degradation of service, including those targeting U.S. banks in 2012/13, General Alexander refers to in his Congressional testimony targets commercial information and communication technology, not industrial control systems. Thus, I distinguish between the terrorist misuse of information and communication technology, and the targeting of industrial control systems.

This section examines the areas where cyberspace and terrorism overlap, an area with an already extensive bibliography (United Nations Office on Drugs and Crime 2012). The enhancement of terrorist organizations capabilities for planning attacks, anonymizing their communications, recruiting, radicalizing and inciting individuals; and financing their operations, presents challenges due to the global reach and always on nature the Internet. The technical realities underlying all aspects of this problem will be emphasized in order to contribute to better informed frameworks and policies.

Spectrum of Cyber Enabled Operations

Influence
• Promotion of violence, recruitment and radicalization of both violent and non-violent sympathizers that will work towards strategic objectives.

Planning
• Facilitate the preparation of acts of terrorism.

Execution
• Real time communications and influence to maximize operational efficiency and feelings of terror in public.

This section described the spectrum across which terrorist may misuse elements of cyberspace focusing on radicalization, recruitment, fundraising/planning, espionage, disruptions and finally armed attack. In the figure above, a spectrum of terrorism misuse of the Internet is shown.

(1) *Cyber Influence*: The misuse of cyberspace to influence populations with propaganda. This could be to create sympathizers to the cause. Included in this category is the process of radicalization and recruitment via the cyber domain.

(2) *Cyber Planning*: Timothy Thomas coined the term cyberplanning as "the digital coordination of an integrated plan stretching across geographical boundaries that may or may not result in bloodshed" (Thomas 2003). Thomas' definition in his work include examples of both influence and execution of attack. One could argue that recruitment and command and control of an operation via cyberspace does not amount to planning. Planning is more akin to intelligence, surveillance and reconnaissance.

(3) *Operational Execution*: The misuse of cyberspace to actually cause physical destruction. This is beyond the realm of the hypothetical when it comes to detonating improvised explosive devices via cellular technologies. What has still not been observed is the terrorist capability to attack industrial control systems via electronic means to cause physical effects.

This section will delve into all of the above categories and conclude with a though experiment of what strategic cyberterrorism might look like.

3.2.1 Cyber Enabled Recruitment and Radicalization

The battle against Islamist and other forms of extremism is being fought not only in the physical realm, but also in the realm of the mind. Cybersecurity experts tend to focus on spectacular worst case scenarios in which terrorists plunge the United States into chaos with a few strokes of a keyboard. Radicalization and recruitment of individuals via the Internet is just as significant of an issue (Braniff and Moghadam 2011). Due to the "always on" nature of the Internet, and the ability to direct information across the globe instantaneously, militants in Somalia and Yemen are able to influence U.S. citizens. The 2010 *National Security Strategy* clearly reflected the growing recognition of the security threat posed by domestic terrorism and emphasized the need to address the problem:

Several recent incidences of violent extremists in the United States who are committed to fighting here and abroad have underscored the threat to the United States and our interests posed by individuals radicalized at home.

Before the availability of Internet technology, U.S. citizens who were sympathetic to Al-Qaida's objectives had a higher cost of entry into a terrorist organization. In today's information society, a plethora of terrorist recruiters are misusing the Internet with success in recruiting U.S. citizens of Muslim faith or Arab decent. Two cases, discussed below, have revealed that the Internet is a hotbed for radicalizing and recruiting individuals.

3.2.1.1 Phases of Internet Radicalization

As discussed below, the Internet is used to recruit and incite people residing in the West to commit terrorist acts. The psychological factors in the making of a terrorist have been analyzed in depth in a multitude of sources already (Borum 2011). My intent here is emphasis rather than breaking down the multitude of factors that could lead to an individual's radicalization either online or offline.

Prior to the widespread distribution of Internet technology, if an individual was not in a place that would expose them to terrorist propaganda, such as Somalia, it would be difficult for a Muslim living in the West to interface with radicals. The Internet changes this, facilitating the radicalization process through its misuse globally. Ordinary Muslims may now have access to content and social networks that are always available online and produced by individuals espousing an Islamist ideology intended to influence people into violent action (Abbasi and Chen 2008).

Internet misuse is a necessary condition for the global radicalization of ordinary people. If a terrorist does not misuse the Internet, then radicalization would not occur. People who would not have otherwise come into contact with extremist content in their local environment, but can now access this information on the Internet, may find validity in the text and begin to support the Islamist cause in some form. If a terrorist does not misuse the Internet, then necessarily radicalization catalyzed or incubated online could not occur. People who would not have otherwise come into

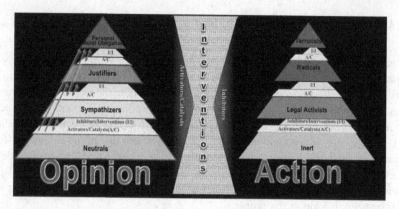

Fig. 3.1 Two pyramid model for radicalization

contact with extremist content in their local environment, but can now access this information on the Internet, may find validity in the text and begin to support the Islamist cause in some form.

To journey from reading to attempting to detonate a car full of explosives in New York City's Times Square is long. Further studies have shown that demonstrate the linkage between ideas and action. For the purpose of this chapter, the pyramid below is used principally to illustrate and contextualize the findings of the McCauley two-pyramid model of radicalization (McCauley 2011). The graphic represents the separation of being radicalize to sympathize with ideas and opinions from the process of being radicalized into action (Fig. 3.1).

The dynamics within the two pyramid model can be correlated with four phases of radicalization according to the New York Police Department (NYPD): pre-radicalization, self-identification, indoctrination and jihadization phases (Silber et al. 2007).

Pre-radicalization: The neutral Internet user neither sympathize nor has motivation to conduct acts of terrorism. Reading terrorist content on the Internet is not a sufficient condition for radicalization. A person must find the content appealing, repeatedly visit a website, and reach out and lend support to the terrorist. Websites, social media, electronic mail and Internet forums are three mediums through which a radical political or religious organization can influence people. Social networks, web sites, and Internet forums are areas on the Internet where people, regardless of their geographic location, can discuss a variety of topics. This includes but is not limited to radical topics in a self-referential environment where dissent is infrequent and when it occurs, is overwhelmed with responses designed to negate the dissenting opinion. A person going into a radicalized chat room or forum with the intention of passively perusing the material or debate the ideas on a website is not misusing the Internet.

Self-identification: During this phase a person may have been catalyzed to begin seeking information about an extremist organization by a real world event. By beginning to browse the extremist web, the individual is exposed to the numerous sites promoting extremist ideologies that misrepresent Islamic theology. When a person first reads and begins to subscribe to the terrorist's ideology, the terrorist is not aware of the individual's metamorphosis into a violent political being. In time a radicalized individual reaches out and offers support to the terrorist via the Internet. The terrorist accepts this, and directs the individual to other websites and terrorists on the Internet. After trust is established between the terrorist and newly radicalized person, the terrorist informs the radicalized individual of other radicalized individuals in the same locale. These other individuals have also been radicalized by the terrorist via his website. This leads to the new radicals utilizing the Internet to discuss actions they can take to assist the terrorist and his cause. Since they are geographically proximate to one another, it is possible for them to continue their meetings in the real world rather than on the Internet. Thus, the terrorist has radicalized people to form a terrorist cell remotely.

Indoctrination occurs when the individual sympathizes begins to devote time to exploring terrorist websites, and forming online relationships with individuals who promote extreme ideologies. Written content or speeches posted on the Internet by a militant may influence non-radicals in a way that leads to the acceptance of militant actions as legitimate recourse against perceived injustice. One expert notes that: "the ability of social network sites to keep an individual embedded in multiple non-overlapping social networks reduces the leverage of any one view over an individual—organizing low-commitment movements such as Occupy Wall Street are far easier, but demanding total commitment to one cause becomes more difficult" (Blair 2013). A radical website serves to lure in an ordinary person who was otherwise looking for information without the intention of joining a terrorist organization. Radical websites mix legitimate content with propaganda designed to disturb a person's psyche.

Violent Extremism: Radicalization is complete when the influenced individual moves from the opinion pyramid into the realm of actively supporting a specific terrorism act, or facilitating it in some material way beyond the realm of ideas (Canna et al. 2012). Radicalization is the transformation of a neutral person from one who is not inclined to commit or support a terrorist act to one who does. This leads to the jihadization phase, in which the online relationship between individuals serves to incite terrorist actions by encouraging violent action, and providing the material required for this action (Silber et al. 2007).

It must be noted that radicalization is not a one-way street. Throughout the process of there are both inhibitors, such as family and friends intervening, and other counter-activators, such as a deeper understanding of a political event that can reverse the individual's course during the radicalization process.

Two examples illustrate the reality of online radicalization for recruitment through ideas and later action. On November 23, 2009 the U.S. Federal Bureau of Investigation announced the largest (unclassified) recruitment operation on U.S. soil. The Al-Shabab organization, an Al-Qaida affiliated group, successfully recruited several young men using the Internet as a propaganda distribution tool. The FBI reported that Al-Shabab does not have any significant on-the-ground presence in the U.S., preferring to create Internet videos targeting a younger crowd of Muslims living in the west (Elliott 2009). The recruits emigrated from Somalia to the U.S. over a decade ago to return to their homeland and engage in combat on behalf of Al-Shabab.

Major Nidal Malik Hasan began to open fire on U.S. military and civilian personnel at Fort Hood, Texas, on November 6, 2009. The gunshots drew most of the media attention to the event however the shooting began at the ideological level. Maj. Hasan's mind was influenced in part by Jihadists exchanging information via the Internet. Online, he was able to network with radicals whom he may have been acquainted with in the offline world. Participating in a self-referential online Islamist environment catalyzed the radicalization process, transforming Maj. Hassan into a terrorist who preferred to influence policy with violence.

There has been much coverage of the Major's ties to the Dar al-Hijrah mosque in Great Falls, Virginia where he attended sermon and held his mother's funeral in 2001. His presence in the Mosque coincided with the attendance of two of the perpetrators of September 11. Further, the radical cleric Anwar al-Awlaki, who has been accused of supporting attacks on troops and supporting terrorist organizations was the Imam at the mosque. While it is uncertain as to whether or not Maj. Hasan had begun to sympathize with Islamist ideology prior to attending services at this mosque, it has become clear from investigations that he continued to stay in contact with Mr. al-Awlaki via the Internet. Indeed, the U.S.-educated radical cleric has been described as an e-recruiter and spiritual motivator. Thus, understanding the general process of Internet misuse and how it may catalyze the radicalization process is important in the context of how terrorists use the Internet.

A future with mobile broadband devices and increasing interpersonal connections is indicative of the need for terrorists to influencing perceptions to achieve effects in the real world effects.

However, such efforts extend well beyond the terrorist efforts to radicalize and recruit individuals to their cause and have broader implications for U.S. operations.

Cyber Technique: Secret Preperatory Communications VoIP is a technology used to make telephone calls either to another computer using a VoIP application, or to a traditional phone line (Federal Communications Commission, *Voice Over Internet Protocol: Frequently Asked Questions*). Although counterterrorism investigators can conduct surveillance on calls that are placed from VoIP services to traditional phone services by monitoring a suspected telephone line, a computer-to-computer VoIP communication can be encrypted using features embedded in VoIP software such as Skype, Viber, or Microsoft's Instant Messenger. Thus, if law enforcement personnel intercept the data stream containing voice data packets, they will not be able to listen in on such encrypted conversations in real-time. Hence, VoIP gives terrorists the secure communications capabilities that can thwart sophisticated law enforcement efforts.

Cyber Technique- Alternate Domain Name Systems: The Internet protocol is a critical Internet resource that allows for universally resolvable URLs as a result of the domain name system (DNS) root system that is managed by the Internet Corporation for Assigned Names and Numbers (ICANN). Although this allows for a free and open Internet to function, the standards and protocols that the ICANN uses to maintain the domain name registries can be used by individuals, ad hoc networks, and nation-states to design and deploy an alternative domain name systems (altDNS) that can either be independent of, or "ride on top" of, the Internet. A corporate LAN, such as ".company name" for internal company use, is an example of the first. When a group wishes to ride over the global DNS root but incorporate its own pseudo top-level domain, core operators of the pseudo domains can use specific software resources to resolve domains that are globally accessible within their alternative DNS system. American audiences can experience what it is like to enter an alternative DNS universe via The Onion Router (TOR) network. Downloading the Onion Router package and navigating to websites one would prefer to visit anonymously (the typical use of TOR), one may point the TOR browser to websites on the ".onion" domain and mingle where the cyber underworld has started shifting the management of its business operations these days to avoid law enforcement and to add another layer of protection to their personas.[1]

Should significant usage of such shadow Internets occur, it could become very challenging for counterterrorist operators to target radicalization networks who now operate on darks corners of the open Internet. The Internet will thus be open to masses of new users who may not have entered the space because of the English language barrier. This presents a significant human capital challenge as the cultural and linguistic challenges facing the counter terrorism community today will only intensify. Thus, even finding adversary propaganda to counter or reverse the radicalization process will become more challenging.

3.2.2 Planning, Command, Control and Communications

The use of information technology in an actual terrorist operations differs from its use to promote ideas and drive otherwise neutral parties into action. Today, terrorists have demonstrated that in all terrorist operations, there is some cyber element contained within it. This may range from the use of encryption technology to protect the communications in the preparatory phases of an attack to the actual command, control and communications during an operation.

Cyber Technique: **Secret Preparatory Communications**: Voice over IP is a technology used to make telephone calls either to another computer using a VoIP application, or to a traditional phone line (Federal Communications Commission,

---

[1] *Disclaimer*: This is for informational use only. Any action undertaken by the reader of this article on the .onion domain is at his/her own risk.

Voice Over Internet Protocol: Frequently Asked Questions). Although counterterrorism investigators can conduct surveillance on calls that are placed from VoIP services to traditional phone services by monitoring a suspected telephone line, a computer-to-computer VoIP communication can be encrypted using features embedded in VoIP software such as Skype, Viber, or Microsoft's Instant Messenger. Thus, if law enforcement personnel intercept the data stream containing voice data packets, they will not be able to listen in on such encrypted conversations in real-time. Hence, VoIP gives terrorists the secure communications capabilities that can thwart sophisticated law enforcement efforts. Encryption technology is another methods terrorists use for secret communications in the preparatory phases of an attack. *Mujaheeden Secrets* is one that includes include 256-bit encryption, variable stealth cipher encryption keys, RSA 2,048-bit encryption keys and encrypted chat-forum-supported instant messaging (Tung 2008). These technologies allow terrorist to plan operations that could go beneath the radar of law enforcement agencies tasked with discovering potential plots.

Cyber Technique: Real Time Cyber Command, Control and Communications
The world has already witnessed the embryonic stage of the sophisticated use of information technology to enable a terrorist operation during an operation. During the siege of Mumbai on November 26–29, 2008. During this attack, members of the Lashkar-e-Taiba organization used information technology to not only shape public opinion and increase terror, but also gain real-time information on the government response mid-incident to drive operational decision making (Gupta and Kumaraguru 2012). Twitter in particular was an effective tool where the public could see the terrorist redirect the operation. In tweet, the terrorists from a central command post monitoring the media noted that "See, the media is saying that you guys are now in room no. 360 or 361. How did they come to know the room you guys are in?... Is there a camera installed there? Switch off all the lights... If you spot a camera, fire on it... see, they should not know at any cost how many of you are in the hotel, what condition you are in, where you are, things like that... these will compromise your security and also our operation..." (Oh et al. 2011). Further, evidence for the use of cyber means to enable operational decision making is observed in the communications related to a decision if the operatives should murder a hostage who was residing in the Taj Hotel. One of the field operatives reported the identity of a hostage to a remote controller via satellite phone. Using a search engine, the remote controller was able to obtain the detailed information about the target: "Terrorist: He is saying his full name is K. R. Ramamoorthy. Handler: K. R. Ramamoorthy. Who is he? ... A designer ... A professor ... Yes, yes, I got it ...[The caller was doing an internet search on the name, and a results showed up a picture of Ramamoorthy] ... Okay, is he wearing glasses? [The caller wanted to match the image on his computer with the man before the terrorists.] Terrorist: He is not wearing glasses. Hey, ... where are your glasses? Handler: ... Is he bald from the front? Terrorist: Yes, he is bald from the front ..." (Oh et al. 2011). Thus, the use of social media has been observed to enhance terrorist planning in the midst of an operation to challenge counter terrorist forces contributing to the response.

Key Points

- There is an important distinction between terrorist misuse of ICT and the targeting of industrial control systems.
- Terrorists make use of ICT in several ways.
- A terrorist capability to attack industrial control systems via electronic means to cause physical effects has not been observed so far.

3.3 Cyber Operations

Spectrum of Cyber Operations

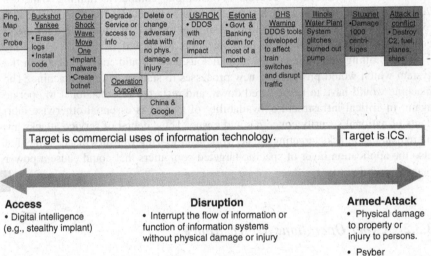

Ping, Map or Probe	Buckshot Yankee • Erase logs • Install code	Cyber Shock Wave: Move One •Implant malware •Create botnet	Degrade Service or access to info	Delete or change adversary data with no phys. damage or injury	US/ROK • DDOS with minor impact	Estonia • Govt & Banking down for most of a month	DHS Warning DDOS tools developed to affect train switches and disrupt traffic	Illinois Water Plant System glitches burned out pump	Stuxnet •Damage 1000 centri- fuges	Attack in conflict • Destroy C2, fuel, planes, ships
			Operation Cupcake	China & Google						

Target is commercial uses of information technology.	Target is ICS.

Access
- Digital intelligence (e.g., stealthy implant)

Disruption
- Interrupt the flow of information or function of information systems without physical damage or injury

Armed-Attack
- Physical damage to property or injury to persons.
- Psyber Operations

3.3.1 Cyber Operation: Distributed Denial of Service Disruption

Above the threshold of criminal activity but below the threshold of cyber attack are incidents and events that, while malicious and disruptive, are aggressive but do not rise to the level of attack. The oft cited cases of distributed denial of service (DDoS) disruptions are an example of cyber crime, not cyber warfare. While instances of cyber espionage may have long term negative consequences for national security, the act of stealing the data itself is not an armed attack.

Despite private-sector arguments to the contrary, industrial espionage is not an act of terrorism or war and would not require a military response by the government.

Instead, a crime has occurred that may have been prevented with better information security. Federal reform to laws such as the Computer Fraud and Abuse Act would to allow the private sector firms to protect themselves by actively responding to thefts of data—to include destroying what was stolen.

The U.S. Department of Defense Dictionary of Military and Related Terms defines non-lethal weapons as "A weapon that is explicitly designed and primarily employed so as to incapacitate personnel or materiel, while minimizing fatalities, permanent injury to personnel, and undesired damage to property and the environment." DDoS disruptions, manipulating data in logistics networks, and other software or hardware incidents would fall into this category.

The kinds of methods that were used in Estonia and Georgia, and the US financial sector in late 2012, certainly did not rise to the level of an armed attack. These disruptions, however, were targeting the network layer of the Internet. This is not true of all denial of service events. So-called "SNMP overloads" are an example of non-network overload DOS attacks. For example, computers running Windows 2000 to program PLCs on an ICS network could be targeted by malicious code that exploited an unpatched vulnerability, causing an "SNMP overload." In this case, a computer's memory, not the network connection, would fail.

By exploiting this vulnerability, a malicious actor would cause a hiccup in the system which would prevent *any* new processes to start on a target machine. The machine would have to be powered down, and restarted in order for it to operate again. In critical infrastructure, availability of system is essential otherwise incidents of national security concern could ensue. Thus, denial of service attacks are more than just attacks targeting the network layer leaving websites inaccessible, but also the application layer of specific targeted computers that could cause a power plant to shut down.

3.3.2 Cyber Operation: Armed-Attack

Existing international legal frameworks provide clarity on how law and policy should treat instances of cyber warfare. The *Tallinn Manual on the International Law Applicable to Cyber Warfare*, perhaps the most comprehensive work on the issue today, offers the definition of a cyber attack as a "cyber operation, whether offensive or defensive, that is reasonably expected to cause injury or death to persons or damage or destruction to objects" (Schmitt 2013).

Cyber events breaching the threshold of armed attack require the use of cyberweapons, which differ substantially from Flame, Zeus, Gauss or other malicious code. While a cyberweapon can be software code designed to attack ICS, it can also be hardware flaws introduced into critical systems. Due to the complexity of ICS, the skill level required to discover vulnerabilities (so-called zero day vulnerabilities), as well as the infrastructure required to find targets, gain access, and execute the attack requires significant financial and human capital. To date, only Stuxnet has risen to the level of a cyber incident that could be considered an armed attack under international law as it caused the physical destruction of objects. One could argue for the Shamoon virus impacting the oil sector is a close second as it destroyed virtual records, which were restored without widespread destruction or physical injury. However, the impact of Shamoon was on the business applications of cyberspace, and not the ICS systems that could cause national security concerns.

Some argue that a terrorist group, with the right team of experts, could conceivably use software designed to gain illicit access to a system could, at the flip of a switch, cause destruction, which is what makes cyber warfare "different." This oft cited claim is groundless. Access software, such as Flame or Duqu, might serve the same function as a laser guiding a weapon to the final target. However, a targeting laser is only part of a weapons system. A missile's payload is the actual object in the weapon system creating destructive effects. Similarly, in the case of a cyberweapons, operators may use previous access to guide a weapon towards a designated target. However, a separate package will have to be developed to exploit vulnerabilities and cause physical effects resulting in death or destruction.

One might further argue that the package could be contained within the set of tools conducting reconnaissance, hence the "cyber attack at a flip of a switch" arguments. However, given the unique characteristics of an ICS, a cyberweapon could not create an effect without being tailor made for a specific target's digital and physical environment. In short, this requires ICS schematics, network maps, teams of coders, cryptographers, and a virtual environment replicating the target on which to test the effects of the weapon before deployment. To argue otherwise is akin to making a claim that a SEAL commander would turn a reconnaissance mission on its first foray into tracking Bin Laden into an all out assault against the complex in Abottabad, and expect a high-likelihood of success. Both instances require diligent preparation prior to execution.

3.3.3   Cyber Target: Industrial Control Systems

Industrial control systems (ICS) are different from commercial ICT applications in business or social environments. ICS are an entirely different because they use technologies that are largely different from in organization and complexity from the technology underpinning the Internet. They are designed to automate complex physical processes on which industry, utilities, transportation management, building controls, automobiles, etc. rely on to function.[2] By their nature, ICS were not designed with security in mind (Kruger 2012). Should ICS processes fail, physical events will stop functioning, leading to damage to equipment, physical destruction, and possibly loss of life.

---

[2] ICSs are composed of SCADA/EMS, DCS, PLCs, RTUs, IEDs, smart sensors and drives, emissions controls, equipment diagnostics, AMI (Smart Grid), programmable thermostats, building controls.

Unlike Internet service and content providers, their focus is on reliability and safety. Modern societies are dependent on their proper functioning. ICSs are comprised of distributed remote access points which allow users to remotely connect to infrastructure connected on a particular ICS network. The systems direct or indirect connections to the Internet allows for the remote monitoring of industrial and critical infrastructure (Mannes 2006). Nations and industries rely on these computer networks to efficiently maintain the machinery that a country runs on. Thus ICS is itself a critical system that allows countries to function (Swearingen et al. 2013). Thus, malicious software designed to cause harm to these systems pose significant threats to human and national security. Currently, terrorists have not demonstrated the necessary capabilities to conduct the vulnerability research and design tools to cause effects in these highly complex systems.

Many ICSs have hardware configurations that are cyber vulnerable and cannot be patched or fixed. For example, the threat to the U.S. power grid is very tangible, and has been so for a very long time, due to the Aurora vulnerability. During a DHS exercise, hackers were tasked with hacking into the information system of a power generator. Succeeding in gaining remote access to the generators SCADA control system, the hackers were able to physically destroy the generator. The Aurora vulnerability, as this exploit is called, lends credence to the suggestion that the manipulation of computer code can be just as effective in destroying critical infrastructure as a missile would. Since utility companies now use SCADA to remotely monitor and access controls for their services, and because SCADA is a ubiquitous technology, U.S. utilities are just as vulnerable to these sorts of attacks. Indeed, several incidents have already occurred in which destruction of the physical elements which an ICS controlled occurred because of poor system design. One such example is the 2009 Sayano-Shushenskaya hydroelectric dam explosion due to a computer misconfiguration that resulted in the destruction of four hydroelectric turbines, the plan, in addition to the cascading effect of environmental damage ("Insulating oil spreads along Siberian river after hydro disaster," RIA Novosti).

Recent events such as Stuxnet have show, they ICS are now becoming a target of sophisticated teams of computing experts. As one expert notes: "In addition to a very broad range of more traditional computer networking attack (hacking) skills, Stuxnet required people who understood mechanical engineering (to determining the likely breaking points of centrifuges (PLC programming (to create the PLC rootkit), electrical engineering (to understand the impacts of manipulating frequency converers, (human-machine interface (HMI) systems, and engineering workstations (to understand how to conceal attack symptoms from system developers)" (Oliver 2013). Additionally, it is not enough to be able to produce the computer code. A terrorist organization would have to develop the testing ground that simulate the target cyber-physical environment to test the malicious software to ensure the desired effects are produced.

In comparison with crime ware or rootkits which are easy to find and purchase for small sum of money, the operational differences between cyber operations targeting ICS and ICT drive up the cost in both human and financial capital. Therefore, a terrorist organization that has the intent of using cyberspace to cause physical effects in the physical world will have to either recruit or train the team of experts required to mount the operation. Hence, although ICS is more likely to be the kind of system terrorist organizations would target in order to create real-world effects akin to the often cited "cyber 9/11," the cost of entry continues to be high. With that in mind, the next session will demonstrate that there is potential of the use of ICT to create physical destruction when the weapon is content and the target is human mind.

3.3.4 Psyber Operations

The misuse of cyberspace by terrorists to create effects that are destructive to person and property is not isolated to industrial control systems, or computer systems. As has been observed in recent protest movements, such as in Iran (2009) the Pittsburg Summit (2009) and Athens (2008), individuals are using converged Internet and cellular technologies, such as Twitter and Facebook, to spontaneously organize themselves into groups that begin with non-violence, but may turn to violent protest. Further, cyber means have caused more than one suicide as a result of an individual being intimidated online (Wiederhold and Riva 2012). One study found that the Internet can facilitate protest and other anti-regime activities through the formation of groups, and that there is an impact of the technology on their subsequent collective actions (Fielder 2013).

Thus, the human mind can be a target of influence to either mobilize, intimidate or terrorize a targeted population. This is what I term psyber-operations: The use of social interactions to mobilize populations without a physical presence to cause physical effects.

The starting point of this concept is that Internet content produces emotions. As discusses above, radicalization of an individual can be the end result of this emotion. Psyber operations is not radicalization. As Aristotle noted: "In forming opinions we are not free: we cannot escape the alternative of falsehood or truth. Further, when we think something to be fearful or threatening, emotion is immediately produced" (Aristotle, *De Anima*). A psyber operation is one in which terrorists could manipulate mass public emotion to create this effect that causes individuals or masses of people to spontaneously move in specific ways in response to messaging. This is not conjecture but has already been observed. Take for example the events transpiring within India in August of 2012. After SMS and social media messages falsely warning of impending Muslim attacks against migrants in across Northeastern India, including major cities such as Bangalore., mass panic and exodus of targeted populations ensued. Indian Prime Minister Manmohan Singh warned, "What is at stake is the unity and integrity of our country" (Yardley 2012). Thus, this is an example of a psyber operation. Hence, what occurs in the content of cyberspace can have a very real impact on a general populations' perceptions of the world around them, leading them to feel terrorized and having broad implications for national security.

Key Points

- DDoS and cyber espionage do not rise to the serious level requiring a military response.
- To date, only Stuxnet has risen to the level of a cyber incident that could be considered an armed attack under international law.
- Although ICS is likely to be terrorist targets to create real-world damage, the cost of entry continues to be high.
- The human is the target of psyber operations.

3.4 A Hypothetical Case of Strategic Cyber Terrorism

Terrorists will target institutions regardless of whether there is a way to do it via cyberspace. Many argue that the cost of entry is low in cyberspace because it is relatively simpler to launch the digital version of a bank robbery, meddle with a hospitals HVAC system, or release the floodgates on a damn. While it is true that one requires significantly less resources to conduct a cyber attack, the reason for this has less to do with the nature of the domain, and more to do poor product development, design and implementation. Software developers, hardware manufacturers and network providers face no liability or responsibility for the systems they produce or operate. As a result they have no reason to deliver secure products to the marketplace. This risk will really begin to manifest as cloud computing takes hold and resulting breaches will destroy multiple points within the healthcare establishment rather than a single hospital. Below are some effects that a cyber attack could have based on brainstorming.

The below thought experiment better illustrates the potential of the strategic use of cyberspace by a terrorist organization during an attack to amplify the effects of a physical attack. The skill level required is high and team based. The overall goal is to maximize carnage, delay and diminish first responder capabilities, cause maximum fear and uncertainty among parents, and overwhelm the ability of government to protect citizens. Much of the operation requires inside knowledge of first responder TTP and planning and prepositioning in advance. Effects could be tailored based on manpower and destructive capability available.

Phase/step of operation	Effect
Phase Zero	A violent extremist organization has successfully recruited an unknown number of operatives to launch an attack within a medium sized city of strategic importance. Some operatives were to be part of the actual attack, while others are sympatric to the cause. Over several months, the plotters used cyber and non-cyber means to plan a hybrid operation that combines cyber and physical means to achieve their organizational objectives
Move Zero	False reports into 911 system flush first responders far from first target [fires/hostage situation, etc.]

(continued)

(continued)

Phase/step of operation	Effect
Phase 1, Stage 1	Bomb at target goes boom
Stage 2	Hack traffic signal controls to snarl traffic and delay first responders from arriving at scene
Stage 2a	Disable cell towers near scene of attack via a distributed denial of service disruption
Stage 2b	Manipulate water pressure in fire hydrant system by spoofing SCADA system monitors to indicate hydrant has full pressure, but there is none at hydrant)
Stage 3	Broadcast video feeds from target area over Internet—stage public executions? Provide commands for phase 2, 3 for forces; Phase 4 forces are embedded in local media (either physically or tapping into their channels and cell phones) and texting status/intel to C2 forces
Stage 3a	Plant false updates/messages in incoming stream to crisis command center
Stage 4	Disrupt the power grid; disable rail/metro system
Phase 2 Stage 5	Attack local area hospitals, disable their back-up generators, hack life support controls in ICU, start killing ER doctors and nurses
Phase 3 Stage 6	Mortar rounds into elementary schools, police stations, fire stations [followed up by IED's at choke points]; truck bombs in local schools disguised as ambulances or school busses
Phase 4 Stage 7	Find where they will have the news conference with Mayor, etc. Preposition snipers; assassinate leaders (or bomb in podium?) on live TV
Stage 8	If an airport nearby, mortar rounds to crater runway at 500' intervals (prevent anyone taking off/landing) hit fuel depot, passenger terminal. Blow up as many planes as possible—especially if you can get them during takeoff/ landing. Also, hit National Guard armory at airport
Stage 9	Hack into sewage treatment plant/water treatment plant controls; create mayhem (longer term health effects—cholera, typhoid, dysentery etc. outbreaks beyond initial attack days to weeks)

The limited insight offered in the hypothetical case study above could become a reality if the application of solutions to specific problems are not realized. Since technological skills and capability do not remain static, it is useful to be aware of the potential for the strategic use of cyberspace by terrorist organizations. Anticipating this danger means affecting the near-term future by increasing investments in cyber technology while beginning to promote legislation that would require all critical infrastructure and key resource operators to comply with a risk based approach to secure both legacy and next generation network and computing environments to the highest standards (Pollet 2002). No defense will be perfect. However, keeping the current status quo between nation-states and terrorist organization within the ICS environments will rely that we continue to maintain and increase the cost of entry to conduct armed-attacks in cyberspace.

Key Point

- In a hypothetical case, terrorists could use a cyber attack to amplify the effects of a physical attack but it would require a high level of skill and preparation.

3.5   Conclusion

Many terrorist organizations are advancing their use of cyberspace to meet their tactical, operational and strategic objectives. This proves cyberpower is becoming increasingly important as a strategic environment for nation-states, and violent non-state actors alike. The intention of this chapter was to conduct an investigation into the role that cyberspace plays in shaping terrorist operations. By examining what is observed in the terrorist use of the domain, I offer that the use of cyberspace by terrorist organizations, and the ability to cause physical effects via cyber are mutually exclusive. Illustrations of the difference between a spectrum of cyber enabled operations and cyber operations showed this difference. The ability of Al-Shabab to recruit US citizens for operations abroad, and Anwar al-Awlaki to radicalize a US service and has drawn attention to the reality of e-recruiters being able to identify, appeal to and radicalize vulnerable individuals. The "always on" two-way transfer of information via the Internet gives terrorist organization the ability to direct information across the globe instantaneously, encrypted and anonymously. We have seen that terrorist planning and execution is increasingly migrating towards cyberspace. Both the political and technical aspects of the Internet complicate policy responses to this emergent threat. The practical importance of all this is to craft appropriate counter-terrorist policies that have the right balance between security and privacy.

Further, we are not at the point in time where terrorists can cause malicious effects of national significance against critical infrastructure. Their human capital and financing, and the complexity of the target set is not sufficient to cause the over-hyped "cyber 9/11." However, overlooked is the potential for psyber warfare. In the near-term, this is the more likely use of cyber to create physical effects. When all these elements are blended together, we get the extreme example of a hypothetical strategic use of cyberspace by a terrorist organization.

Further Reading

Cebula JJ, Young LR (2010) A taxonomy of operational cyber security risks
Hildick-Smith A. Security for critical infrastructure SCADA systems. http://www.sans.org/reading_room/whitepapers/warfare/1644.php. Accessed 27 Apr 2013
Kruglanski AW, Fishman S (2006) The psychology of terrorism: "syndrome" versus "tool" perspectives. Terrorism Polit Violence 18(2):193–215
Sugarman DB, Willoughby T (2013) Technology and violence: conceptual issues raised by the rapidly changing social environment. Psychol Violence 3(1):1
Torres Soriano MR (2012) The vulnerabilities of online terrorism. Stud Conflict Terrorism 35(4):263–277
Weiss J (2012) Ensuring the cybersecurity of plant industrial control systems. Power 156(6):26

References

Abbasi A, Chen H (2008) Analysis of affect intensities in extremist group forums. Terrorism Informat 18(2):285–307

Blair D (2013) Back to the future: understanding radicalization through a social typology of media, past and present. Topics for operational considerations: insights from neurobiology & neuropsychology on influence and extremism—an operational perspective, strategic multi-layer assessment periodic white paper

Borum R (2011) Radicalization into violent extremism I: a review of social science theories. J Strat Secur 4(4):2

Braniff B, Moghadam A (2011) Towards global jihadism: al-Qaeda's strategic, ideological and structural adaptations since 9/11. Perspect Terrorism 5(2)

Canna S., St. Clair C, Chapman A (2012) Neurobiological & cognitive science insights on radicalization and mobilization to violence: a review. Strategic multilayer assessment. JS/J-3/DDGO OSD/ASD (R&E)/RFD/RRTO

Clapper JR (2012) Unclassified statement for the record on the worldwide threat assessment of the US Intelligence Community for the Senate Select Committee on Intelligence. Office of the Director of National Intelligence, Washington, DC

Elliott A (2009) Charges detail road to terror for 20 in U.S. New York Times, p A1

Federal Communications Commission. Voice over internet protocol: frequently asked questions: http://www.fcc.gov/voip/. Accessed 27 Apr 2013

Fielder JD (2013) The Internet and dissent in authoritarian states. In: Yannakogeorgos PA, Lowther AB (eds) Conflict and cooperation in cyberspace: the challenge to national security. Taylor & Francis, New York, pp 161–194

General Keith B (2013) Statement of General Keith B. Alexander, Commander, United States Cyber Command/Director, National Security Agency before the Senate Committee on Appropriations

Gupta A, Kumaraguru P (2012) Twitter explodes with activity in Mumbai blasts! A lifeline or an unmonitored daemon in the lurking? https://repository.iiitd.edu.in/jspui/bitstream/123456789/26/1/IIITD-TR-2011-005.pdf

Hardy K, Williams G (2014) What is 'cyber-terrorism'? Computer and internet technology in legal definitions of terrorism. In: Chen T, Jarvis L, Macdonald S (eds) Cyberterrorism: understanding, assessment, and response. Springer, New York

Jarvis L, Nouri L, Whiting A (2014) Understanding, locating and constructing cyberterrorism. In: Chen T, Jarvis L, Macdonald S (eds) Cyberterrorism: understanding, assessment, and response. Springer, New York

Kohlmann EF (2006) The real online terrorist threat. Foreign Aff 85:115

Kruger DA (2012) Thwarting large scale ICS reconnaissance and attacks

Lewis JA (2002) Assessing the risks of cyber terrorism, cyber war and other cyber threats. Center for Strategic & International Studies, Washington, DC

Mannes A (2006) The terrorist threat to the Internet. In: Forest JJF (ed) Homeland security: protecting America's targets. Vol. III: critical infrastructure. Praeger Security International, Westport, pp 339–353

McCauley C (2011) Group desistence from terrorism: dynamics of actors, actions, and outcomes. Presented at the Royal Institute for International Relations (Egmont Institute), Brussels. www.egmontinstitute.be/speechnotes/11/111010/Clark-McCauley.pdf. Accessed 25 June 2013

RIA Novosti (2009) Insulating oil spreads along Siberian river after hydro disaster. http://en.rian.ru/russia/20090818/155846126.html. Accessed 20 Aug 2009

Oh O, Agrawal M, Rao HR (2011) Information control and terrorism: tracking the Mumbai terrorist attack through twitter. Inform Syst Front 13(1):33–43

Oliver EP (2013) Stuxnet: a case study in cyber warfare. In: Yannakogeorgos PA, Lowther AB (eds) Conflict and cooperation in cyberspace: the challenge to national security. Taylor & Francis, Boca Raton, pp 127–160

Pollet J (2002) Developing a solid SCADA security strategy. In: Sensors for industry conference, 2002. 2nd ISA/IEEE, IEEE, pp 148–156

Schmitt MN (ed) (2013) Tallinn manual on the international law applicable to cyber warfare. Cambridge University Press, New York

Silber MD, Bhatt A, Analysts SI (2007) Radicalization in the west: the homegrown threat. Police Department, New York

Swearingen M, Brunasso S, Weiss J, Huber D (2013) What you need to know (and don't) about the AURORA vulnerability. Power 157(9):52

Thomas TL (2003) Al Qaeda and the internet: the danger of 'cyberplanning'. Parameters 112–123

Tung L (2008) Jihadists get world-class encryption kit. http://www.zdnet.com/jihadists-get-world-class-encryption-kit-1339285480/

United Nations Office on Drugs, & Crime (2012) The use of the Internet for terrorist purposes. United Nations Publications

Wiederhold BK, Riva G (2012). Online social networking and the experience of cyber-bullying. Annual review of cybertherapy and telemedicine 2012: advanced technologies in the behavioral, social and neurosciences, vol 181, p 212

Yardley J (2012) Panic seizes India as a region's strife radiates. The New York Times, p A1

Chapter 4
Putting the 'Cyber' into Cyberterrorism: Re-reading Technological Risk in a Hyperconnected World

M.R. McGuire

4.1 Introduction

The perception that "cyberspace is used by terrorists to spread propaganda, radicalise potential supporters, raise funds, communicate and plan" (UK Cabinet Office 2012) has become a central tenet of government policy across the world. Such claims have been enthusiastically endorsed by law enforcement agencies who constantly remind us that terrorists have "a clear interest in hacking skills" and in combining "real attacks with cyber attacks" to produce a threat that is inexorably "rapidly expanding" (HS Newswire 2010). By contrast, many academics and strategic commentators have argued that cyber terrorism is a construct which may have been somewhat overinflated. They suggest that the little concrete evidence there is around cyberterrorism indicates either that truly devastating attacks are too expensive and complex to conduct effectively (cf. Conway 2007, 2012) or that our fears about cyberterrorism have over-inflated its real threat (Weimann 2004; Singer 2013; Bowman-Grieve 2014) Others have been more direct in their critique, suggesting cyberterrorism is a convenient myth (Green 2002), a term of art that has as much to with political expediency as with material strategic risk.

Such doubts are clearly seen in the context of threat assessments of cyberterrorism where two critical questions have emerged. The first centres upon the supposed novelty of the offence. That is, whether the involvement of Information Communication Technology (ICT) indicates a new and substantive category of terrorist acts, or whether cyberterrorism is an empty category, one which has only gained credibility from the portentous, (but ultimately misleading) name attached to it (cf. Whiting et al. 2014). A second variety of challenge centres more directly upon risk—the extent to which terrorist uses of ICT might translate into substantive harm (where this includes harm either to human victims or to infrastructures). In this

M.R. McGuire (✉)
Department of Sociology, University of Surrey, Surrey GU2 7XH, UK
e-mail: m.mcguire@surrey.ac.uk

T.M. Chen et al. (eds.), *Cyberterrorism: Understanding, Assessment, and Response*, DOI 10.1007/978-1-4939-0962-9_4, © Springer Science+Business Media New York 2014

chapter, I want to consider a far less discussed (though arguably more basic) question about the potential risks of cyberterrorism. This centres directly upon the 'what-it-is' which defines the offence—i.e. (information) technology and its relationships to the intents and aims of motivated individuals. It is somewhat surprising that developed analyses of technology as a tool for furthering terrorist causes remain lacking—especially given its role as an apparently necessary condition for the cyberterrorist construct. In what follows, I aim to consider the relationship between terrorism and the use of technology in more detail and to critically challenge some of the assumptions around what (and how) the latter contributes to the former. Central to this analysis will be some recurring confusions about the criminogenic potentials of technology in general—in particular the extent to which (as this is often now put) technology 'enables' offending, at least in any substantive causally agentic sense. I will argue that it is only by developing a more coherent understanding of the socio-technic relations which underpin cyberterrorism that a robust evaluation of its threats can be made.

Key Points

- Governments across the world have expressed concerns about the terrorist use of cyberspace.
- Academic and other commentators tends to be more circumspect about the cyberterrorism threat.
- Lacking so far has been any substantive analysis of what technology actually is: the focus of this chapter.

4.2 Technological Crime

Information technology related offending has been bestowed a seemingly unique status within the criminological field. For, unlike crimes which use technology incidentally, this is crime which is fundamentally *dependent* upon technological artefacts. This dependency upon technological, as well as human, agency has already generated a number of conceptual problems around cause and culpability for other (supposedly) novel forms of ICT based offending such as 'cyber' stalking or 'cyber' bullying (cf. McGuire 2007, 2012). Where the 'cyber' prefix is applied to terrorist activity an even more uncertain exercise in criminal taxonomy arguably results. That there are risks posed by increased access to ICT has never been in doubt. As early as 1988, the Morris worm (Schmidt and Darby 2001)—one of the first viruses to be successfully transferred across networks—had indicated the extent to which ICT might offer a resource for misuse that was palpably different from traditional offending. When coupled with destructive ideologies and a determination to act upon these, a 'doomsday' mechanism for harm and criminality was perceived to have emerged—one which, at the extreme, threatens a kind of 'digital armageddon'

(Parks 2003; Clarke and Knake 2010). The true force of the resulting threat has been vigorously debated (See for example, Yannakogeorgos 2014; Wilson 2014; Conway 2014; Stohl 2014) but without more detailed consideration being paid to the *means* which both define and facilitate this offence, it is hard to see how useful conclusions can be drawn. After all, citing ICT when characterising the cyberterrorist threat seems no more satisfactory a form of explanation than saying that WW2 was won 'because of' superior military technology or that television 'causes' violence. Whether modelling or risk assessing cyberterrorism, a far better understanding of the way human agents use technology seems required—in particular, how technology can be causally agentic to an action.

Our willingness to invoke technology as a 'cause' is not limited to claims about cybercrime. There has been a widespread tendency to perceive technology as having a determining effect upon social life, with the association between historical epochs and particular technologies (iron age, industrial age, information age etc.) counting as one obvious example of this. This willingness to accept that technological change in some sense 'determines' social change has also been a recurring theme of many more sophisticated accounts of economic and social phenomena. Marx' famous declaration in the Poverty of Philosophy that, "the hand-mill gives you society with the feudal lord; the steam-mill society with the industrial capitalist" (1847:202) has often been taken as one of the paradigmatic assertions of what has been called 'technological determinism' (cf. Bimber 1990). In fact Marx' views on technology were a great deal more subtle than this. Rather, he argued for a properly developed 'critical' theory of technology, one able to acknowledge the contributions of technology to social life whilst also locating these within structures of power which technology extends or reinforces (cf. Feenberg 2002). Though Marx never fully developed such a theory himself, his challenge has been one that was taken up (in very different ways) by later theorists such as Heidegger (1949), Marcuse, Ellul, Habermas, Feenberg and Steigler amongst many others.

Crucial to the critical theory Marx proposed was a rejection of 'instrumental' views of technology—the idea that technology is a neutral object, something 'out there' waiting to be used by humans—with good or bad intent (Feenberg 2002). By rejecting instrumentalism about technology, Marx insisted upon its function as a *social* object, something that is not just a product of social processes but which actively shapes those who use it. Yet in spite of the challenges to instrumentalism posed by Marx and later critical theorists within the Frankfurt School (notably Marcuse and Habermas), this view remains the default position on technology. A locus classicus of technological instrumentalism is of course to be found in the claims of the gun lobby, which rejects any idea that there is a gun 'culture' which might itself influence gun use. Instead, it clings resolutely to the familiar mantra that 'guns don't kill people, people do', thereby seeking to minimize regulation of gun technologies. By contrast, the cyberterrorist threat has generated a far greater readiness to attribute causal power to technology. The obvious inconsistencies here are one indication amongst many others of just how uncertain our understanding of the interface between human and technical agency is, and how poorly risk assessments of technology have been conceptualised to date.

The willingness to accede disproportionate causal power to ICT flies in the face of plausible evidence about criminal uses of previous technologies—even very early examples. We know for example that naval technologies were fundamental to the spread of piracy throughout the Mediterranean in the ancient world (Konstam 2008). Similarly it was not just the discovery of gold in the New World that helped spread piracy across the Atlantic but the advent of new navigational devices such as the compass (ibid). And the advent of the stirrup did not just change the nature of warfare (White 1964) but, when linked with the new road technologies of the eighteenth century onwards, facilitated a significant rise in property crime. And as with cyberterrorism, it even generated a 'new' criminal type—the highwayman. Nor can the influence of communications technology upon crime be exclusively associated with the internet era. For example, the Roman Cursus Publicus, or postal system, not only facilitated wider communication but also widespread criminal activity (Lemke 2013) much like the development of printing led to a major rise in forgery and fraud and the consequent development of our current copyright legislation system (cf. Deazley et al. 2010). Equally, if not more striking, were the contributions to criminality of the new telegraph and telephone networks of the 19th and early 20th centuries. This was not limited to murder, theft or fraud but also the furthering of subversive causes equally destructive to the social order as anything cyberterrorism has yet produced. For example, during the Chartist uprisings of the 1840s the authorities expressed regular concerns that these new communications networks were being used to co-ordinate anti-state subversion. Indeed, John Lewis Ricardo—the chairman of Electric Telegraph Company—was so concerned about threats against telegraph clerks from Chartist 'terrorists' that he demanded police protection (Mather 1953).

Yet for all these historical precedents there was never any sense at the time that defining criminality in terms of specific technologies was a useful thing to do. This striking departure from contemporary obsessions cannot be put down to any lack of coherent thinking about technology at the time. Though it is true that the term 'technology' did not become widely used until the nineteenth century, classical concepts of technology—such as *techne*—arguably allowed for far more sophisticated thinking than is currently found. In particular *techne* suggested that technology should be associated with *human* doing or making, not just with the artefacts that result (cf. McGuire 2012:12ff). Commentators on more recent technologies have been equally unwilling to coin any special terminology for technological offending such as 'printing crime', 'telephone crime' or 'bicycle crime'. This cannot be because the impacts of such technologies upon society, or upon offending has been any less significant than the internet. There are good reasons to suppose that new communications technologies like the telegraph network were just as revolutionary and had just as sensational an impact upon the public imagination as the internet. A key question then emerges. What explains these inconsistent perceptions of technological crime and what implications does this have for our understanding of cyberterrorism and the threat it poses?

Key Points

- Cyberterrorism is fundamentally dependent upon information communication technology (ICT) both as a concept, and for its execution.
- The relationship between technology and criminal activity is imperfectly understood.
- One sign of this are the disproportionate criminal impacts attributed to ICT when compared to other equally risky technologies.

4.3 The 'Cyber' in Cyberterrorism

The sense that ICT produces a criminality 'unlike' other forms of offending (technological or otherwise) appears to rest upon two basic assumptions:

(I) Spatio-temporal Scale—ICT based threats are 'different' because they further wider spatio-temporal distributions of criminal activity.
(II) Destructive Scale—ICT based threats are 'different' because they further potentially more harmful or destructive criminal activities.

When the use of ICT is coupled to the cyberterrorist trope these arguments acquire even greater force—with at least three (progressively more serious) forms of support it has been linked with (see amongst many others, Weimann 2004; Wykes and Harcus 2010; Brickey 2012; Bachmann 2014; Chaps. 5, 6 and 7 this volume).

(1) ICT as an organising, communicating or radicalising tool.
(2) ICT as a tool for facilitating an attack upon other ICT—i.e. national networks, or digital resources.
(3) ICT as a tool for facilitating significant human injury or other damage—the 'digital armageddon/pearl harbour view.

There seem to be important interrelations amongst these potential activities. For example a web fora might be used to distribute tools such as malware for an attack on networks. Or a network attack could (we are told) lead to physical destruction, such as malware being used to make a plane 'drop from the sky' or a DDoS attack upon a power station causing system failure and consequent destruction.

Given the sheer range (and potential impacts) of these deployments of ICT it is important to be clear that both of the above assumptions which support them—Spatial Scale and Destructive Scale—can be challenged. For example, the kinds of spatial redistributions of offending suggested by the first assumption are not unique to ICT. Rather, such redistributions have been witnessed many times within the history of communications technologies. And arguably many of these have been no less notable in terms of scale—for example, both the telegraph and postal networks created globally connected communication systems. It also seems clear that there are many other technologies which parallel, if not exceed the destructive potentials of ICT. Chemical or biological technologies constitute perhaps the obvious example here, though threats raised by far less sophisticated technologies should also not be overlooked. Striking support for this can be seen in the fact that one of the technologies that was key to the successful 9/11 attack was not the internet, but simple pocket knives.

In spite of their implications, such objections have not been widely considered. One result has been a readiness to ignore evidence around the genuine threat landscape constituted by cyberterrorism—not least the failure to identify even one unambiguous cyberterrorist attack (cf. Conway 2011). This means that the high-risk status attributed to cyberterrorism depends more upon the possible than the actual. That is, upon counterfactual claims such as '*if it were the case* that some major ICT based attack were to occur then *it might be the case* that cyberterrorism threatens catastrophic outcomes'. Of course appeals to counterfactuals are not without justification within risk assessments. It makes sense that security and law enforcement take them seriously since we expect those employed to protect us to guard against possible as well as actual risk. Yet it is of course also true that in the realm of the possible almost anything might be 'possible'.

A further (hidden) premise is therefore required to explain why we appear so willing to invest in protecting against the potentials of cyber terror rather than other technology based threats that may be far more devastating (such as global warming or genetic modification). This premise ultimately depends upon a particular weighting of the probabilities involved—one which implies that cyberterrorism is 'more possible/serious' than other technology based terrorist threats. But is this weighting justified, and can definitive probabilities be distributed in such a way? The evidence is not promising—especially given how poorly the probabilities around technology based risks are currently understood. Take for example attempts to develop the technique of 'Probability Risk Assessment' (PRA), which aims to "define and quantify the probability that an adverse event will occur" (Taylor et al. 2002). PRA was pioneered within the hi-tech environment of NASA, but almost immediately faced difficult questions. For example, during the development of the Shuttle programme a probablistic risk assessment commissioned by the USAF estimated there to be a 1 in 35 chance of a solid rocket booster failure in the Challenger Shuttle (Bedford and Cooke 2001). However NASA discounted this and came up with their own (very different) 1 in 100,000 figure (Bedford and Cooke ibid)—a telling indication of the subjectivities underlying such estimates. These huge disparities in weighting are an obvious warning about trying to define definitive metrics of risk—as the tragic outcome of the Challenger miscalculation emphasized. Effective PRA also depends upon a capacity to calculate the prior probabilities of risks and this, in turn, requires substantive background data. Unfortunately, given the relative novelty of cyber threats major data gaps exist which mean that PRA is not typically carried out in cybersecurity scenarios (Taylor et al. ibid). The repeated failures of cyber experts to predict many of the large scale, significant hacks which have occurred or the misplaced predictions of cyberterrorist attacks which never materialised, emphasizes why such caution is sensible.

Key Points

- ICT-based threats have been fore-grounded over other technology threats because of their spatial and temporal reach, and destructive potentials.
- Other technologies, however, also exhibit these properties.
- The lack of data around cyber threats means that risk analysis is forced to depend upon probability estimates.
- Probability estimates face significant methodological challenges.

4.4   Technology, Agency and Intent in the Law

There is an alternative to the uncertain art of defining probabilistic measures of cyberterrorist threats. Rather than focussing upon risk directly, this approach towards prevention would take the more indirect approach of analysing continuities between technology and cyber terrorist aims. For, by placing greater emphasis upon the material contributions of ICT to cyberterrorism far more reliable threat assessments may be attainable. After all, if ICT is 'the' key factor in furthering this threat, a better understanding of this relation seems likely to be more useful than analogies based upon incomplete probability weightings.

Key to developing this line of thought effectively is a more cogent sense of technological *causation*—the extent to which a technology contributes towards realising specific goals. At present however this is not a relation that is very well understood. Take for example the legal context—surely a central resource for clarifying how the question of technological agency can be handled. A first, important point to note here is that, within most jurisdictions, cyberterrorist offences do not require any necessary connection to technology for them to count as a distinctive category of crime. Instead, such acts are usually prosecuted under more general definitions of terrorism. For example within UK law, terrorism is defined under section 1 of the Terrorism Act, 2000, with the Anti-Terrorism, Crime and Security Act, 2001 adding extra provisions, Part of the definition is harm based (subsection 2) and it is only here where anything like a concept of cyberterrorism emerges since any action is deemed to count as 'terrorist' if it "is designed seriously to interfere with or seriously to disrupt an electronic system" (TA 2000 sub-section (2)(e), See Chap. 1, this volume for a discussion of the legal basis to cyberterrorism). The inadequacy of this legal conception is evident enough for it is clearly permits many actions which may have no relation to terrorism (such as a hacktivist style trespass) to be treated as terrorist acts (ibid). US law is more replete in this area (both in terms of volume and provisions), but remains equally vague about the role technology plays in defining cyberterrorism as an offence. The term is introduced without definition under the deterrence and prevention of cyberterrorism provision in s814 of the USA PATRIOT Act, 2001 and is associated with outcomes such as illicit access to computers or malware transmission (cf. s1030 of Title 18 of the PATRIOT Act[1]). But such actions again seem to blur with many other offences against computers which would *not* be classified as terrorist, though, uniquely, s1030 does stipulate misuse of computers which could lead to physical injury, or threats to public health and safety (s1030 5B, (iii) & (iv)). In general then, not only is there no requirement for a cyberattack to cause injury for it to be defined as 'terrorism' (ibid)—the precise causal contribution of technology required for this to be classed as an offence is also usually very unclear.

As it stands, most legal conceptions of the use or misuse of technologies like ICT are framed in 'instrumentalist' terms, as acts almost wholly dependent upon the intent of an actor. The UK CPS guidelines make this very clear in the case of weapons technologies, stating that, "Although some weapons are more serious than others the nature of the weapon will not be the primary determinant, as this will depend on its intended use" (CPS 2010). The complications law faces in clearly associating culpability with specific technological outcomes seem related to more general complications around what has been termed the 'duality of artefact function' (Kroes and Meijers 2006)—the observation that an artefact's function often supervenes as much upon an agent's intentions as the end for which it was designed. Mitcham made a similar distinction between the *intrinsic* or *extrinsic* uses of an artefact (1994:164) and we can easily see how object functionality can be shifted from one objective to another, simply by changes in thinking. Thus, with the right intention, a ladder offers more than a means of replacing a roof-tile—it can also facilitate a burglary. Likewise, a bottle ceases to be a mere receptacle for liquids when it is smashed and pointed at someone. Thus, the standard legal basis for establishing culpability—an agent's carrying out of an *actus reus* of an offence, while concurrently having an appropriate *mens rea*—appears to be significantly complicated where cause and intention are mediated through technology.

Another way in which the redundancy of technology for legal purposes can be seen is where the causal picture behind an offence is complex. For example where there are a range of tools potentially implicated in an offence. Suppose, for example, a victim of a stabbing is taken to a hospital by the assailant. On the way their vehicle is hit by a truck and the stabbing victim then suffers a life threatening blow to the head from the windscreen. When they finally arrive at the hospital its A&E department is so busy it is unable to treat the victim immediately. It is later established that the victim would have survived if she had received immediate care. There is a tangle of possible causes where technology seems to play a role in furthering the outcomes here—the action of the knife, the impact of the vehicle and (ironically) the subsequent *lack* of any technological intervention at the hospital. It is not that the law is unable to accommodate multiple causes—as R. v Cheshire established, defining a dominant cause is not necessary, provided a jury can be satisfied that an accused's acts can be said to have made a 'significant contribution' to an offence.[2] But of

---

[1] Added by the Cyber Security Enhancement Act of 2002, and implemented under the title of the (more familiar) Homeland Security Act of 2002.
[2] Beldam, LJ Rv Cheshire (1991) 1 WLR 844.

course determining 'significance' in a cause remains vague—and even more so if it is technology which has served as the factor thought to have made a cause 'significant'. One possible way of firming these relations up was recently touched upon in the UK Law Commission in its draft Bill on Involuntary Homicide in 1996 (LC 1996). This acknowledged that flexibility was essential when assigning responsibility for causation where an 'intermediary factor' is present. However this does not seem to allow for technology to serve as an 'intermediary factor' since a causal role can usually only be granted where it involves a 'juristic person' i.e. a social entity, composed of human actors to which a legal personality can be ascribed (a corporation is one obvious example here).

The heavy emphasis placed by law upon intention in assessing culpability raises difficult questions for the distinctiveness of cyberterrorism as an offence—at least if (as it seems it should be) technology is central to its definition. Firstly, if intention carries so much weight in determining the offence we might reasonably ask—why is technology relevant at all? Conversely, if the status of cyberterrorism *is* tied to the fact that technologies like the internet help to 'cause' offending of a serious nature, what explains the inconsistency of law in making one variety of technological misuse a harm that carries legal sanctions whilst many others do not? Take for example the misuse of other more 'low-tech' tools or artefacts. There are good arguments to suppose that these can sometimes pose more frequent risks, and cause greater material harm. For example, if prosecutions are taken a measure of legal significance the fact that just 22 individuals were convicted under the UK Computer Misuse Act between 2002 and 2012 (CO 2013) does not suggest that misuse of ICT poses a very high degree of risk. By contrast, though 20,000 plus individuals in the UK were injured in 2002 as a result of encounters with coffee tables (RoSPA 2010), there has never been any sense that coffee tables or their manufacturers pose any kind of technological risk.

Perhaps one of the starkest indications of inconsistency in legal and political thinking about technological culpabilities can be seen in the disproportionate volume of legislation involving ICT when compared to other technologies. We might well wonder why there has been such a comparatively high volume of legislation (and prosecutions) around something like social networking when compared to that involving (say) nuclear technologies., especially given the voluminous evidence of the far greater harms produced by the latter. For example emissions from the Sellafield nuclear plant alone have been associated with rates of childhood leukaemia amongst 0–14 year olds in North Wales which stand at 28 times the UK national average (cf. Busby 2004).

I have argued elsewhere that these are not just problems of legal scope, but of a far wider conceptual failure. For if our best system of defining wrongs and determining their sanctions (i.e. the law) is now inadequate to manage the emerging shift in relationships between humanity and technology then it seems clear that new kinds of thinking are required. To see what this might involve and how our criminal justice systems might be reconceptualised to cope with such shifts it is time to return again to the question of what technology 'does' in the context of cyberterrorism.

Key Points

- An alternative to risk assessing in terms of probability weightings is to focus directly upon the technology which both defines and facilitates a threat.
- This requires a clear sense of technological causation: something lacking at present.
- The law, for example, is 'blind' to technological causes, acknowledging only intention as the primary marker of culpability.

4.5 Technology, Causation and Cyberterrorism

So how might risk assessments of cyberterrorism effectively accommodate technological causes? To answer this it is worth revisiting some standard ways of thinking about causality. Though there are many theories of causation (see Pearl 2000 for some of them) a standard approach is to require, first that there be some *mechanism* linking a cause C with its effect, E and second that C should make some *difference* to E (Darby and Williamson 2011). Prima facie, the emphasis placed upon mechanism in this analysis accommodates technological causes very well—especially when applied to cyberterrorism or other 'cyber' offences. For the relevant mechanism—ICT—appears to be obvious enough. But closer inspection suggests matters may not be quite so straightforward. One problem is that there is no *single* mechanism identified where ICT is invoked. Rather, ICT involves many kinds of technological forms and artefacts. Even 'the internet' is not a single mechanism, but a multiple array of artefacts such as URL software, servers, workstations, cabling and so on. And even if 'the internet' *were* taken as the mechanism of relevance, it is by no means clear that this, rather than something else, could be definitively shown to have been what 'made the difference' in any purported 'cyberterrorist' incident. I will return to this point shortly.

A second, related difficulty is the lack of any single or characteristic range of 'differences' or effects which might serve to define cyberterrorism offences. As already suggested, the effects/causal outputs which have been associated with 'cyberterrorist' offences seem to be very broad. Should cyberterrorism be linked to causal outputs such as disabling or destroying key infrastructures such as a power grid? Or are illicit actions involving communications, co-ordination, or radicalisation the more relevant causal process? In each case the way that ICT 'makes a difference'—i.e. causally furthers the outcome seems quite different. Nor would restricting focus to a singular causal process such as terrorist communication simplify matters, for this too might be facilitated via a multiplicity of technical solutions, none involving precisely the same mechanism. Where ends are more complicated—as with terrorist 'co-ordination'—defining how ICT makes a causal difference becomes even more confusing. For not only must the technology now facilitate some (unspecified) form of information exchange, it must also (in some even more vague way) 'further' terrorist action on the basis of this communication. But 'furthering' might involve anything from a full scale deployment of terrorist resources to the more mundane decision to visit a supermarket for sandwiches. Where associations are made between the use of ICT and harmful or destructive outcomes, further troublesome and tenuous relations emerge. For example, could it really be said that the use of ICT to cause direct physical destruction (such as the downing of an aeroplane, or the compromise of a utility) involves the same kinds of causal process as radicalizing someone via a video posted online?

An obvious worry emerges at this stage. Whilst causal explanation in the social sciences is notoriously complex, and may indeed involve multiple processes, attempts to introduce a further set of causal factors—now involving technology—threatens to disrupt useful explanation entirely. For what results are forms of explanation where effects which have **no** common causal basis/mechanism are linked to a ragbag of differing inputs which also have no commonality other than being grouped together under a convenient label. This matters because in science (whether natural or social) a lack of uniformity in causal relations has usually been taken to indicate a need for caution when attributing common origins or identities. A well recorded instance of this was seen within the prescientific claim that, because pepper and fire appeared to exhibit similar effects (i.e. to 'cause' the sensation of heat), both must be the product of the same thing—the heat-bearing substance 'phlogiston' (cf. Conant 1950). Phlogiston was eventually abandoned as a genuine physical entity once it was realised that any perceptions of a common underlying mechanism to these forms of heat were illusory. For, the heat of a chilli was found to be an effect produced by chemical processes, whilst fire's heat arose from molecular motion. Conversely, one of the most productive and successful aspects of the scientific enterprise has been the way that ostensibly *different* phenomena can be unified under a common explanation where a common causal base can be found. A familiar example is the discovery of gravity. The suggestion that an apple falling can be explained in terms of a identical mechanism as a planet rotating may seem obvious to us now, but would have been regarded as nonsensical at one point. It was not until the mathematics of gravitational attraction had been worked out that 'gravity' was accepted as a real constituent of the world.

The construct of cyberterrorism thus appears to rest upon very unclear causal footings and so, at best, to involve a variety of 'pre-scientific' explanation. At worst the suspicion must be that it constitutes a wholly pseudo-scientific category of explanation. For, though it may be uncontroversial to accept that there are usually 'multi-variate' bases for social processes or outcomes, this does not licence the removal of all meaningful constraints in explaining them. Unless there is to be a free-for-all which renders social science trivial, explanations of the social world require at least some form of causal uniformity. For example, if we say that 'poverty causes ill health' or 'gender causes discrimination in the workplace' the causal process is not required to be singular (i.e. poverty can be a sufficient, but not necessary cause of ill-health since other things may cause this too). But it is required that there are some commonalities for the explanations to be good ones.

The question then is how 'common' must we require the causal commonalities involved in cyberterrorism to be for it to constitute a substantive, (social) scientifically tractable threat? One increasingly popular option for conferring such uniformity upon the assemblage of activities related to cybercrime (including 'cyberterrorism') is the practice of describing technological agency in terms of the concept of 'enablement'. That is, some piece of technology T is said to be causally implicated in an effect E if T 'enables' E. This has become a commonplace approach within law enforcement and governmental accounts of technological based explanation (which almost inevitably comes down to issues around ICT rather than other technologies). Thus, we now see talk about the enablers of identity crime, enablers of violence (ACC 2011), enablers of organised crime (GACOC 2012) or enablers of hi-tech crime (ACPO 2009). The widespread distinction between computer enabled and computer dependent offences appears to endorse this terminology—though it is really intended to distinguish between traditional offending which uses ICT (is 'enabled' by it) and contemporary offending which could not be conducted without a computer (is 'dependent' upon it). And this appears to be evidence of a terminological confusion, rather than a useful clarification of the way in which enablement might provide a causal uniformity to ICT's role in furthering cybercrime/ cyberterrorism.

Sure enough, as soon as the question of how enablement serves as a unifying causal basis for cyberterrorism (or indeed cybercrime in general) is pressed, the concept begins to unravel. At least three problems are worth noting:

Enablement is a circular concept. Explaining technological causation in terms of enablement appears to quickly collapse into circularity or, worse, empty tautology. For most attempts to define enablement do this by using terminology which, effectively, reproduces the concept to be defined within the definition. Take for example (HO 2011), where an enabler is defined as … "an instrument, process or organisation that facilitates or assists in the opportunity to commit (crime)". There is clearly little or no difference between an 'enabling' mechanism, or one which 'facilitates' or 'assists' an action. Since useful definitions usually require new or substantive information as predicates, most definitions of enablement therefore appear no more informative than saying the meaning of 'red' is red. Contrast this with a substantive (non tautological) definition—that 'red' is a perception of a particular wavelength of light.

Enablement based explanations threaten triviality. A second problem is that enablement seems too generously loose a concept in that it allows almost any prior aspect of a process to be a 'cause'. The writer Douglas Adams once gave an apocryphal example of this in highlighting the growing hysteria around the 'influence' of the internet upon crime (Adams 1999). He pointed to a group of bank robbers who plan their raid in a motorway cafe over a cup of tea and asked 'did the cafe have an enabling role in the outcome'? If the raid 'could not have happened' without the meeting it appears to make sense to say that it did. Indeed it could even be said that their raid was enabled by drinking the tea, since it is was this that helped place the details of the raid into their heads. However absurd, there is nothing in the concept of enablement which appears to restrict such associations.

Enablement is not causation. A third and perhaps decisive objection to reading what ICT contributes to cyberterrorism in terms of enablement is that enablement need not involve anything which is obviously causal. Consider the example of someone who throws a lighted match into some bushes. Just as it is going out, a second person throws some petrol onto it, with the result that the neighbouring house burns down. Whilst the first person 'enabled' the fire to occur, it was the second person who caused the house to burn down. It seems then that enablement is a signal only of correlation—and as any social scientist knows, correlations are not causes. Nor are such objections mere matters of verbal pedantry. A number of psychological experiments have been conducted using similar examples to test whether we think differently about cause and enablement in legal contexts (cf. Frosch et al. 2007). Results indicate that not only can most people distinguish between something which causes an event, and someone which merely 'enables' it to occur. Crucially, they also tend to judge that causers are more responsible for an outcome and therefore more liable for punishment than enablers (ibid).

The conceptual and practical problems around using enablement to ground technological causation seem to be decisive and suggest that we need to cast our net more widely for an account of technologies causal power that could feed usefully into risk assessments of cyberterrorism. One promising direction lies in the phenomenological challenge to instrumentalist views. Rather than accepting that technology is socially neutral, or rooted in subject-object distinctions between us and 'it', the phenomenological perspective has helped set the agenda for a more plausible sense of its agentic aspects. A key theme of this 'post-human' approach is sociotechnic connectivity and even physical fusion—ways in which the body begins to become indistinguishable from technology. These entanglements between technologies and the human create, according to Latour, new kinds of causal subjects—the actant (cf. Latour 1994; Brown 2006). The subtle forms of agency associated with actants can be seen in a range of reciprocally transformative effects they induce— for example those seen in the claim that, "you are another subject because you hold the gun, (and) the gun is another object because it has entered into a relationship with you" (1999:179) Donna Haraway, who has located these 'techno-social' fusions in more overtly body-centric terms goes further, arguing that we are all, "theorized and fabricated hybrids of machine and organism; in short, we are cyborgs." (1991:150, see also Clark 2006).

Key Points

- Cyberterrorism involves a complex variety of causal effects as well as mechanisms.
- The experience of science warns us that we should be cautious in asserting common identities where the underlying causal picture is too fragmented.
- Notions of 'enablement' do not help us resolve this problem of technological causation.
- It may be more promising to look at how technology combines with the body to produce wholly new kinds of agent.

4.6 Extension, Hyperconnection and Hyperspatialised Terror

Whilst the posthuman approach offers a more promising direction for defining how human agency becomes intertwined with technological agency it remains unclear how this might be used to risk assess technology-based threats such as cyberterrorism. In this section I will consider what I argue to be a more economical, functional approach to human-technic relations than that offered by either posthuman or instrumentalist views. The position is one I have outlined previously (McGuire 2012) and has its origins in the views of one of the first 'philosophers of technology', Ernest Kapp. As long ago as the nineteenth century, Kapp had argued that our technologies should be thought of as "kinds of (human) organ projections" (1877), so that "in the tool, the human continually produces itself" (ibid, pp. 44–45). For example, bent fingers find their technic parallel in hooks, just as the function of a cupped hand in gathering water can be more completely realised by the technology of a wooden or a ceramic bowl. Freud offered an even more explicit claim about the nature of our 'technological organs', theorising them in terms of 'prosthetics' which have come to offer humanity various evolutionary advantages. He argued that:

> With every tool (man) is perfecting his own organs, whether motor or sensory, or is removing the limits to their functioning. Motor power places gigantic forces at his disposal, which, like his muscles, he can employ in any direction… With the help of the telephone he can hear at distances which would be respected as unattainable even in a fairy tale. (Freud 1962:90–1)

Similar views can be found in more recent work by the anthropologist Arnold Gehlen (1965) or, perhaps more familiarly, in McLuhan (1964), who argued that, "all technologies are extensions of our physical and nervous systems" (p. 90). Like Kapp, McLuhan saw an analogy between technological extensions and our limbs— to use one of his famous examples, the wheel 'extends' the foot, just as the hammer 'extends' the arm.

Viewing technology in terms of concrete bodily relations like extension is not just a way of evading the practical and conceptual difficulties around enablement. A particular advantage of the extension line in dealing with technology offences like cyberterrorism is that it seems far better in accounting for causality. With technological extension, causality remains centred upon the human agent, though with the difference that they can do and experience things that were previously hard, perhaps impossible. The extension of my arms and muscle power by a hammer means that I can drive in nails more powerfully than before, much like the internet helps me communicate more widely, organise more diversely, or direct my destructive intentions more completely than could be achieved by my (unextended) body. Technological extension is also more amenable to wider analysis—for example we can qualify our extensions in terms of further variables which clarify how an extension enhances our causal powers. One example of relevance here is the distance or range from our bodies at which technological artefacts extend our capacity to act (cf. McGuire 2012). The causal power of ICT can then be analysed in terms of the way that it extends our capacity to interact with objects or individuals 'at a distance'. That is, at spatial ranges beyond our normal bodily reach or at temporal distances beyond our immediate sphere of access and retrieval (as in our interactions with data). This conception echoes other familiar sociological characterizations of our modern world—for example, the idea that ICT serves as an instrument of 'distanciation'(Giddens 1990) or as a way in which time and space can be 'compressed' (Harvey 1989) By adding this qualification we can also begin to unify many seemingly diverse technologies by way of the distance at which their effects are felt—whether the artefact is a mundane, familiar one like a saucepan, or an advanced one like a particle accelerator.

Adopting an extensional view of technology emphasizes why the early conceptual framework associated with ICT has proved so obstructive to effective evaluations of the risks posed by cyberterrorism and cybercrime in general. For it becomes clearer why the 'cyber' in cyber offending should never have been taken to signify a 'cyberspace'—where this involved some kind of distinct spatial realm, with its own laws and threats. Rather, the development of the internet involved precisely the same space as that which we already inhabit, except that our spatial experiences have been extended in various ways. That is, these now involve a wider range of causal and agentic possibilities than could be experienced in the social spaces that existed prior to ICT.

Accepting this wider analysis of technological agency allows us to move towards a more sophisticated set of conclusions about the causes and impacts of cyberterrorism. Detached from any seemingly necessary association with ICT, the impacts of extended spatial location and reach become the central focus of cyberterrorist threat assessment. Rather than focusing on 'kit'—i.e. ICT itself—it emphasises why our attention would be better directed at the new kinds of spatio-temporal experience which characterise our age. In particular, the emerging state of hyperconnection which has arisen from the extensions offered by ICT. A hyperconnected world (cf. McGuire 2007, 2012) is one which offers us all the potential to communicate and to interact with anyone, anywhere at anytime. As has been pointed out elsewhere (Fredette et al. 2012; Anderson and Rainie 2012; Ganascia 2013), it is also a world where connections are always 'on'; where more and more things are connected together; where information is continuously recorded and increasingly accessible. But hyperconnection is not exclusively realised by the internet. It also now arises through our ever more ubiquitous digital platforms (whether this is just the mobile phone in everyones pocket, a pair of 'Google glasses', or more direct body/technic fusions such as chip implants). In my 2007 (see also McGuire 2008) I pressed a specific criminological question about the implications of all this—namely, what are the consequences of a hyperconnected world for criminal behaviour? One possible response is that if the spatio-temporal extensions to social interaction are taken seriously a wholly new kind of social space—a 'hyperspace'—must now be seen as emerging and with that a spatially enhanced set of opportunities for criminality—a 'hypercrime'. On this basis, if threats such as cyberterrorism are analysed as risks which emerge from the 'hyperspatial' world we now inhabit it soon becomes evident why ICT offers only a preliminary explanatory factor in analysing its very new threat landscapes. The now familiar cybercrime scenario of a single individual, armed with little more than a computer virus who can, in principle, direct harm towards any place or person, from anywhere, at anytime is certainly one aspect of this landscape. But any potentials for catastrophic harm which also arise are better seen as a direct outcome of hyperconnection, rather than ICT *simpliciter*.

On this basis it also becomes clear why malware distribution or network attacks are unlikely to constitute the primary range of threats posed by a hyperconnected world. Rather, with hyperconnection at the centre of our risk models a far more varied (and potentially hard to manage) set of scenarios can begin to be discerned. For, in a hyperspatial world, virus and network attacks simply become one part of a richer palette of techniques which may exploit extended causal reach to foster terror. One well discussed set of examples of this kind have centred upon the intensive forms of personalisation information technology has opened up. The world of big data required to support targeted consumerism is precisely one of hyperspatialised access and this means that it is as equally accessible to the determined terrorist as it is to the marketing executive. And with this, come a number of potentially novel ways of disseminating terror. Increasingly fine-tuned targeted attacks upon specific company systems and networks are one example which has already been witnessed (cf. Shiels 2011). However, exploiting hyperconnection for precision targeting of individuals, whether for intelligence, assassination or other goals may offer an even more tempting set of options. One striking recent example of this was demonstrated by a US cybersecurity researcher who was able to identify the names of up to 12 current or former members' of the elite unit which carried out the bin Laden raid of 2011 (Singer 2013). Of equal concern was the way he was able to determine their families' names and their home addresses. This information was acquired by exploiting a relatively unsophisticated form of hyperconnectedness—the plurality of personal traces left across the multiple digital platforms we use. In this case, social networking sites were used to obtain pictures of friends and family members in t-shirts that displayed unit logos together with information about specific training classes they had attended (Singer ibid).

The increasing use of location based social media applications offers further opportunities for remote access and disruption by terrorists. US and UK military officials have warned soldiers to be aware that innocently uploading photos from their smartphones to Facebook could provide geocoded data that could be used to determine their unit's position (Rodewig 2012). Other systems such as Foursquare, where individuals 'check in' at new positions also provide a wealth of information and spatial patternings that could be of use to a determined terrorist. Similarly photos uploaded to Flickr, or data on the Facebook 'timeline' could also offer hyperspatialised 'location-tags' which result in the friends or families of military targets being blackmailed, kidnapped or even killed. Nor is there any reason to suppose that terrorists would restrict their interests to purely military personnel. Influential, professional members of society (for example those responsible for managing key infrastructures) could also be targeted in the same way. Indeed, given that one aim of terrorism is to spread random violence and terror, such targeting might be profitably directed at almost any of us, individually or collectively. Thus, more obvious activities such as intelligence gathering could be complemented by reputational forms of attack and sabotage. For example, 'bringing down' a five star general by circulating private misbehaviours could be as effective a way of disrupting military operations as killing him. Similarly, coercing a middle manager of a power station into sabotage by blackmailing him could result in as serious a compromise to security as any virus planted on the station's network.

As just stressed, it is crucial to be clear that the internet is now only one of many tools which facilitate the misuse of hyperconnectivity. Terrorists also have ample access to other devices such as GPS and satellite technologies which offer their own options. These have already been used in any number of damaging ways—for example via techniques such as 'jamming' (which can disrupt surveillance of a car's movements; 'rebroadcasting' (or 'meaconing') a GNSS signal (to enable a misreporting of a position) or 'spoofing' (also useful for deceiving tracking devices) (RAE 2011). And with over 6% of European GDP now estimated to be directly dependent upon GPS and satellite navigation systems (RAE ibid) there may also be risks that such techniques are used to inflict low intensity forms of economic sabotage. A further, even more dramatic set of threats offered by hyperconnection can be seen in the phenomenon of Machine to Machine (M2M) or Machine to Machine to Human (M2M2H) connectivity (cf. Cha et al. 2009). Such technology is becoming increasingly central to the operation of traffic cameras, asset & cargo tracking, utility metering and vending machines amongst many other applications. An especially important context is their use within healthcare, where medical applications that work with sensors are now routinely attached to patient's bodies (Fredette et al. 2012), so allowing doctors and nurses to remotely monitor or to diagnose them continuously. It is not hard to see how this could allow less well meaning individuals to intercept, divert or even 'takeover' such devices in order to cause death or injury (see for example the proof of concept 'pace-maker hack' discussed in Kirk 2012). Similarly, the increasing use of RFID tagging to track children (cf. Kravets 2012) also creates disturbing options for hyperspatialised terror by spatially extending their physical locations.[3] And with the advent of what has been called an 'internet of things'—where every kind of object from fridges to the clothing we wear is networked together—an as yet unpredictable world of terrorist possibility potentially emerges (cf. van Kranenburg 2008). In this world a variety of ways in which minor chaos is inflicted upon social order can be imagined—whether this involves systematic shutdowns of local central heating systems, inducing malfunctions to on-board car computers, or even disruptions to washing machine cycles. However mundane such inconveniences appear to be at first glance, co-ordinated or sustained attacks upon these aspects of everyday life might result in far more damage to our social order than any spectacular 'one-off' style attack.

A final benefit of deferring to hyperconnection, rather than to ICT when threat assessing cyberterrorism, is that it also allows us to discern a range of less immediately obvious risks. In particular it helps us appreciate that our shift into the hyperspatial is not just about joining together very distant locations—but very close ones too. That is, just as ICT permits causal interaction with very distant objects, there are

---

[3] The recent reported hack of a baby monitor (Seltzer 2013) offers an especially disturbing 'proof of concept' of the way that hyperspatialisation can bring terror into the heart of our homes.

other varieties of 'hyperspatial' extension offered by bio-chemical technologies which now permit us to connect to and manipulate very 'near' objects such as molecular or chemical entities. Wholly new risk scenarios such as 'bio-hacking'—where new chemical substances or lifeforms can be modified 'in the basement' (Wohlsen 2011)—thereby emerge. And with this come new and disturbing scenarios of infection and biological attack—scenarios likely to prove far more deadly than any computer virus. The (apparent) lack of any 'cyber' in this should not be taken to mean that what we currently call 'cyberterrorism' is not coextensive or continuous with such risks. For one thing, any manipulation of matter cannot usually be done in the absence of ICT—significant computing power may be required for genetic manipulations and modifications. Overall though, such reflections should emphasize why ICT is but one part of the wider technological process of hyperspatialisation, where manipulation of objects at both near and far distances becomes a new social norm. The result for any analysis of cyberterrorism should be to remind us that effective risk management requires us to understand how hyperconnection fuses and blurs technology—just as extension blurs and fuses the human with the technic. The outcomes of this process may not just be stranger and more dangerous than we have imagined—but stranger and more dangerous than we can imagine. Moreover as McLuhan once suggested, terrorists primary aim—of spreading fear or panic—is also vastly furthered by hyperconnectivity since, "terror is the normal state of any (such) society, for in it everything affects everything all the time" (1962:32). Focusing analysis of cyberterrorist risks upon hyperconnection rather than ICT may only be in its infancy—but it seems to offer a better sense of the new modalities of terrorism than the technological fetishism which has dominated debates so far.

Key Points

- Analysing technology in terms of bodily extension offers a better account of its causal power than the concept of 'enablement'
- The phenomenon of 'hyperconnection'—where social relations transcend traditional spatio-temporal limits to become increasingly interlinked—provides a more robust basis for theorizing cyberterrrorism than its associations with ICT.
- Devices such as geocoding manifest one kind of option for terrorist action which a hyperconnected world provides.

Further Reading

Blyth T (2003) Terrorism as technology: a discussion of the theoretical underpinnings. Knowl Tech Pol 16(1):45–55
Brey P (2000) Theories of extension as extension of human faculties. In: Mitcham C (ed) Metaphysics, epistemology and technology, research in philosophy and technology, vol 19. Elsevier, London

Chan W, Simester A (2011) Four functions of mens rea. Camb Law J 70(2):381–396
Cockfield A (2004) Towards a law and technology theory. Manitoba Law J 30:383–415
Feenberg A (2002) Transforming technology—a critical theory revisited. OUP, Oxford
McGuire M (2012) Technology, crime and justice. Routledge, London

References

ACC (2011) Enabler activities, organised crime in Australia. Australian Crime Committee report
ACPO (2009) ACPO E-crime strategy. Association of Chief Police Officers, August 2009
Adams D (1999) How to stop worrying and love the internet. Times 29 August 1999
Anderson J, Rainie L (2012) Millennials will benefit and suffer due to their hyperconnected lives. Pew Research Center's Internet & American Life Project
Bachmann S (2014) Hybrid threats, cyber warfare and NATO's comprehensive approach for countering 21st century threats. Amicus Curiae 88:14–17
Bedford T, Cooke R (2001) Probabilistic risk analysis: foundations and methods. Cambridge University Press, Cambridge
Bimber B (1990) Karl Marx and the three faces of technological determinism. Soc Stud Sci 20(2):333–351
Bowman-Grieve L (2014) Cyberterrorism and moral panics: a reflection on the discourse of cyberterrorism. In: Jarvis L, Macdonald S, Chen T (eds) Terrorism online. Routledge, Abingdon
Brickey J (2012) Defining cyberterrorism: capturing a broad range of activities in cyberspace. Westpoint CTC Sentinel, vol 5, p 8
Brown S (2006) The criminology of hybrids: rethinking crime and law in technosocial networks. Theor Criminol 10(2):223–244
Busby C (2004) Nuclear pollution, childhood leukaemia, retinoblastoma and brain tumours in Gwynedd and Anglesey Wards near the Menai Straits, North Wales 2000-2003. Report 04/1B;2. Green Audit, Aberystwyth
Cha I, Shah Y, Schmidt A, Leicher A, Meyerstein M (2009) Security and trust for M2M communications. Vehicular Technology Magazine, IEEE
Clark A (2006) Natural-born cyborgs: minds, technologies, and the future of human intelligence. OUP, Oxford
Clarke R, Knake R (2010) CyberWar: the next threat to national security and what to do about it. Ecco/HarperCollins, New York
CO (2013) Computer misuse act 1990 productions. Crown Office and Procurator Fiscal Service
Conant J (ed) (1950) The overthrow of phlogiston theory: the chemical revolution of 1775–1789. Harvard University Press, Cambridge
Conway M (2007) Cyberterrorism: hype and reality. In: Armistead L (ed) Information warfare: separating hype from reality. Potomac Books, Inc., Washington, DC, pp 73–93
Conway M (2011) Against cyberterrorism. Comm ACM 54(2):26–28
Conway M (2012) What is cyberterrorism and how real is the threat? A Review of the Academic Literature, 1996–2009, pp 277–303
Conway M (2014) Three arguments against cyberterrorism: technological complexity; the image factor; and, the accident issue. In: Cyberterrorism, a multidisciplinary approach, Springer
CPS (2010) Sentencing manual: knives and offensive weapons. UK Crown Prosecution Service, London
Darby G, Williamson J (2011) Imaging technology and the philosophy of causality. Philos Technol 24:115–136
Deazley R, Kretschmer M, Bently L (eds) (2010) Privilege and property: essays on the history of copyright. Open Book Publishers, Cambridge
Feenberg A (2002) Transforming technology. Oxford University Press, Oxford

Fredette J, Marom R, Steinart K, Witters L (2012) The promise and peril of hyperconnectivity for organizations and societies. Chapter 1.10 the global information technology report, World Economic Forum 2012

Freud S (1962) Civilization and its discontents. Trans. James Strachey. Norton, New York

Frosch CA, Johnson-Laird PN, Cowley M (2007) It's not my fault, Your Honour, I'm only the enabler. In: McNamara DS, Trafton JG (eds) Proceedings of the 29th Annual Cognitive Science Society. Cognitive Science Society, Austin, p 1755

GACOC (2012) Organized crime enablers, Global Agenda Council on Organized Crime. World Economic Council

Ganascia JG (2013) View and examples on hyper-connectivity. European Commission working paper

Gehlen A et al (1965) Anthropologische Ansicht der Technik. In: Freyer H (ed) Technik im Technischen Zeitlater. J Schilling, Dusseldorf, pp 101–118

Giddens A (1990) The consequences of modernity. Stanford University Press, Stanford

Green J (2002) The myth of cyberterrorism. Washington Monthly

Harvey D (1989) The condition of postmodernity. Blackwell, Oxford

Heidegger M (1949/1977) The question concerning technology. In: Lovitt W (ed & trans.) The question concerning technology and other essays. Harper & Row, New York, pp 3–35

HO (2011) Fighting fraud together: the strategic plan to reduce fraud. National Fraud Authority 12 Oct 2011

Kapp E (1877) Grundlinien einer Philosophie der Technik. George Westermann, Braunschweig

Kirk J (2012) Pacemaker hack can deliver deadly 830-volt jolt. Computerworld 17 October 2012

Konstam A (2008) Piracy: the complete history. Osprey Publishing, Westminster

Kravets S (2012) Tracking school children with RFID tags? It's all about the Benjamins. Wired 7 September 2012

Kroes P, Meijers A (2006) The dual nature of technical artefacts. Stud Hist Philos Sci 37(1):1–4

Latour B (1994) On technical mediation—philosophy, sociology, genealogy. Common Knowl 3(2):29–64

LC (1996) Law Commission, legislating the criminal code: involuntary manslaughter: item 11 of the sixth programme of law reform: criminal law: report no 237, HC (1995-96) 171, clause 4(2)(b) back

Lemke L (2013) .The cursus publicus in the 4th century through the lens of the Codex Theodosianus. Shifting frontiers in late antiquity X conference, Ottawa, Ontario, March 2013

Marx K (1847/1975) The poverty of philosophy, in collected works, vol. 6. Lawrence & Wishart, London, pp 105–212

Mather F (1953) The railways, the electric telegraph and public order during the Chartist period. History 38:40–53

McGuire M (2007) Hypercrime: the new geometry of harm. Routledge, London

McGuire M (2008) From hyperspace to hypercrime: technologies and the new geometries of deviance and control. Papers from the British Criminology Conference, vol 8

McGuire M (2012) Technology, crime and justice: the question concerning technomia. Routledge, London

McLuhan M (1962) The Gutenberg galaxy: the making of typographic man. University of Toronto Press, Toronto

McLuhan M (1964) Understanding media: the extensions of man. McGraw Hill, New York

Mitcham C (1994) Thinking through technology, the path between engineering and philosophy. University of Chicago Press, Chicago

HS Newswire (2010) FBI: cyber-terrorism a real and growing threat to U.S. Home Security Newswire 5 March 2010

Parks C (2003) Cyber terrorism: hype or reality? J Corp Account Finance 14(5):9–11

Pearl J (2000) Causality. Cambridge University Press, Cambridge

RAE (2011) Global navigation space systems: reliance and vulnerabilities. Royal Academy of Engineering, London

Rodewig C (2012) Geotagging poses security risks. US Army News 7 March 2012

ROSPA (2010) Home and leisure accident surveillance system. See: http://www.hassandlass.org. uk/query/MainSelector.aspx

Schmidt C, Darby T (2001).The what, why, and how of the 1988 Internet worm. See: http://www. snowplow.org/tom/worm/worm.html

Seltzer L (2013) Baby monitor hack shows danger of default passwords. ZdNet 14 August 2013

Shiels M (2011) Targeted cyber attacks an 'epidemic'. BBC 2 June 2011

Singer PW (2013) The cyber terror bogeyman. Armed Forces J

Stohl M (2014) Dr. Strangeweb: or how they stopped worrying and learned to love cyber war. In: Chen T, Jarvis L, Macdonald S (eds) Cyberterrorism: understanding, assessment, and response. Springer, New York

Taylor C, Krings A, Alves-Foss J (2002) Risk analysis and probabilistic survivability assessment (RAPSA): an assessment approach for power substation hardening. In: Proc ACM workshop on scientific aspects of cyber terrorism. UK Cabinet Office, Washington, DC. http://www.cabinetoffice. gov.uk/sites/default/files/resources/uk-cyber-security-strategy-final.pdf

UK Cabinet Office (2012) Written evidence from the Ministry of Defence. Defence Select Committee 20 Feb 2012

van Kranenburg R (2008) The Internet of Things: a critique of ambient technology. Institute of Network Cultures working paper

Weimann G (2004) Cyberterrorism, how real is the threat? USIP report 119, December—2006 terror on the Internet: the new arena, the new challenges. U.S. Institute of Peace Press, Washington, DC

White L Jr (1964) Medieval technology and social change. Oxford University Press, Oxford

Whiting A, Nouri L, Jarvis L (2014) Understanding, locating and constructing cyberterrorism. In: Chen T, Jarvis L, Macdonald S (eds) Cyberterrorism: a multidisciplinary approach. Springer, New York

Wilson C (2014) Cyber threats to critical information infrastructure. In: Chen T, Jarvis L, Macdonald S (eds) Cyberterrorism: a multidisciplinary approach. Springer, New York

Wohlsen M (2011) Biopunk: DIY scientists hack the software of life. Current, New York

Wykes M, Harcus D (2010) Cyber-terror: construction, criminalisation & control. In: Yar M, Jewkes Y (eds) Handbook of internet crime. Willan, Cullompton

Yannakogeorgos P (2014) On the terrorist misuse of the internet. In: Chen T, Jarvis L, Macdonald S (eds) Cyberterrorism: a multidisciplinary approach. Springer, New York

Chapter 5
Dr. Strangeweb: Or How They Stopped Worrying and Learned to Love Cyber War

Michael Stohl

5.1 Introduction

I begin with a story which introduces many of the themes highlighted in this chapter. In February 1986 I was invited to present a talk to the Defense Intelligence College at Bolling Air Force Base in Washington, D.C. on the topic of state and state sponsored terrorism.[1] The audience consisted of a few other invited academic specialists (European and American) on terrorism and about 500 representatives of the armed forces, Departments of State and Defense and the intelligence community. My hosts expected that the talk would focus on Muammar Gaddafi and perhaps Saddam Hussein, as well as others linked in the popular imagination to the support of various Palestinian and Arab groups employing terrorism against Israel, the Arab States and Western European countries during the previous decade. Instead, I focused my talk on the superpowers and international terrorism. My arguments for doing so, articulated in the talk, were that: (1) we could learn much more about decisions to employ terrorism by focusing on the known decision processes and calculations of state decision makers than we could extrapolate from the as yet unknown decision processes of the insurgent terrorist; (2) further, that states were far more effective and dangerous employers of terrorism than were insurgents because they possessed much greater resources and abilities; and, (3) that the then predominately bipolar structure of the international system provided the framework within which international behaviours were framed. While the conflict between the superpowers was the main focus of security analysts during the cold war, and the lens through

---

[1] Stohl, M. (1985) presented at the Defense Intelligence College Symposium on Terrorism, Washington, DC, December 3, 1985. Later published as Stohl, M. 1988. "States, Terrorism and State Terrorism: The Role of the Superpowers" in Slater, R. and Stohl, M. (eds.) *Current Perspectives on International Terrorism*, Macmillan, London, and St. Martin's Press, New York, pp. 155–205.

M. Stohl (✉)
Department of Communication, UC Santa Barbara, Santa Barbara, CA 93106-4020, USA
e-mail: mstohl@comm.ucsb.edu

T.M. Chen et al. (eds.), *Cyberterrorism: Understanding, Assessment, and Response*, DOI 10.1007/978-1-4939-0962-9_5, © Springer Science+Business Media New York 2014

which many of the conflicts within and between other states were viewed, the behaviors and assumptions about them also created and reinforced the norms of behavior which guided states and other actors within the system.

This was well understood and illustrated by the development of the nuclear regime. When the development and possession of nuclear weapons, which initially decided great power status during this period, appeared on the verge of becoming accessible to a greater number of states, the superpowers began to negotiate both test ban and non-proliferation treaties to enable a greater management of the nuclear threat. Thus, by practising certain forms of behaviour (which I argued constituted terrorism consistent with the then definition of the US Department of State) and condoning and supporting such behaviour by other state and non- state actors of which they approved, the superpowers contributed to the overall level of terrorism in the international system. In addition, the argument contended that by virtue of their political and military power as superpowers, they had the greatest capacity and interest in controlling the level of terrorism in the system. While each superpower would have preferred that their adversaries refrain from the use of terrorism, they each continued to employ, sponsor and turn a blind eye to terrorism by themselves and their surrogates in its different forms while decrying its use by others.

The talk produced a very negative reaction in that room and only a few members of the audience challenged or even discussed the theoretical arguments I presented. Most simply chose to berate me for suggesting that United States and Soviet Union behaviours could be discussed in parallel. Eventually, one member of the audience, who identified himself as an employee of one of the Intelligence agencies, admonished his colleagues to consider the arguments and appreciate their potential for understanding the process of terrorism. I recognized the speaker. He had been my instructor in the Fortran computer programming language when I was a graduate student. When the session ended I sought him out and after thanking him for his intervention asked him why he had left the university and how he had found his way to the intelligence community. His answer: "You know how much I love computers, computing and data? Who has the largest computers, the greatest computing power and the most access to data to analyse and lets me play with the toys every day?"

This chapter will argue that there are many parallels to my 1985 observations about states, terrorists, and terrorism that have unfolded in the development and discussion of threats of cyber terrorism and cyber war during the past quarter century. It will commence by tracing the parallels between cyber war and cyber terrorism on the one hand and state terrorism and terrorism on the other. The chapter will conclude by considering the implications of the undermining of the very norms necessary to both build cooperation and trust relationships and to meet the challenges posed by cyberwar.

Key Points

- There are many parallels between contemporary debate on cyber-war and cyberterrorism, on the one hand, and, on the other, discussions around state terrorism and terrorism.
- Great powers shape the behaviours and norms within the international system.

5.2 Cyber Terrorism and Cyber War

The discussion of cyber terrorism and cyber war is initially confounded by the definitional conflict which surrounds the concept of terrorism itself. While almost all definitions of terrorism highlight the communicative constitution of violence, many definitions of terrorism begin from the perspective that the state cannot be terrorist and therefore include in the definition the phrases (or ones very similar) "by subnational groups" or "unlawful acts."[2] The consequence is that violence intended to intimidate and conducted by non-state actors is defined as terrorism; violence intended to intimidate but conducted by states against other states is war (although quite clearly states understand the utility of the threat and use of violence to produce not only destruction but also fear, the other components of most definitions of terrorism); and, violence intended to intimidate civilian populations is defined as law enforcement or an abuse of power. I argue that an actor neutral definition of terrorism which focuses on the acts themselves provides much greater analytic utility for understanding the process of terrorism. Therefore, I define terrorism as the purposeful act or the threat of the act of violence to create fear and/or compliant behavior in a victim and/or audience of the act or threat. The key words are *purposeful*, *violence*, *fear*, *victim*, and *audience*.

What is the result when you introduce the concept of cyber to that of terrorism? White (1998:3) submits that Barry Collin introduced the concept of cyber terrorism in the 1980s and defined it as "the intentional abuse of a digital information system, network, or component toward an end that supports or facilitates a terrorist campaign or action." So conceived, cyber terrorism would include any activity by a group designated terrorist that involved computers, information and the internet, ranging from the creation of a web site for propaganda or recruitment to the destruction of critical infrastructure. This is consistent with the work of Arquilla and Ronfeldt (1998:8) who ignore the distinction between terrorism and war and define these as: "Cyberwar—a concept that refers to information-oriented military warfare" which is becoming more evident at the military end of the spectrum; and "Netwar [which] figures prominently at the societal end of the spectrum where the language is normally about small-scale contingencies." Arquilla, Ronfeldt and Zanini (1999:82) further note that "netwar is more likely to involve nonstate, paramilitary, and irregular forces—as is the case of terrorism." According to Arquilla and Ronfeldt (1999:4) "evidence is mounting about the rise of network forms of organization and about the importance of "information strategies" and "information operations" across the spectrum of conflict, including among ethno nationalists, terrorists, guerrillas and activists." The key to both cyberwar and netwar is that "[n]either concept is simply about technology; both refer to comprehensive approaches to conflict based on the centrality of information—comprehensive in that they combine organizational, doctrinal, strategic, tactical and technological innovations, for offense and defense (Arquilla and Ronfeldt 1998:9)." This is a helpful distinction as far as the power of the use of information in terms of political power is concerned, but Arquilla and Ronfeldt serve to muddy the waters by not only employing the concept of

---

[2] For an illustration see the debate between Wight (2012) and Stohl (2012).

warfare to describe non-violent activities but by also failing to distinguish between non-state actors, terrorists and states who use both information and the power of network forms of organization to advance their political aims or challenge prevailing power and authority structures. Their identification of the power of information and its central role in contemporary warfare is, however, very important and we return to that discussion below.

The approach suggested more than a decade ago by Dorothy Denning, while still suffering from a failure to disentangle actors and acts, is a more useful place to start. Denning (2000:10) argues that: "Cyberterrorism is the convergence of terrorism and cyberspace. It is generally understood to mean unlawful attacks against computers, networks and the information stored therein when done to intimidate or coerce a government or its people in furtherance of political or social objectives....[A]n attack should result in violence against persons or property, or at least cause enough harm to generate fear." Denning (2000:1) suggests that examples of cyber terrorism would include those incidents that result in casualties, property damage or "severe economic loss." "Serious attacks against critical infrastructures could be acts of cyberterrorism, depending on their impact. Attacks that disrupt nonessential services or that are mainly a costly nuisance would not." Stark (1999:8–9) proffers a definition similar to Denning's that attempts to capture both the conventional and cyber aspects of cyber terrorism but note-worthily does not discriminate by the legal status of the perpetrator. Stark writes: "[C]yber-terrorism is defined as the purposeful or threatened use of politically, socially, economically or religiously motivated cyber warfare or cyber-targeted violence, conducted by a non-state or state-sponsored group for the purposes of creating fear, anxiety, and panic in the target population, and the disruption of military and civilian assets." Stark (1999:9) also argues that it is the target that defines the nature of cyber terrorism, i.e. cyber terrorism involves any attack against information systems and does not necessarily have to involve the use of computers to do so. As John Murphy suggests, the question may thus arise as to whether and how cyber terrorism should be differentiated from conventional terrorism. He asks and answers, "does the prospect of computer network attacks by terrorists constitute something "really different," or does it amount only to a new technique of attack for terrorists raising no new issues of law and policy? The answer, it appears, is that the possibility of computer network attacks does raise some new issues, although many of the old conundrums still pertain (1999:3–4)."

In the literature on cyber terrorism the issue is certainly not settled and many different discussions still do not explicate whether cyber terrorism is any use of digital information technology by designated groups, or whether it requires the elements identified by Denning and Stark before an action is classified as a cyber-terrorist attack. The definitions of Denning and Stark provide an important theoretical foundation because they require the differentiation of cyber terrorism from cybercrime and from how terrorists and criminals employ cyber technology to organize, communicate, finance, recruit and gather information to further their aims. In short, while it is important to understand and monitor how and when organizations which employ terrorism adopt those aspects of digital technology that will enable them to operate and grow with a greater degree of efficiency, we must recognize that, in this

sense, terrorist groups are simply exploiting modern tools to accomplish the same
goals they sought in the past. The adoption of new technologies does not create a
new category of behavior as is illustrated in the analyses of Conway (2005), Grabosky
and Stohl (2003) and Thomas (2003) who each discuss the different categories of
organizational behavior that new digital technologies and organizational tools enable
for enhanced organizational capabilities (see also Chap. 4, this volume).

There continues to be a predictable cycle of cyber sector and government press
releases that are routinely reported in the mainstream media and within trade sector
publications which highlight the security threats posed. This cycle includes information about various digital security sector trade conferences highlighting the latest
malware and their software "fixes"; annual "digital war games" such as Def Con
held in Las Vegas each summer where hackers compete, demonstrate and ply their
skills in disrupting digital devices; and reports of the major computer security firms
such as McAfee, Symantec, and Kaspersky outlining the year's Cyber Crime and
Security Breaches. Each of these highlights existing security flaws and routinely note
the unwillingness of individuals, corporate and government actors to take even minimal steps to improve their security profiles, preferring in almost all cases convenience
and ease to enhanced security procedures such as strong or encrypted passwords,
limited access to file, software and hardware sharing, and other simple preparations
for home or business computers that involve the initial settings on the operating software, routers, wireless devices, firewalls etc. (see Kent and Steiner, 2012).

As discussed previously (Stohl 2006) the voluminous academic and popular literature as well as press releases on cyber terrorism also contain much that is sensa-
tionalist, not only to garner attention to sell security projects but also to move
political agendas. "The most popular term, 'electronic Pearl Harbor', was coined in
1991 by an alarmist tech writer named Winn Schwartau to hype a novel. For a while,
in the mid-1990s, 'electronic Chernobyl' was in vogue. Earlier this year, Sen.
Charles Schumer (D-N.Y.) warned of a looming 'digital Armageddon'. And the
Center for Strategic and International Studies, a Washington think tank, christened
its own term, 'digital Waterloo' (Green 2002)."[3] By 1999 Crypt newsletter noted
that "Electronic Pearl Harbor" and variations of it could be found in over 500 cita-
tions for the phrase in on-line news archives, military research papers and press
releases. After 9/11, the fear of a digital 9/11, cyber 9/11 or al Qaeda cyber-attacks
generally replaced the idea of a digital or electronic Pearl Harbor. Richard Clarke, a
major user of the term digital Pearl Harbor before 9/11 (Stohl 2006) for example,
along with the FBI, discussed fears with reporters that Al Qaeda would employ the
web to cause bloodshed. "Cyber-Attacks by Al Qaeda Feared, Terrorists at Threshold
of Using Internet as Tool of Bloodshed (Gellman 2002)." Nonetheless, the term
digital Pearl Harbor has yet to disappear as its use continues to resonate with policymakers. In October 2012 Secretary of Defense Leon Panetta, in the context of
announcing that the Department of Defense was updating its rules of engagement
and procedures that guide a potential military response to a cyber-attack, became

---

[3] See also Debrix (2001).

the latest senior American government official to warn of the possibility of a cyber-Pearl Harbor (Bumiller and Shanker 2012). Interestingly this was headlined in the Wall Street Journal as U.S. Defense Chief Warns of Digital 9/11 (King 2012). What Panetta actually said was: "This is a pre-9/11 moment (Panetta 2012)."

Paul Kurtz, a cyber-security expert who, at the time, was being considered for the position of cybersecurity coordinator in the new Obama administration, introduced the term "cyber Katrina (Epstein 2009)" in February 2009 and urged the creation of a Cyber Security FEMA style organization to enable federal response to the disasters that were sure to come. Two months later Senators Rockefeller and Snowe introduced a bill to create the Office of the National Cybersecurity Advisor and Senator Snowe pressed the need for the office saying "if we fail to take swift action, we, regrettably, risk a cyber-Katrina (Aquino 2009)." Nonetheless, while the potential of cyber terrorism continues to exist and individuals and corporations as well as governments are consistently embarrassed, inconvenienced and damaged by security breaches by criminals which cause havoc and billions of dollars in insurance losses and productivity, none of the doomsday scenarios have yet to occur.

Key Points

- Differentiating cyberterrorism from cyberwar is made more challenging by the disagreement that surrounds the term 'terrorism'.
- An actor-neutral definition of terrorism—and therefore cyberterrorism—is preferable.
- The threat of cyberterrorism is contested, although perpetuated by a range of economic and political interests.
- Hyperbole, captured by 'electronic pearl harbours' metaphors and their equivalent, continues to run through political discourse.

5.3 Cyber War

While the media and general public have witnessed the increasingly shrill headlines and continued concern about cyber terrorism without much consideration of the differences between terror, crime and hacking detailed above,[4] states have been investing increasing resources in the development of their own cyber war capabilities at the same time as they have encouraged the private sector to engage in cyber security. Until the last decade, much of this had gone unnoticed by the general public and, for the most part, states did not discuss threats emanating from other states. An exception came in the fall of 2001 when the Bush administration began their 18 month

---

[4] See also Stohl 2007.

campaign to declare war on Iraq and proclaimed the connection between Saddam Hussein and Al Qaeda. Joshua Dean (2001) reported the assertions of terrorism analyst Yonah Alexander of the Potomac Institute connecting Iraq and cyber terrorism who declared that Iraq had been secretly developing a cyber-arsenal called Iraq Net since the mid-1990s. Alexander asserted that IraqNet consisted of a series of more than 100 Web sites spread across domains globally and claimed that Iraq Net was designed to overwhelm cyber-based infrastructures by distributed denial of service and other cyber-attacks. Alexander's doomsday scenario predicted that, "under an Iraqi attack on the nation's critical infrastructure, telephone systems would crash, freight and passenger trains would collide, oil refineries would explode, the air traffic control system would be undermined and cities would suffer from blackouts… Saddam Hussein would not hesitate to use the cyber tool he has," Alexander said. 'It is not a question of if but when' (Dean 2001). George C. Smith (2002) immediately scoffed at the likelihood of the existence of Iraq Net by arguing:

> that Iraq couldn't even support its ".iq" TLD (top-level domain service) in the mid-1990s. Assertions of the construction of a mighty computer **Destructor** capable of remotely broiling U.S. real estate seem counter-intuitive[5] … but are more exhilarating reading.

Smith also noted that "Iraq Net" was an unlikely "moniker" for the supposed weapon. As with the Bush administration's repeated assertions of the existence of Iraqi WMD, one might offer a most generous evaluation for the existence of Iraq Net, the Scot's verdict of not proven. However, as the verdict requires some evidence rather than simply accusations, it is more accurate to indicate that to this date no evidence has ever been presented to substantiate the claims. Interestingly, the Iraq net story played out almost entirely within the Washington Beltway, being recirculated on government news webs but not circulated thorough the mainstream media. It is interesting to speculate as to why this particular instance of hyperbole, unlike so many others went unrepeated. Perhaps, as Smith (2002) indicated above, the claim was so amateurish that the experts and security firms who frequently distribute such claims avoided association with the claim for fear of ridicule.

For the mainstream media the idea of Cyber War, rather than simply Cyber Terrorism, came to the fore with the media coverage of the Russo-Estonian War of 2007, often cited as the first Cyber War (Richards 2009,). The New York Times headlined "In Estonia, what may be the first war in cyberspace (Landler and Markoff 2007)" and The Guardian led with "Russia accused of unleashing cyberwar to disable Estonia (Traylor, 2007)." The Cyber-attacks were in response to the relocation of a Soviet World War II memorial on April 27 which engendered protests by ethnic Russian Estonians in which 1,300 people were arrested, 100 people were injured, and one person died. Media reported on the 3 week struggle by Estonian authorities to defend their country. U.S. government officials fanned the flames. As Landler and Markoff (2007) note, Linton Wells 2nd, U.S. deputy assistant secretary of defense for networks and information integration suggested that, "This may well turn out to be a watershed in terms of widespread awareness of the vulnerability of modern society."

---

[5] Sic, as written in the original.

While the Estonians argued that an Internet address involved in the attacks belonged to an official working in the administration of Russia's president, Vladimir Putin, the Russian government denied a role in the attacks. The attacks, primarily distributed denial of service attacks (DDOS), appeared to attempt to impede the functioning of the country's digital infrastructure as well as the Web sites of the president, the prime minister, Parliament and other government agencies, and Estonian banks and daily newspapers. However, in this "cyberwar," as Hansen and Nissenbaum (2009) note, "the attackers were not able to—or interested in—penetrating critical digital infrastructures that regulate electricity, finance, energy, or traffic. Forcing a bank to close down online services for an hour might be hard to constitute as "war" and as the Daily Mail laconically noted, "to be frank, in Estonia no one died' (Daily Mail 2007)."

The second cyber war occurred during the following year within the context of a conventional war between Georgia and Russia. The cyber component was similar to the Russian attack on Estonia; DDOS attacks and the defacement of web pages. Estonia sent technical experts to assist Georgia in the defense of their web backbone. Carroll, who dubs the war Cyber War 2.0, describes the interesting strategic decision by the Georgians, who did not receive more than diplomatic support from the West during the physical war.

> At one point… multiple government websites were down or inaccessible for hours. This led them to make perhaps the most strategic move to date in cyber warfare. This impressive move came when the Georgian Government decided to relocate President Mikhail Saakashvili's web site to a web site hosting service in Atlanta, Georgia in the United States. The strategic thinking surrounding this move was twofold. First, the Russian cyber attackers would surely think twice about attacking a web site hosted on servers located in the United States. Secondly, if the Russian cyber attackers were to go after the President's web site hosted on U.S. soil, that action might bring the United States into the conflict (Carroll 2008).

Nonetheless, because of the relatively trivial nature of the targets of the cyber-attacks and perhaps because of the two small nations which were the victims, these first two "cyber-wars" did not create large fears and concerns within the general public and media and public interest waned almost immediately.

However, in the past year, North Korea, China, the United States, Russia and Israel have all been implicated in cyber behaviors that have garnered much greater attention and concern. In spring 2012 the United States took responsibility for the Stuxnet worm, produced through a joint US-Israeli government effort. Stuxnet targeted the Iranian nuclear development effort by disabling the centrifuges used to generate the nuclear fuel (Sanger 2012). Kaspersky Labs identified a campaign which they indicated appeared to emanate from Russia called Red October in January 2013 and further information made available in March 2013 indicates that Red October may have been more dangerous than was originally reported as Kaspersky had later discovered that the perpetrators appeared to have had access to the keys for major cryptography systems which were employed as protection by the European Union, NATO and the German government (Judge 2013; Perlroth 2013). Sanger et al. (2013) detail the most recent state cyber-attacks directed at the New York Times, identified by the security firm Mandiant as originating with the Chinese People's Liberation Army (PLA) and which were subsequently found to have also been directed at the Washington Post and the Wall Street Journal. South Korea has also accused North Korea of initiating attacks on computer systems which paralyzed some banks and television stations. The malware employed in the attacks has been labelled "DarkSeoul" (Choe 2013). We will return to the implications of these three events below, but first it is important to place these events and the current concern with cyber war and its implications in context.

Warner (2012:782) argues that concern with cyber war (and cyber security) is not new but has developed over the past half century. He points to the National Security Agency "war game" ELIGIBLE RECEIVER in 1997 as a signal point but one that occurred three decades after the concern with thinking about cyber war by the US military had commenced. That thinking identified key concerns which Warner (2012:782) summarizes as:

- Computers can spill sensitive data and must be guarded (1960s)
- Computers can be attacked and data stolen (1970s)
- We can build computer attacks into military arsenals (1980s and 1990s)
- Others might do that to us—and perhaps already are (1990s)

Stevens (2012:151) submits that while Rattray argued that "the 1990s were characterized more by a focus on 'the use of perception management than with digital attacks on information infrastructures', more recent work has tended to concern itself with the deterrence of 'cyber attacks', understood as adversarial computer-mediated actions against critical information infrastructures (CII) and other ICT-networked national assets, including those of the military and security services."

Most importantly, what we see, most clearly and transparently in the United States, is the elevation of the cyber component of military strategy. The military has long been concerned with the use of cyber tools for improving what was characterized in the 1960s as C3: Command, Control and Communication. This concept has transitioned through a number of stages corresponding to advances in digital technologies. Its second stage was C3I (Cimbala 1984), Command, Control, Communication and Information, and then C4I, Command, Control, Communication, Computers and Information to today's C4ISTAR Command, Control, Communications, Computers, Intelligence, Surveillance and Reconnaissance. The concern throughout has been to marry the command and control capabilities of the digital to the physical force capabilities of the "traditional" military functions while also understanding and developing the distinctive utilities of both the digital and physical force capabilities. As Giacomello (2004:391) argues:

Professional military around the world are used to judge the effectiveness of weapons systems according to the "break things, kill people" principle... Under certain circumstances, however, even employing bytes (the basic units of all CNO) may lead to the same results. If CNO target the critical application software of certain infrastructures, they may well yield a BTKP outcome.... If the main outcome of those attacks had been the SCADA (Supervisory Control and Data Acquisition) management systems of critical infrastructure, the potential physical damage would have been considerable.

And, as Stevens (2012:149) reminds us, John Arquilla and David Ronfeldt in their oft-cited 1993 article, 'Cyberwar is Coming!' differentiated between strategic-level 'netwar', which constitutes a 'societal-ideational' conflict mediated by networked ICTs, and 'cyberwar', which connotes an operational-tactical form of information conflict between organized state militaries. Guitton (2013) submits that the there was a perception by states, and particularly the US, that the cyber environment has grown more threatening over the next decade and therefore, "The US Government responded to their perception of a latent threat from information systems by issuing policy. The first cyber strategy was published in 2003 and the budget requested to secure the cyberspace increased since then to reach the high figure of $3.2 billion in 2011 of $3,729 billion of the requested expenditure for the next fiscal year (2013:21–22)."

In the context of that budget request, the United States signaled a dramatic escalation in its commitment to cyber war in 2010. First, after much discussion, initiated by Secretary of Defense Robert Gates, it created US Cyber Command in May 2010 and second, shortly thereafter followed publication of the Pentagon's New Cyberstrategy by U.S. Deputy Secretary of Defense William Lynn III in Foreign Affairs (Lynn 2010).

General Keith Alexander, who in 2010 was the Director of the National Security Agency (NSA), which had been created in 1952, was named to head Cyber Command while also maintaining his position as the Director of NSA. The National Security Agency has two main missions, to collect signals intelligence and to protect U.S. information systems. Much about the NSA is classified and for most of its history has been hidden from public view much less scrutiny. Bamford (1983), who has become the foremost scholar of the NSA, has argued that it has been so secretive that its acronym jokingly has been pronounced as standing for No Such Agency.

The NSA is divided into two major missions: the Signals Intelligence Directorate (SID), which produces foreign signal intelligence information, and the Information Assurance Directorate (IAD), which protects U.S. information systems (Bamford 1983, 2001). General Alexander was quite assertive in espousing the new command's responsibilities. "We have to have offensive capabilities, to, in real time, shut down somebody trying to attack us (Nakashima 2010)." Clearly, placing General Alexander at the head of the two commands effectively combines the defensive and offensive cyber capabilities under one command and reflects the transformation in cyber war doctrine. Deputy Secretary of Defense Lynn (2010) provided the public presentation of the new cyber strategy. Lynn argued that "As A DOCTRINAL[6] matter, the Pentagon has formally recognized cyberspace as a new domain of warfare. Although cyberspace is a man-made domain, it has become just as critical to military operations as land, sea, air, and space." Earlier in the year Sanger and Shanker (2013) argued that the new Pentagon strategy was premised on a secret internal Obama administration review which concluded that the President could lawfully engage in pre-emptive cyber-attacks in the event that the U.S. confronted an imminent threat. After the Lynn article appeared, Stephen Webster (2012) argued that "The capabilities being sought would allow U.S. cyber-warriors to "deceive, deny, disrupt, degrade and destroy" information and computers around the globe."

---

[6] Capitals in original.

In brief, the United States, having previously engaged in the creation of the offensive weapons, Stuxnet, Duqu, Flame and Gauss (GReAT 2012), was announcing an important transformational strategy. The United States formally and publicly made the transition from a cyber-defense position anchored by the formal National Security Agency missions of gathering intelligence and protecting critical infrastructure in a primarily defensive posture enabling C4ISTAR (Control, Communications, Computers, Intelligence, Surveillance and Reconnaissance, see Cimbala 2005) to a force structure and strategy that affords equal status to offensive capabilities and their applications within conflict. It is important to understand the step level jump that Stuxnet and its family of malware produced by the United States (and Israel) represents:

> Stuxnet could spread stealthily between computers running Windows—even those not connected to the Internet. If a worker stuck a USB thumb drive into an infected machine, Stuxnet could, well, worm its way onto it, then spread onto the next machine that read that USB drive. Because someone could unsuspectingly infect a machine this way, letting the worm proliferate over local area networks, experts feared that the malware had perhaps gone wild across the world (Kushner 2013).

What this means is that if critical infrastructure, the web and all machines, devices etc. are indeed kept separate stuxnet cannot spread to critical infrastructure-but the reality is that people, corporations, terrorist groups and governments find it too inconvenient to follow the basic rules of protection.

And even more importantly, it means that the United States has unleashed a new generation of weapons which are more ambitious than any weapons previously employed by any states, criminal enterprises or other non-state actors. General Alexander previously had compared cyber-attacks with weapons of mass destruction and, his recent statements more clearly indicate that the US is planning for even greater offensive applications of the new mode of warfare. Aiding in the new command's new offensive intentions was the announcement in January 2013 that Cyber Command's 900 personnel would be augmented by 4,000 new hires, despite cuts in other segments of the Pentagon's budget that were mandated by the newly in force sequester agreement (Bumiller 2013). While the NSA budget remains classified, its budget is generally recognized to be the largest component of the intelligence budgets. Since 9/11, moreover, billions of new allocations have flowed to the agency and it has dramatically expanded its physical footprint to accommodate the growth (Bamford 2012). It is clear that there is no non-state actor which is capable of putting together the resources, both in terms of personnel and hardware, that the United States has committed to the enterprise and indeed there are few, if any, states, that could match the enormous investment that the United States has now made in cyber war, both offensively and defensively. The fruits of those efforts can be seen through Stuxnet which targeted the Iranians to destroy their nuclear development. As yet, we do not know the purpose of Gauss but it, Flame and Duqu clearly target military, diplomatic and financial resources and provide an enormous quantity of information for the NSA to evaluate. The United States has also developed a classified set of weapons, and protocols for using them, and distributed them throughout the US military and intelligence establishment, making clear the intention to employ the offensive advantage it has at present (Nakashima 2011).

We also know that the Chinese have made significant investments and efforts in cyber espionage, both commercial/industrial as well as military/diplomatic. The Russians have expended great efforts and Red October indicates that they have focused their efforts on military/diplomatic cyber-espionage. Guitton (2013:22) argues that the securitisation of cyberspace in Europe has reached the doctrinal level, but not the allocation of resources. However, other states have established a cyberwar presence. Lewis and Timlin (2011:3–4) identified 33 states that include cyber-warfare in their military planning and organization and argue that public information is available on 12 states that have established or plan to establish military cyber-warfare organizations within the next year. The consequence of all these state investments in cyber war capabilities are clear: The genie is out of the bottle and the states have, by their public behaviors, endorsed the use of the weapons.

> **Key Points**
>
> - Despite the hyperbole attracted by cyberterrorism, states have been investing increasingly heavily in their cyber war capabilities for more than a decade now.
> - These capabilities went largely unnoticed until the early twenty-first century and high profile events in Estonia, Georgia and Iran.
> - The US, and other major international players have become increasingly interested in offensive cyber capabilities.

5.4   Implications and Conclusions

It is clear thus that there are many parallels to observations about states, "terrorists" and terrorism that have unfolded in the development and discussion of threats of cyber terrorism and cyber war during the past quarter century. Just as states decried the use of terrorism by non-state actors while also supporting or turning a blind eye to the use of terrorism by non-state actors of whom they approved, states have condemned cyber terrorists while building up their own capacities to engage in destructive cyber behaviors.

Jason Healey (2011) provides additional evidence of these parallels. Healey provides an argument for the need to establish "The Spectrum of State Responsibility" when attributing a cyber-attack:

> The *spectrum of state responsibility* is a tool to help analysts with imperfect knowledge assign responsibility for a particular attack or campaign of attacks with more precision and transparency. This spectrum assigns 10 categories, each marked by a different degree of responsibility, based on whether a nation ignores, abets, or conducts an attack. The spectrum starts from a very passive responsibility—a nation having insecure systems that lead to an attack—up to very active responsibility—a national government actually planning and executing an attack.

The ten categories[7] fall into three sets of responsibility: passive, actively ignoring or abetting, and direct involvement in ordering or conducting activity. In the talk referenced at the beginning of this chapter (Stohl 1985) I proposed, in addition to Coercive diplomacy three parallel categories of state terrorism in international affairs: Surrogate terrorism in which the state gave passive consent by what I referred to as acquiescence, Surrogate terrorism in which there was direct support by the state, and clandestine terrorism in which the state directly participated. What both the Healey and Stohl spectrums of responsibility have in common is that they illustrate how behaviors that states, in general, condemn when done by their opposition and by non-state actors are "legitimated" by labeling. The unintended consequence is that these behaviours, regardless of how they are labeled, serve to undermine the norms necessary for building cooperative state and international community behaviour to confront cyber threats not only to military establishments, but also to other national critical infrastructures: transportation, power, water, food distribution systems and institutional as well as personal financial security systems dependent more and more on web based transactions.

Deibert (2011) addresses the implications of Russian and Chinese inability to compete with the investments that the United States has made in CyberWar. He argues "they will look at asymmetric techniques, including potentially cultivating criminal networks, or encouraging so-called patriotic hacking in which citizens themselves wage cyberattacks." Combining this with the observations of Hollis (2011:3) that:

> Hacker wars between (often quite talented) patriotic amateur hackers, cyber militias, and organized criminal gangs have become a widely accepted de facto form of nation-state conflict over the past 20 years (for example: Israeli vs Arab/Muslim (Sept 2000), India vs Pakistan, US vs China (April-May 2001), Russian vs Estonia (April-May 2007), etc...).

---

[7] The Spectrum of State Responsibility

1. State-prohibited. The national government will help stop the third-party attack
2. State-prohibited-but-inadequate. The national government is cooperative but unable to stop the third-party attack
3. State-ignored. The national government knows about the third-party attacks but is unwilling to take any official action
4. State-encouraged. Third parties control and conduct the attack, but the national government encourages them as a matter of policy
5. State-shaped. Third parties control and conduct the attack, but the state provides some support
6. State-coordinated. The national government coordinates third-party attackers such as by "suggesting" operational details
7. State-ordered. The national government directs third-party proxies to conduct the attack on its behalf
8. State-rogue-conducted. Out-of-control elements of cyber forces of the national government conduct the attack
9. State-executed. The national government conducts the attack using cyber forces under their direct control
10. State-integrated. The national government attacks using integrated third-party proxies and government non-state actors. These behaviors thus serve to undermine the norms which underlie the international law regime

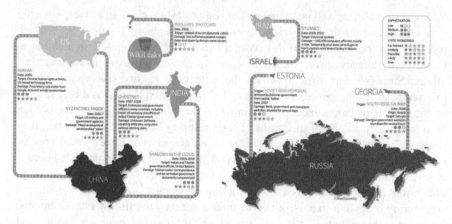

Fig. 5.1 Cyber Attacks by Country by Giles 2010

Jim Giles (2010) question of whether states are unleashing the dogs of cyber war appears to be sadly behind the curve. He usefully provides the following graphic to illustrate the level of activity (Fig. 5.1).

Neither the attacks nor the investments they represent have gone unnoticed by the larger world community of states. Many states have recognized the danger of the genie being allowed out of the lamp and are struggling to find mechanisms to try to put it back in. However, as with the nuclear genie, the cyber genie once out of the lamp, is unlikely ever to be returned. The head of the UN International Telecommunications Union (ITU) has called for a treaty to prevent 'cyberwar', which would act to reduce states' inclination to launch cyber first-strikes against other states, a proposal supported by Russia, China and many non-aligned countries, although not the United States (Stevens 2012:163). O'Connell (2012) argues that the United States would be far better served by devoting increased resources to the development of a comprehensive cyber security treaty that de-militarizes cyberspace and emphasizes law enforcement cooperation and improved defence and suggests that "It is time, therefore, to turn to cyber disarmament and a focus on peaceful protection of the Internet. The motto should be: a good cyber defence is good cyber defence."

It remains the case that individual hackers and criminal enterprises provide a continuing threat to business systems, banks and social networks. Networked infrastructure such as power stations, water resources and transportation systems also remain vulnerable. Whether that threat rises to the level of cyber terror rather than criminal behavior remains contested terrain. As of the present, a cyber terrorist event by a non-state actor has still not actually occurred. The United States and Israeli Stuxnet attack on Iran's nuclear development would have been categorized as cyber terrorism had it been initiated by a non-state actor, as similarly would have been the activities of Chinese, Russian and North Korean actors launching their cyber attacks over the past year. As with the case of terrorism in general, such attacks when conducted by states are by convention designated by more conventional labels such as war, coercive diplomacy or espionage. Nonetheless, the behaviours or acts are the same.

In the United States, unlike the rest of the OECD nations, much of the physical and digital infrastructure is in private rather than government hands. The recent Snowden leaks have once again reminded the public that the US state, while not owning the digital infrastructure, has full access to its capabilities for its own purposes (including accessing the same private information that individuals worry that cyber terrorists will acquire). The US government has not yet made the assertion that it is necessary, for security purposes, to attempt to place these resources in public rather than private hands and in the contemporary political environment would unlikely succeed in doing so in any case.

What is apparent is that the United States is more comfortable in its superior resource and capabilities position. In terms of Cyber-War, the Obama administration has raised to the doctrinal, the preemptive warfare doctrine first enunciated by the Bush Administration. The likely consequence is a cyber-arms race for the foreseeable future. Given US investments and strategic announcements, the Chinese and the Russians are unlikely to unilaterally disarm or invest great resources in preventing non-state actors, whether criminal or political, from employing cyber weapons against the United States or other states unless their own interests are threatened. This further undermines potential and needed positive norms of state responsibility as outlined by Healey (2011). The consequence of the great powers' individual actions, however unintentional, collectively serves as an endorsement of Stanley Kubrick's and Terry Southern's satirical insights on nuclear war. As the chapter title signals, "they" have stopped worrying and learned to love cyberwar.

Key Points

- States continue to condemn 'cyberterrorism' while building up their own cyber capabilities, just as they condemn the 'terrorism' of their enemies rather than their selves and their allies.
- A consequence of this inconsistency is the undermining of the norms required for international cooperation.

Further Reading

Bamford J (1983) The puzzle palace. Penguin, New York

Bamford J (2001) Body of secrets: anatomy of the ultra-secret National Security Agency. Doubleday, New York

Bamford J (2012) The NSA is building the country's biggest spy center (watch what you say). In: Wired 15 March 2012. http://www.wired.com/threatlevel/2012/03/ff_nsadatacenter/all/

Cimbala SJ (1984) U.S. strategic C3I: a conceptual framework air university review November/December 1984. http://www.airpower.au.af.mil/airchronicles/aureview/1984/nov-dec/cimbala.html

Cimbala SJ (2005) Transformation in concept and policy. Joint Force Q 38(Summer 2005)

Stevens T (2012) A cyberwar of ideas? Deterrence and norms in cyberspace. Contemp Secur Pol 33(1):148–170. http://dx.doi.org/10.1080/13523260.2012.659597

Stohl M (2006) Cyber terrorism: a clear and present danger, the sum of all fears, breaking point or patriot games? Crime Law Soc Change 46(4–5):223–238
Warner M (2012) Cybersecurity: a pre-history. Intell Natl Secur 27(5):781–799. http://dx.doi.org/10.1080/02684527.2012.708530

References

Arquilla J, Ronfeldt D (1998) The Zapatista Social Netwar in Mexico. Rand, Santa Monica
Arquilla J, Ronfeldt D (1999) The advent of netwar: analytic background. Stud Conflict Terrorism 22:3
Arquilla J, Ronfeldt D, Zanini M (1999) Networks, netwar and information age terrorism. In: Lesser A, Hoffman B, Arquilla J, Ronfeldt D, Zanini M (eds) Countering the new terrorism. Rand, Santa Monica, pp 39–84
Aquino S (2009) Should Obama control the Internet? In: Mother Jones 2 April 2009. http://www.motherjones.com/politics/2009/04/should-obama-control-internet
Bamford J (1983) The puzzle palace. Penguin, New York
Bamford J (2001) Body of secrets: anatomy of the ultra-secret National Security Agency. Doubleday, New York
Bamford J (2012) The NSA is building the country's biggest spy center (watch what you say). In: Wired 15 March 2012. http://www.wired.com/threatlevel/2012/03/ff_nsadatacenter/all/
Bumiller E (2013) Pentagon expanding cybersecurity force to protect networks against attacks. The New York Times 27 January 2013. http://www.nytimes.com/2013/01/28/us/pentagon-to-beef-up-cybersecurity-force-to-counter-attacks.html?_r=0
Bumiller E, Shanker T (2012) Panetta warns of dire threat of cyberattack on U.S. The New York Times 11 October 2012. http://www.nytimes.com/2012/10/12/world/panetta-warns-of-dire-threat-of-cyberattack.html?pagewanted=all&_r=0
Carroll W (2008) Cyber War 2.0—Russia v. Georgia. 13 August 2008. Available via DefenseTech. http://defensetech.org/2008/08/13/cyber-war-2-0-russia-v-georgia/#ixzz2PJhri1hS
Choe S-H (2013) Computer networks in South Korea are paralyzed in cyberattacks. The New York Times 23 March 2013. https://www.nytimes.com/2013/03/21/world/asia/south-korea-computer-network-crashes.html
Cimbala SJ (1984) U.S. strategic C3I: a conceptual framework air university review November/December 1984. http://www.airpower.au.af.mil/airchronicles/aureview/1984/nov-dec/cimbala.html
Cimbala SJ (2005) Transformation in concept and policy. Joint Force Q 38(Summer 2005) 28–33
Conway M (2005) Terrorist "use" of the internet and fighting back. Paper prepared for presentation at the conference Cybersafety: safety and security in a networked world: balancing cyber-rights and responsibilities. Oxford Internet Institute (OII), Oxford University, Oxford, 8–10 Sept 2005. http://www.oii.ox.ac.uk/research/cybersafety/extensions/pdfs/papers/maura_conway.pdf. Accessed 1 Feb 2006
Crypt Newsletter (2009) http://www.soci.niu.edu/~crypt/other/harbor.htm
Dean J (2001) Nation unprepared for cyber war, experts say December 17, 2001. Government Executive. http://www.govexec.com/defense/2001/12/nation-unprepared-for-cyber-war-experts-say/10725/
Debrix F (2001) Cyberterror and media-induced fears: the production of emergency culture. Strat J Theor Cult Polit 14(1):149–168
Deibert R (2011) Tracking the emerging arms race in cyberspace. Bull Atom Scient 67:1
Denning DE (2000) Activism, hacktivism, and cyberterrorism: the Internet as a tool for influencing foreign policy. http://www.nautilus.org/info-policy/workshop/papers/denning.html. Accessed 4 Feb 2000
Epstein K (2009) Fearing 'Cyber Katrina,' Obama candidate for Cyber Czar urges a "FEMA for the Internet". Business Week 18 February 2009. http://www.businessweek.com/the_thread/techbeat/archives/2009/02/fearing_cyber_k.html

Gellman B (2002) Cyber-attacks by Al Qaeda feared: terrorists at threshold of using internet as tool of bloodshed, experts say. Washington Post 27 June 2002:A01. http://www.washington-post.com/ac2/wp-dyn/A50765-2002Jun26. Accessed 1 Dec 2005

Giacomello G (2004) Bangs for the buck: a cost-benefit analysis of cyberterrorism. Stud Conflict Terrorism 27:387–408

Giles J (2010) Are states unleashing the dogs of cyber war? NewScientist 16 December 2010. http://www.intellectualtakeout.org/library/chart-graph/cyber-attack-country

Grabosky P, Stohl M (2003) Cyberterrorism. Reform 82:5–13

GReAT (Global Research & Analysis Team) (2012) Gauss abnormal distribution. http://www.securelist.com/en/analysis/204792238/Gauss_Abnormal_Distribution

Green J (2002). The myth of cyber terrorism. Washington Monthly. http://www.washington-monthly.com/features/2001/0211.green.html. Accessed 1 Feb 2006

Guitton C (2013) Cyber insecurity as a national threat: overreaction from Germany, France and the UK? Eur Secur 22(1):21–35

Hansen L, Nissenbuam H (2009) Digital disaster, cyber security, and the Copenhagen School. Int Stud Q 53:1155–1175

Healey J (2011) The spectrum of national responsibility for cyberattacks. Brown J Int Aff 18(1):43–56

Hollis, D (2011) Cyberwar case study: Georgia 2008. Small Wars J. http://smallwarsjournal.com/jrnl/art/cyberwar-case-study-georgia-2008

Judge P (2013) CeBIT: Red October had EU and German crypto codes—Kaspersky. TechWeek Europe7March2013.http://www.techweekeurope.co.uk/news/cebit-2013-red-october-encryption-kaspersky-109713

Kent J, Steiner K (2012) Ten ways to improve the security of a new computer United States Computer Emergency Response Team. http://www.us-cert.gov/

King R (2012) U.S. Defense Chief Warns of Digital 9/11. 11 October 2012. http://blogs.wsj.com/cio/2012/10/11/u-s-defense-chief-warns-of-digital-911/

Kushner D (2013) The real story of Stuxnet: how Kaspersky Lab tracked down the malware that stymied Iran's nuclear-fuel enrichment program Spectrum: Mar 2013. http://spectrum.ieee.org/telecom/security/the-real-story-of-stuxnet

Landler M, Markoff J (2007) In Estonia, what may be the first war in cyberspace. New York Times Monday 28 May 2007. http://www.nytimes.com/2007/05/28/business/worldbusiness/28iht-cyberwar.4.5901141.html?pagewanted=all

Lewis JA, Timlin K (2011) Cybersecurity and cyberwarfare. CSIS, UNIDIR, Washington DC

Lynn III WJ (2010) Defending a new domain: the Pentagon's cyberstrategy. Foreign Affairs Sept/Oct 2010. http://www.foreignaffairs.com/articles/66552/william-j-lynn-iii/defending-a-new-domain

Nakashima E (2010) Pentagon considers preemptive strikes as part of cyber-defense strategy. The Washington Post 28 August 2010. http://www.washingtonpost.com/wp-dyn/content/article/2010/08/28/AR2010082803849.html

Nakashima E (2011) List of cyber-weapons developed by Pentagon to streamline computer warfare. The Washington Post 31 May 2011. http://www.washingtonpost.com/national/list-of-cyber-weapons-developed-by-pentagon-to-streamline-computer-warfare/2011/05/31/AGSublFH_story.html

O'Connell ME (2012) Cyber security without cyber war. J Conflict Secur Law 17(2):187–209

Panetta L (2012) Remarks by Secretary Panetta on Cybersecurity to the Business Executives for National Security, New York City U.S. Department of Defense Office of the Assistant Secretary of Defense (Public Affairs). News Transcript 11 October 2012. http://www.defense.gov/transcripts/transcript.aspx?transcriptid=5136

Perlroth N (2013) Security firm discovers cyber-spy campaign. The New York Times 14 January 2013. http://bits.blogs.nytimes.com/2013/01/14/security-firm-discovers-global-spy-campaign/

Richards J (2009) Denial-of-service: the Estonian Cyberwar and its implications for U.S. National Security. International Affairs Review 18:1. http://www.iar-gwu.org/node/65

Sanger DE (2012) Obama order sped up wave of cyberattacks against Iran. The New York Times 1 June 2012. http://www.nytimes.com/2012/06/01/world/middleeast/obama-ordered-wave-of-cyberattacks-against-iran.html?pagewanted=all

Sanger DE, Shanker T (2013) Broad powers seen for Obama in cyberstrikes. The New York Times 3 February 2013. http://www.nytimes.com/2013/02/04/us/broad-powers-seen-for-obama-in-cyberstrikes.html?pagewanted=all&_r=0

Sanger DE, Barboza D, Perlroth N (2013) Chinese army unit is seen as tied to hacking against U.S. The New York Times 18 February 2013. http://www.nytimes.com/2013/02/19/technology/chinas-army-is-seen-as-tied-to-hacking-against-us.html?pagewanted=all&_r=0

Smith GC (2002) Compumetrically speaking, chapter 2. 10 January 2002. https://vmyths.com/column/2/2002/1/10/

Stark R (1999) Cyber terrorism: rethinking new technology. Department of Defense and Strategic Studies, Washington, DC

Stevens T (2012) A cyberwar of ideas? Deterrence and norms in cyberspace. Contemp Secur Pol 33(1):148–170. http://dx.doi.org/10.1080/13523260.2012.659597

Stohl M (1985) States terrorism, and state terrorism. Paper presented at the Defense Intelligence College Symposium on Terrorism, Washington, DC, 3 December 1985

Stohl M (1988) States, terrorism and state terrorism: the role of the superpowers. In: Slater R, Stohl M (eds) Current perspectives on international terrorism. Macmillan, London, pp 155–205

Stohl M (2006) Cyber terrorism: a clear and present danger, the sum of all fears, breaking point or patriot games? Crime Law Social Change 46:223–238

Thomas TL (2003) Al Qaeda and the Internet: the danger of "cyberplanning". Parameters 33(1):112–23, From Carlisle http://www.army.mil/usawc/Parameters/03spring/thomas.pdf. Accessed 1 Feb 2006

Traynor, I (2007) Russia accused of unleashing cyberwar to disable Estonia The Guardian Wednesday 16 May 2007. http://www.guardian.co.uk/world/2007/may/17/topstories3.russia

Warner M (2012) Cybersecurity: a pre-history. Intell Natl Secur 27(5):781–799. http://dx.doi.org/10.1080/02684527.2012.708530

Webster SC (2012) Pentagon may apply preemptive warfare policy to the Internet. The Raw Story 29 August 2010. http://www.rawstory.com/rs/2010/08/29/pentagon-weighs-applying-preemptive-warfare-tactics-internet/

White CKC (1998) Cyber-terrorism: modem mayhem. U.S. Army 639 War College, Carlisle Barracks, Pennsylvania. http://stinet.dtic.mil/dticrev/a345705.pdf. Accessed 1 March 2006

Chapter 6
Reality Check: Assessing the (Un)Likelihood of Cyberterrorism

Maura Conway

6.1 Introduction

A January 2013 article on the prominent technology news website ArsTechnica headlined 'Security Pros Predict "Major" Cyber Terror Attack This Year' reports upon the results of a survey of computer security professionals at the October 2012 Information Systems Security Association conference in Anaheim, California. The survey found that of 105 attendees surveyed, 79 % believed, "there will be a 'major' cyberterrorism event within the next year." Read the piece more closely however and it emerges that what the survey respondents actually believe is that there will be some sort of large-scale attack on the information technology powering some element of America's critical infrastructure (i.e. the electrical grid, energy sector, financial institutions, etc.). In fact, the survey didn't mention cyberterrorism; it "didn't give a definition for a major cyber attack" at all. "We left that to the security professionals to interpret for themselves," a representative from the company that conducted the survey is reported as saying; "[t]he general idea of the question was 'is something big going to happen?'" (Gallagher 2013). Unfortunately, the assumption that any 'big' attack with a cyber-component may be deemed 'cyberterrorism' is commonplace as is the assertion that cyberterrorism is just around the corner. There is no doubt that cyber insecurity and thus cyber threats are serious, increasing, and warrant attention, including from IT professionals, media, scholars, and policymakers. It is certainly the case that, globally, critical cyber infrastructures are insufficiently secured and are thus highly vulnerable to attack. However, the widespread assumption that such an attack will be of a cyberterrorist sort completely omits the calculations likely to be made by terrorists in weighing the costs and benefits of cyberterrorism versus other methods available to them.

M. Conway (✉)
School of Law and Government, Dublin City University, Glasnevin, Dublin, Ireland
e-mail: maura.conway@dcu.ie

T.M. Chen et al. (eds.), *Cyberterrorism: Understanding, Assessment, and Response*,
DOI 10.1007/978-1-4939-0962-9_6, © Springer Science+Business Media New York 2014

Such calculations are at least as important, if not more so, than the technological aspects of cyberterrorism. Just because IT professionals, journalists, policymakers, and some scholars tend to narrow their thinking to and thence privilege the technology, it should not be assumed that terrorists are of a similar mind. The technology is only half the story, in other words; this chapter addresses the other half (compare with Wilson 2014).

My approach here is two-pronged. I begin by briefly revisiting definitional issues (see Conway 2002a, b, 2003a, 2007, 2012; Hardy and Williams 2014; Jarvis et al. 2014). This is necessary, because any 'reality check' on cyberterrorism—such as that offered in this chapter—requires a reminder that terrorism is not merely 'something big', hence cyberterrorism may not be defined as 'something big in cyberspace.' Having underlined the importance of the 'terrorism' in cyberterrorism, the greater part of the chapter is taken-up with a comparison of cyberterrorism with car bombing that again privileges a terrorism over a technology approach. This is a useful comparison, it is posited, because those hyping the cyberterrorism threat have a tendency to equate opportunity with outcome rather than reflecting upon whether something that *could* happen is in fact *likely* given the potential perpetrators' motives, capabilities, and ends.

Key Points

- Critical cyber infrastructures globally are insufficiently secured and vulnerable to attack.
- Fears of cyberterrorism, however, focus upon technological potential rather than the motives of terrorists: on the 'cyber' rather than the 'terrorism'.
- Focusing on the importance of the 'terrorism' aspect offers a reality check in relation to the threat posed by cyberterrorism.

6.2   Underlining the 'Terrorism' in Cyberterrorism

It is today commonplace when dealing with computers and the Internet to create new words by placing the handle 'cyber,' 'electronic,' or 'information'—often shortened to simply 'e' or 'i'—before another word. This may appear to denote a completely new phenomenon, but often it does not and confusion ensues. Cyberterrorism is the convergence of cyberspace and terrorism. Not the convergence of cyberspace and 'something big' or even the convergence of cyberspace and 'something bad'—although, as will be illustrated below, a cyber-attack would probably need to be both 'big' and 'bad' to be properly deemed cyberterrorism. But the convergence of cyberspace and *terrorism*, the latter of which is something, albeit subject to a high level of definitional contestation, that has a long history and a basic outline shape. First, in order for an attack to be classified as terrorism, it must have a political motive; that an attack is carried out via the Internet does not make this requirement any less necessary. To fail to recognise the importance of motive is to seriously mischaracterize what it is that constitutes terrorism. The second necessary requirement for traditional or 'real world' terrorism is violence or the threat of violence. The problem that arises here is that although 'real world' political violence—and violence more generally—is very heavily studied, virtual 'violence' is a relatively new phenomenon and thus under-researched. It is clear enough that the destruction of another's computer with a hammer is a violent act, but should destruction of the data contained in that machine, whether by the introduction of a virus or some other technological means, also be considered 'violence'? (Gordon and Ford 2002:640). And even if destruction of data or systems meets the 'violence' threshold, can disruption do likewise? Two well-known definitions of cyberterrorism are compared below with respect to their treatment of motive, violence, and a number of other points germane to the follow-up comparison between cyberterrorism and Vehicle-Borne Improvised Explosive Devices (VBIED) attacks.

The US Naval Postgraduate School's Professor Dorothy Denning's definitions of cyberterrorism are probably the most well-known and respected. Denning's (2007:124) most recent definition of cyberterrorism is as follows:

> highly damaging computer-based attacks or threats of attack by non-state actors against information systems when conducted to intimidate or coerce governments or societies in pursuit of goals that are political or social. It is the convergence of terrorism with cyberspace, where cyberspace becomes the means of conducting the terrorist act. Rather than committing acts of violence against persons or physical property, the cyberterrorist commits acts of destruction and disruption against digital property.

Denning (2007:125) goes on to say that:

> To fall in the domain of cyberterror, a cyber attack should be sufficiently destructive or disruptive to generate fear comparable to that from physical acts of terrorism, and it must be conducted for political and social reasons. Critical infrastructures…are likely targets. Attacks against these infrastructures that lead to death or bodily injury, extended power outages, plane crashes, water contamination, or billion dollar banking losses would be examples.

Another well-known definition was proposed by Mark M. Pollitt in his article 'Cyberterrorism: Fact or Fancy?' (1998) in which he unified a definition of cyberspace with a well-known definition of terrorism. For Pollitt, cyberspace may be conceived of as "that place in which computer programs function and data moves." He employed the definition of terrorism contained in Title 22 of the United States Code, Section 2656f(d): "The term 'terrorism' means premeditated, politically motivated violence perpetrated against non-combatant targets by sub-national groups or clandestine agents, usually intended to influence an audience." Pollitt arrived at the following definition of cyberterrorism by combining these two: "Cyberterrorism is the premeditated, politically motivated attack against information, computer systems, computer programs, and data which results in violence against non-combatant targets by sub-national groups or clandestine agents" (Pollitt 1998:9).

Denning's and Pollitt's definitions share similarities, but also significant differ-ences. A crucial point on which Denning and Pollitt are in agreement is that an act may not be classified as cyberterrorism absent a (socio-)political motive. Even very large scale attacks carried out for purposes of, say, self-enrichment, one-upmanship, or similar are thus excluded. With regards to the impacts of a cyberterrorist attack however, Denning's definition appears wider than Pollitt's as she explicitly distinguishes between traditional terrorism's physical violence against persons and property as opposed to cyberterrorism's "acts of destruction and disruption against digital property." Pollitt, on the other hand, refers fairly unambiguously to activity that "results in violence" against persons (see also Schmitt 2013:123; Hardy and Williams 2014). Both definitions nevertheless prohibit classification of everyday terrorist uses of the Net (e.g. for social networking, radicalisation, researching and planning, financing, and other purposes) as cyberterrorism as these are not in themselves either directly violent or massively disruptive or destructive. Both definitions also rule out (distributed) denial of service ((D)DoS) attacks and similar. An additional issue covered by both definitions are the wider intimidatory or coercive purposes of terrorism and thence also cyberterrorism. An interesting case in this respect is recent revelations, contained in previously classified intelligence reports, of al-Qaeda's interest in hacking into and disabling US drones' satellite links and remote controls (Whitlock and Gellman 2013). If successful, this would not in itself be terrorism however, in the same way as IRA bombings were counted as terrorist acts, but IRA bank robberies were largely not. This is because the former had a terror-inducing and thus directly coercive purpose, but the latter were largely a funding mechanism. For interference with a drone to be classified as an act of cyberterrorism under either of the two definitions under discussion here, I suggest, al-Qaeda operatives would need to hack into and take control of a drone and then successfully re-route and re-aim it to cause civilian fatalities.

The fourth pertinent issue worth drawing attention to in regard to definition is Denning's requirement that for an attack to be labelled cyberterrorism it should be undertaken by 'non-state actors'. This contrasts with Pollitt's approach that mentions 'clandestine agents', in addition to 'sub-national groups'. If the 2010 Stuxnet attack on Iran's Natanz nuclear facility was a joint operation by the United States and Israel (Denning 2012), then it might be conceived as cyberterrorism on Pollitt's definition. It is, however, ruled out as such by Denning's, and the same may be said for the 2007 cyber attacks on Estonia (Rid 2013:6–7). Both the Estonia attacks and Stuxnet were nevertheless described in the press and elsewhere—including by the Estonian government—as instances of cyberterrorism (see, for example, Agence France Presse 2007; Baltic News Service 2007; Lloyds 2014). The fifth and final definitional issue I want to address is Denning's and Pollitt's differing perspectives on the role of cyberspace in cyberterrorism. Denning is clear in her definition that cyberterrorism must use cyberspace as the method of attack and not just its target. This clearly distinguishes her approach from Pollitt's as the latter's definition would appear to include, for example, a car bomb attack on an Internet hub while Denning's emphatically does not (see also Macdonald et al. 2013:9). This distinction is, I suggest, as important in respect of the cyber component of the definition of cyberterrorism as the motive and violence issues are to the terrorism component of same. In fact, Pollitt's definition would appear to allow for the label of cyberterrorism to be retrospectively applied to a whole range of attacks, including bomb attacks on electricity sub-stations, telephone exchanges, etc., undertaken decades prior to the invention of the term. This is the main reason why Denning's definition is preferred over Pollitt's in this chapter.

It should be clear at this stage that carefully categorising cyber attacks using a well-thought-out definition excludes a great many types of activity typically held-up by journalists, policymakers, and others as cyberterrorism from being conceived as such. Journalists, for example, regularly mix mention of cyberterrorism with terrorist 'use' of the Internet, hacktivism (i.e. activist hacking), hacking, and even cyberwar, as if these activities are all on a par with each other or even indistinguishable. Newspaper headlines such as 'Cyber Terror is the New Language of War' (Dorgan 2013), 'Cyber Spies Terror War; MoD and Treasury Targeted' (Riley 2011), and 'Terrorists "Gaining Upper Hand in Cyber War"' (Sengupta 2010) are prevalent. Taking the terrorism components of cyberterrorism seriously rather than myopically focusing on its cyber aspects provides considerable clarification. Application of Denning's criteria having eliminated everything from website defacements to Stuxnet from the domain of cyberterrorism, there is nonetheless a range of cyber activities that, were they to have a political motive and a message-generation component and that resulted in massive disruption or violence, could—would?—be termed cyberterrorism. So why haven't we yet seen any such attacks?

The position adopted in this chapter is that there are a number of factors that distinguish cyberterrorism from 'real world' terrorism that cause cyberterrorism to remain an outside threat. Cyber-based activities, it will be argued herein, don't tend to work as terrorism, and the domination of debate in this area by 'The IT Crowd' (Singer and Friedman 2014)—rather than, if you like, 'The Terrorism Studies Crowd'—has skewed assessment of risk. From a terrorism perspective, the costs largely outweigh the significantly less than assured destructive capacities and publicity benefits likely to accrue to a cyberterrorist attack (compare with Wilson 2014). This chapter concentrates on four major factors that weigh against the likelihood of cyberterrorism occurring: (i) cost factor; (ii) complexity factor; (iii) destruction factor; and (iv) media impact factor. Denning has observed that "For a politically-motivated cyber-attack to be considered an act of cyber-terror, it would have to be serious enough to actually incite terror on a par with violent, physical acts of terrorism such as bombings" (Denning 2012:678). Each of these factors will therefore be considered not just in respect of cyberterrorism, but also in respect of 'Vehicle-Borne Improvised Explosive Devices' (VBIEDs) or, in common parlance, 'car bombs.' No act of cyberterrorism has ever yet occurred, car bombing, on the other hand, has a long and bloody globe-spanning history and continues to prove a spectacularly attractive terrorist option (Davis 2008). Following a detailed weighing-up of the pros and cons of cyber-attack versus car bombing the conclusion arrived at is that traditional low-tech 'real world' terrorist attacks will continue to be more effective and therefore 'attractive' than their cyber variant for some time to come.

6.3   Cyberterrorism Versus VBIED Attacks

This section compares instances of car bombing with non-instances of cyberterrorism. This has some difficulties as an approach, as one might imagine. It is rather difficult to compare things that have an actual existence and can therefore be described, counted, costed, etc. and those that do not. The seeming implausibility of such an undertaking notwithstanding, the insistence of journalists, policymakers, IT security professionals, and others that catastrophic cyberterrorism is imminent requires analysis and counter-argument. Those involved in the cyberterrorism debate cannot draw on either history or experience to bolster their positions, as a major cyberterrorist incident has never yet occurred. For this reason, different scenarios or stories about the possible course of future events are providing the grounds on which decisions must be made. The upshot of this is that a multitude of actors with their various, and often divergent, interests are competing with each other by means of their versions of the future, which are particularly subject to political exploitation and instrumentation (Deibert 2010:118). Cyberterrorism has thus taken on a rather grandiose 'sci-fi' character. The comparison below is therefore by way of a reality check in which some of those potential attacks that would fit Denning's definition of cyberterrorism are compared with a form of terrorism that is so contemporarily 'doable' that in some countries and regions it has come to be mundane or commonplace: VBIED attacks.

'Vehicle-Borne Improvised Explosive Device' (VBIED) is the term used to describe a 'home-made' as opposed to off-the-shelf explosive device housed and delivered in a vehicle. The most common type of VBIED is a car bomb (see, for example, Table 6.1), but a range of other vehicles from bicycles to boats have been employed. Some analysts even consider the planes on 9/11 as VBIEDs, albeit these were not carrying explosives additional to their fuel. Car bombs are remarkably effective weapons as they offer a highly innocuous way to transport large amounts of explosives and/or flammable material to a target while the content of the vehicle's fuel tank lends the blast additional power and the body of the vehicle itself produces copious shrapnel.

Table 6.1 Documented civilian casualties from suicide VBIEDs in Iraq, 20 March 2003–31 Dec. 2010

	Suicide bike or scooter bomb	Suicide car bomb	Suicide truck or minibus bomb	Suicide fuel tanker bomb	Total suicide VBIED[a]
Events (n[%])	15 (2 %)	532 (53 %)	49 (5 %)	6 (1 %)	664 (66 %)
Civilian deaths (n[%])	194 (2 %)	4358 (36 %)	906 (7 %)	625 (5 %)	7072 (58 %)
Civilian injuries (n[%])	442 (1 %)	12224 (40 %)	2967 (10 %)	1690 (6 %)	19989 (65 %)
Civilian casualties (n[%])	636 (1 %)	16582 (39 %)	3873 (9 %)	2315 (5 %)	27061 (63 %)
Injured-to-killed ratio	2:3	2:8	3:3	2:7	2:8
Mortality in victims (%)	31 %	26 %	23 %	27 %	26 %

Adapted from Table 1 (p. 907) in Hsiao-Rei Hicks et al. (2011)
[a]Results do not total across suicide bomb subtypes because not all suicide VBIEDs were described in adequate detail to identify vehicle sub-type

In recent years, suicide VBIEDs have been used extensively, including in Iraq (see Table 6.1), Afghanistan, and elsewhere. Other countries or conflicts in which VBIEDs have been widely deployed include Colombia, India, Israel, Lebanon, Northern Ireland, Pakistan, Russia, and Sri Lanka. VBIED attacks have been chosen for comparison with cyberterrorism in this chapter precisely because of their long history, wide geographical spread, and contemporary ubiquity, but also because this form of attack is neither the easiest nor the most complex type of terrorism. It is not the cheapest or the most expensive. It is neither the flashiest nor the most attention-getting. It might be described as mid-range terrorism and thus an appropriate comparator.

The four factors with respect to which VBIED attacks and cyberterrorism are compared below are those that have been evidenced by experience to matter, to varying extents, to almost all terrorists. Put another way, these are the factors, it is suggested, that would be taken into account by terrorists in the early stages of planning an attack and evaluating the desirability of cyber versus more traditional methods. In terms of the comparison, some of the arguments may strike the reader as more convincing than others; I'm less interested however in the merits of each comparison taken separately than in the compelling nature of considering them in tandem.

6.3.1 Cost Factor

Even though exact figures are difficult to obtain, one thing is clear, car bomb construction is cheap. The first World Trade Centre attack in 1993 killed six people and injured more than a thousand; the truck bomb is estimated to have cost $400 to construct (Giacomello 2004:397). In April 1995, the Oklahoma City bombing, which prior to 9/11 was the largest terrorist attack on US soil in history, killed 168 people. It is estimated to have cost less than US$5,000, which was outlaid for fertiliser, fuel, and van rental fees (Michel and Herbeck 2001:176). The 9/11 attacks—although not strictly VBIED attacks—were also relatively cheap to carry out; the *9/11 Commission Report* estimated that it cost just $400,000–$500,000 in total

financing over nearly 2 years, including living expenses for and other payments to
the 19 hijackers (2004:172; see also Wilson 2014). VBIED attacks are commonplace in on-going conflicts, such as in Iraq and Afghanistan. The US Department of
Defense's Joint Improvised Explosive Device Defeat Organisation (JIEDDO) estimated that the average cost to construct a car bomb in Afghanistan in 2006—the
most recent year for which such information is (publicly?) available—was just
$1,675 (Ackerman 2011).

If the exact cost of VBIED construction is difficult to estimate due to the diversity of components used, significant cost disparities depending on where the vehicle
and/or other components are purchased, and so forth, the challenge of estimating
the cost of a potential cyberterrorism attack is exponentially greater. Giampiero
Giacomello nevertheless engaged in a speculative analysis that addressed precisely
this issue in 2004. In his 'Bangs for the Buck: A Cost-Benefit Analysis of
Cyberterrorism,' Giacomello considered the cost of two common cyberterrorism
scenarios: a cyber attack on a hydroelectric dam and a cyber attack on air traffic
control systems. He estimated the cost of the dam attack at $1.2–1.3 million with
potential fatalities of between 50 and 100 and the cost of the air traffic attack at
$2.5–3 million with the potential for 250–500 casualties (Giacomello 2004:397–
398). The dam attack, he pointed out, "would look like an attractive investment, if it
were not the case that a suicide bomber would cause roughly the same amount of
casualties at a fraction of that cost" (Giacomello 2004:397). Now consider that
according to the author of the definitive analysis of Stuxnet, testing for that attack
"must have involved a fully-functional mock-up [uranium enrichment test bed]
operating with real uranium hexafluoride" (Langner 2013:20). This puts the cost of
just a portion of that attack at (conservatively) tens of millions of dollars. There is
every appearance therefore that Giacomello got it right when he concluded that on
the basis of financial considerations alone "cyberterrorism would be a highly inef-
ficient solution for terrorists, due to high costs and meagre returns" (2004:388).

6.3.2   Complexity Factor

VBIEDs are relatively simple to build and deliver. Bicycles, scooters, motorcycles,
cars, vans, mini-buses, trucks, and tankers are everywhere. Many people own small
vehicles and so are already in possession of an important component of the finished
device; larger vehicles can be bought, rented, or stolen. In terms of a delivery mechanism, VBIEDs are highly innocuous and therefore difficult to guard against.
Fertiliser is the other major component of many VBIEDs. Large amounts of it can
still be purchased easily (and relatively cheaply) due to its wide legitimate use in
agriculture, despite governments' efforts to place curbs on sales of large amounts
due to its explosive capacities. A great many groups and individuals have the necessary expertise to themselves construct and/or to educate others how to construct
VBIEDs. These include members or former members of terrorist organisations,
such as Hamas, Hizbollah, the Liberation Tigers of Tamil Eelam (LTTE), and the

Provisional IRA, and increasing numbers of violent jihadi bomb-makers active in Afghanistan, Iraq, and elsewhere. Individuals with no known links to any terrorist organisation have also demonstrated the capacity for VBIED-construction; these include Timothy McVeigh and Terry Nichols, the perpetrators of the Oklahoma City bombing, and Anders Breivik, who deployed a VBIED against government offices in Oslo, Norway on 22 July, 2011 that killed 8 people and injured over 200.

There has been heightened concern amongst policymakers, law enforcement agencies, and others since the 9/11 attacks regarding the proliferation of "how to" information online devoted to explaining, amongst other things, the technical intricacies of making VBIEDs. In fact, as early as 1997, the US Department of Justice had concluded that the availability of bomb-making information played a significant role in facilitating terrorist and other criminal acts (pp.'s 15–16). Today, there is easy online access to various types of forums and content containing bomb-making information. The level of threat posed by this remains a source of debate with some commentators insisting that legislation must be put in place to outlaw such online content, and others pointing out both that this material is already easily accessible in bookstores and libraries (Leonard 2013) and also that much of the information is unreliable or simply wrong (Kenney 2010). Sophisticated terrorist organizations do not need to rely on the Internet for developing their bomb-making skills, but disaffected individuals prepared to use terrorist tactics to advance their politics, of whatever stripe, appear to have increasing recourse to online content. While Faisal Shazad, the failed Times Square car-bomber, is said to have travelled to acquire his bomb-making skills in Pakistan where he received 3–5 days of training (Hoffman 2010:3), Anders Breivik produced a new type of fertiliser bomb through combining knowledge from different recipes he located on the Internet (Aasland Ravndal 2012:17). The main point here is that rudimentary bomb-making skills can be easily and quickly obtained in a number of different ways. On the other hand, the failed Times Square attack, along with the failed car bomb attacks planned and carried out by medical doctors in central London and at Glasgow airport in June 2007, shows that even relatively unsophisticated real-world attacks have a level of difficulty and are routinely unsuccessful. Cyberterrorism can be expected to have an exponentially greater margin of difficulty.

In a March 2010 speech, then FBI Director (2001–2013) Robert Mueller observed "Terrorists have shown a clear interest in pursuing hacking skills. And they will either train their own recruits or hire outsiders, with an eye toward combining physical attacks with cyber attacks." That may very well be true, but 'wanting' to do something is quite different from having the ability to do the same. Violent jihadis' IT knowledge is not superior to the ordinary publics. Research found that of a random sampling of 404 members of violent Islamist groups, 196 (48.5 %) had a higher education, with information about subject areas available for 178 individuals. Of these 178, some 8 (4.5 %) had trained in computing, which means that out of the entire sample, less than 2 % of the jihadis came from a computing background (Gambetta and Hertog 2007:8–12) And not even these few could be assumed to have mastery of the complex systems necessary to carry out a successful cyber-terrorist attack. Journalists therefore need to stop elevating so-called 'script-kiddies' to potential cyberterrorists and insinuating that just because some group has the capacity to establish a website, distribute content online, and/or engage in DDoS attacks the next step is a major attack by them using the Internet. This threat framing has taken on renewed salience in the wake of recent 'attacks' by the al-Qassam Cyber Fighters and the Syrian Electronic Army, which have been repeatedly characterised as cyberterrorism.

Many people respond to the above arguments by saying that if one doesn't have the requisite know-how in-house, an alternative option is to hire "outsiders" to undertake a cyberterrorism attack on one's behalf. This would force the terrorists to operate outside their own trusted circles and thus leave them ripe for infiltration however. Moreover, even if contact with "real" hackers was successful, the terrorist group would be in no position to gauge their competency accurately; they would simply have to rely on trust. This would be very personally and operationally risky (Conway 2003b:10–12). Turning to the possibility of online crowd sourcing as a response to these types of challenges then; if proxies could be employed to actually commit acts of cyberterrorism, terrorists would improve their ability to avoid culpability or blame altogether. The problem with this is two-fold: first, it would require gathering a 'crowd' which would, in turn, require fairly wide dissemination of information about the activity to be undertaken thus opening-up the very real possibility of the attack plans coming to the attention of the authorities. Second, the terrorists would lose control over when, where, how, or even *if* the attack took place. This might be advantageous in terms of instigating low-level 'real world' (e.g. jihadi-inspired lone actor terrorism) and cyber operations (e.g. (D)DoS attacks), but is not a suitable method for undertaking a major cyberterrorism operation. Furthermore, while the potential anonymity provided by crowd sourcing might protect the instigators from being detected, it would also lose them their credit for the attack. On the basis of technical knowhow alone, then, cyberterrorism is not feasible.

6.3.3 Destruction Factor

Stuxnet is the only cyber attack to date that is agreed to have caused actual physical destruction. This, moreover, was to a system and not to human beings. VBIEDs, on the other hand, have a long and very widely proven history of destruction of lives and property. "Trucks and vans can easily deliver the explosive equivalent of the bomb load of a B-24 (the workhorse heavy bomber of the Army Air Forces in World War Two) to the door step of a prime target. Even the average family SUV with 10 cubic feet of cargo space can transport a 1000-pound bomb" (Davis 2008:8). Indeed, some authors go so far as to portray the September 11 attacks as simply a scaled-up version of the 1993 van-bombing of the World Trade Centre. Basically, the entire range of ground transportation options is available for attacks based on the same fundamental principles. The destruction to lives and property that can be wrought by such devices is, unsurprisingly, potentially massive.

One of the deadliest such attacks was carried out by radical Islamists in closely-timed suicide truck bomb attacks on the US Marine barracks and French members of the Multinational Force in Lebanon on 23 October 1983 in Beirut. The combined death toll from the attacks was 305. The already-mentioned Oklahoma City Bombing killed 168 people, including 19 children and three pregnant women, injuring nearly 700 others. The "single worst terrorist incident" of the Northern Irish 'Troubles' took place on 15 August, 1998 in the town of Omagh in County Tyrone (Police Ombudsman for Northern Ireland 2001:1). On that Saturday afternoon, the Real IRA—a dissident offshoot of the Provisional Irish Republican Army—parked and subsequently detonated a car filled with 500 lbs of fertiliser-based explosive in the town, killing 29 people, including a woman pregnant with twins, and injuring some 250 others. The Northern Ireland conflict was characterised by a long string of car bombings that began in Belfast in 1972, but that has since been eclipsed by the alacrity with which the VBIED has been deployed in the Iraq conflict. It is estimated that some 664 *suicide* VBIED attacks alone took place in Iraq between March 2003 and December 2010 (see Table 6.1). Nine separate car bombs exploded in Baghdad on a single Sunday in October 2013. The blasts, which hit eight different Shiite-majority areas in and around the Iraqi capital, killed at least 54 people and wounded more than 90. The pan-Arab news channel Al-Arabiya reported that at the time of the blasts the Iraqi government had actually restricted many Baghdad residents from using their cars in an attempt to thwart car bombings (Al-Arabiya 2013).

The 'worst' terrorist attacks are generally conceived as those that have the highest number of fatalities and injuries associated with them. The destruction of human lives is not the only type of destruction associated with VBIED attacks however, many of which also cause enormous property damage. In addition to the fatalities associated with it, the Oklahoma City bombing blew the front from the targeted Alfred P. Murrah building and "caused major damage to adjacent structures, touched off car fires, and blew out glass windows and doors in a three-square-mile area on the north side of downtown Oklahoma City" (Oklahoma City Police Department 1995:1). While the Omagh bomb killed the greatest number of people in a single terrorist attack in Northern Ireland, the property destruction associated with it was minimal compared to that wrought by the Provisional IRA's 1992–1996 mainland bombing campaign. Total combined property damage arising from the 1991 Baltic Exchange truck bomb, 1992 Bishopsgate Road dump truck bomb, 1996 Canary Wharf car bomb, and 1996 Arndale Centre van bomb was estimated to exceed $5 billion (Davis 2008:133–137). Anders Behring Breivik's 2011 car-bombing of the government quarter in Oslo severely damaged the building in which the Prime Minister's office was housed and surrounding buildings. Discussion is on-going in Norway at time of writing as to whether the four most badly damaged buildings (i.e. H-block, Y-block, R4, and S) should be preserved and refurbished or demolished and replaced. The cost of preserving and refurbishing H-block and Y-block alone has been estimated at over $100 million (Sandelson and Smith 2013).

Giacomello's 'Bangs for the Buck' article considered not just the cost in terms of preparation for a cyber attack and lives lost, but also the cost of a "Cyber attack on computer systems regulating regional electric power, combined with physical attacks on transmission and distribution network." The potential outcome of the latter were described as "Regional electricity shortages that persist for a week; health risks from heat/cold; interruption of production schedules; destruction of physical capital" (Giacomello 2004:399) with an estimated total potential cost of $25 billion. A combined physical and cyber attack as just described, it should be noted, would be greatly more complex to successfully carry out than either a standalone cyber attack or a standalone physical attack. Furthermore, the same article contains an estimate for potential costs associated with "Widespread terror against key elements of public economy across nations (malls, restaurants, movie theatres, etc.)" at fully ten times that of the complex combined physical and cyber attack. It is speculated in the article that "widespread terror" of the sort just described would result in a significant and sustained decline in economic activity in public spaces and an associated drop in consumer confidence that could have potential costs of $250 billion (2004:399). Indeed such "widespread terror" has already been generated in many countries by the use of relatively cheap VBIEDs, while also having devastating impacts on lives and property and inflicting, in addition, huge financial costs on governments, insurers, and others, as illustrated herein. An additional important point made by Giacomello and germane to this analysis is with respect to the electricity blackout that afflicted the north eastern United States and eastern Canada on 14 August 2003:

> If, one the one hand, it proved that the North American power grid could be compromised with vast repercussions, on the other, it showed that, contrary to some appearance, modern societies and economies are also more resilient. Although the blackout affected 50 million people, there were very few injuries or fatalities. Most people reacted calmly and hospitals and emergency services continued to function properly (2004:400).

Granted the above blackout, and those that affected a host of European countries in summer 2003, were relatively short-lived with most lasting for a maximum of 1–2 days; they are illustrative however of the relative lack of destruction generally arising from lights-out events.

6.3.4   Media Impact Factor

Schmid and De Graaf, characterize terrorism as a form of violent communication. In fact, "without communication," they argue, "there can be no terrorism" (1982:9). This explains the large literature on the intersection of media and terrorism and the oft-repeated claim that media and terrorists enjoy a symbiotic relationship. In his text, *The Anatomy of Terrorism*, David Long opined that, "The media's mission to cover the news and the terrorist's ability to "create" news have led to a symbiotic relationship between the two, one in which the media not only convey the news but help the terrorists create it (1990:119; see also Hoffman 2006:195). Long goes on to employ the metaphor of theatre to explain terrorism; Mark Juergensmeyer drawing on the same metaphor suggests that we view terrorism not as a tactic but as what he calls "performance violence," which has two major components. First, such acts are dramas designed to have an effect on their audiences. In the case of terrorist violence, those who witness it via the news media are part of what occurs. Second, according to Juergensmeyer, the term "performance" also implies the notion of "performative," which refers to certain kinds of speech that are able to perform social functions (i.e. their utterance has a performative impact).

> Like vows recited during marriage rites, certain words not only represent reality but also shape it: they contain a certain power of their own. The same is true of some nonverbal symbolic actions, such as the gunshot that begins a race, the raising of a white flag to show defeat, or acts of terrorism (2000:124).

The performative and propagandistic nature of terrorist acts is central to many of the available definitions of terrorism. According to Schmid and De Graaf:

> Terrorism cannot be understood only in terms of violence. It has to be understood primarily in terms of propaganda. Violence and propaganda have much in common. Violence aims at behaviour modification by coercion. Propaganda aims at the same through persuasion. Terrorism is a combination of the two (1982:14).

The events of 9/11 underscored that moving images are crucial for a truly spectacular terrorist event. The attacks on the World Trade Center were a fantastic piece of performance violence: a lavish visual event. More traditional VBIED attacks are also impactful; they advertise themselves. Not only do they kill and injure those in their vicinity and destroy surrounding buildings, but they are loud: their sound can often be heard for miles. They can also generate a percussive wave that can often be felt at long distances. And, in our mobile telephone-saturated world, such attacks increasingly have spectacular live moving images associated with them. This gives rise to a number of associated or sub-factors: VBIED attacks generate live on-the-scene reporting, which makes compelling viewing and thus attracts large audiences; these attacks must be reported, even in authoritarian states; they are not generally apprehended nor can they generally be reported as accidents. The problem with respect to cyberterrorism, from a terrorism perspective, is that many of the hypothesised attack scenarios, from shutting down the electric power grid to contaminating a major water supply, fail on all of the above accounts. In terms of theatricality, such attacks would likely have no easily captured spectacular (live) moving images associated with them, something we—as an audience—have been primed for by the 9/11 attacks. The only commonly forwarded cyberterrorism scenario that would have this performance value would be interfering with air traffic control systems to crash planes, but hasn't it been shown that planes can be much more easily employed in spectacular 'real world' terrorism? And besides, is it not the case that all of the infrastructures just mentioned and others besides are much easier and more spectacular to simply blow-up?

On a related note, but perhaps even more importantly, a terrorist event that has the possibility of being portrayed as an accident is a failed attack. Consider the observation that:

> Publicity would be also one of the primary objectives for a terrorist attack. Extensive coverage has been given to the vulnerability of the US information infrastructure and to the potential harm that could be caused by a cyberattack. This might lead terrorists to feel that even a

marginally successful cyberattack directed at the United States may garner considerable publicity. Some suggest that were such a cyberattack by a terrorist organization to occur *and become known to the general public*, regardless of the level of success of the attack, concern by many citizens may lead to widespread withdrawal of funds and selling of equities [my emphasis] (Rollins and Wilson 2007:5).

In testimony before a US Senate committee Howard Schmidt, the Obama administration's onetime Cybersecurity Coordinator, made a similar observation: "...during NIMDA and Code Red, we to this day don't know the source of that. It could have very easily been a terrorist..." (US Senate Committee on the Judiciary 2004:28). These observations betray a fundamental misunderstanding of the nature and purpose(s) of terrorism, particularly its attention-getting function. A terrorist attack with the potential to be hidden, portrayed as an accident, or otherwise remain unknown is unlikely to be viewed positively from a terrorism perspective. One of the most important aspects of the 9/11 attacks in New York from the perpetrators' viewpoint was surely the fact that while the first plane to crash into the WTC could have been accidental, the appearance of the second plane confirmed the incident as a terrorist attack in real time (as, of course, did subsequent events in Washington DC and Pennsylvania). This is a characteristic of all VBIEDs; stationary vehicles do not generally explode absent their containing explosives and being triggered to do so. If one considers that, in addition, many contemporary VBIED attacks are at the same time suicide attacks, it becomes clear that deniability (as suggested in, for example, Collins and McCombie 2012:89) is not a major concern of many contemporary terrorists nor has it ever been. On the contrary, "[c]oercion requires attribution", which explains why "terrorists spend as much time marketing their exploits as they do fighting, bombing, assassinating, and so on" (Gartzke 2013:46–47).

Key Points

- The costs of cyber attacks are difficult to estimate, but are potentially vastly higher than their non-cyber equivalents such as VBIEDs.
- Terrorist groups lack the mastery to carry out successful cyber attacks which are exponentially more challenging than non-cyberterrorism.
- The destructive potential of non-cyber attacks such as car bombings can be far more readily materialised than cyber attacks.
- Terrorism's power is linked to its theatricality. Cyber attacks lack this symbolic dimension and therefore will be less desirable than conventional attacks.

6.4 Conclusion

Stuxnet cannot be classed as an act of cyberterrorism on the basis of either of the definitions of cyberterrorism described in this chapter's opening section. It is, however, connected to the cyberterrorism debate given that it is accepted by many to be the most consequential cyber attack to have yet occurred. It was, by all accounts, an enormously complex attack to get right, involving for its development and deployment an estimated 10,000 person hours of coding by a team or teams of individuals and costing anywhere from millions to tens of millions of US dollars (Halliday 2010; Langner 2013:20; US Senate 2010; Zetter 2010). In fact, such was the complexity and cost of this undertaking that it is generally agreed that it could not have been carried out by any entity other than a state or states (Langner 2013:20; see also Gross 2011; Halliday 2010). The damage caused by the Stuxnet worm to the Iranian nuclear programme is said to have put it back at least 2 years (Langner 2013:15) and thus was a major event not only in the cyber realm, but in international affairs more generally.

Now let's consider the Boston Marathon bombing. If the VBIED attacks described throughout this paper were of a mid-range sort of terrorism in terms of their complexity, cost, and destructive outcomes, the Boston Marathon attack was of the lowest-level type of 'real world' terrorism imaginable. At a cost of $100–$180 each (Bucktin 2013; Wallack and Healy 2013), the two pressure-cooker bombs were considerably less expensive than a VBIED in even Afghanistan. The complexity of both the bombs themselves and the overall attack strategy was low. Given their design, the Tsarnaev brothers may have based the devices construction on instructions contained in al-Qaeda in the Islamic Maghreb's (AQIM) English language magazine *Inspire*, which is freely available on the Internet (Leonard 2013). The cheap financial cost and low level of sophistication of the attack notwithstanding, it cost two young women and a child their lives and 14 others their limbs, and is estimated to have caused upwards of $333 million in property damage, lost sales, medical costs, etc. (see Dedman and Schoen 2013 for breakdown). So while the Stuxnet attack was complex and high-cost, the Boston Marathon attack was easy and low-cost. And while Stuxnet caused disruption and destruction, it caused no direct harm to human beings. The starkest difference between Stuxnet and the Boston Marathon bombings however was their widely differing media impacts. A search of 'All English Language News' on Lexis-Nexis on 20 October 2013 returned 881 items with 'Stuxnet' in the headline, but 2,482 items with 'Boston Marathon Bombing' in the headline. Put another way, a conservative estimate puts the amount of media coverage afforded the Boston Marathon attack at almost triple that of Stuxnet, illustrating once again that it is perfectly possible for cheap and easy attacks to trump their costly and complex counterparts.

It may be true, therefore, that from a technological perspective, "Stuxnet has proved that cyber terrorism is now a credible threat" (Collins and McCombie 2012:89). Not from a terrorism perspective however. As Dunn-Cavelty (2011) has pointed out, "careful threat assessments…necessarily demand more than just naval-gazing and vulnerability spotting. Rather than simply assuming the worst, the question that must be asked is: Who has the interest and the capability to attack us and why?". Cyberterrorism should not therefore ever be considered in isolation from more traditional forms of terrorism as if its cyber component renders it separate to the latter; thence the focus on careful definition and comparison in this chapter.

In their 2002 paper, Brenner and Goodman pose the question: "Why has cyber-terrorism not yet manifested itself? And follow-up with: "This is concededly something of a mystery. There are no reliable answers as to why cyberterrorism remains an as-yet unrealized phenomenon" (Brenner and Goodman 2002:44). On the contrary, as illustrated in this chapter, there are at least four pretty straightforward and convincing reasons for why no act of cyberterrorism has ever yet occurred. VBIED construction is cheap. Cyberterrorism scenarios vary hugely in their potential size and scope and for this and other reasons are thus hugely difficult to cost; having said this, even the most conservative analyst would probably be forced to agree that no major cyberterrorism attack is likely to cost less than the average price of construction of a VBIED. Cost need not be a determining factor however; the complexity issue is a different matter. VBIED construction is relatively easy. The components are widely available and the know-how accessible via personal connections, bookstores, libraries, and online. The know-how necessary to cause the necessary levels of disruption, destruction, or even violence for a cyber attack to be deemed cyberterrorism is unlikely to be readily available to terrorists and therefore risky to obtain. The potential for destruction of a cyberterrorism attack is difficult to estimate too, but the available evidence suggests that wide disruption or destruction, not to say fatalities, would be costly and difficult to achieve. Cheap and easy methods, such as VBIED attacks, can be widely destructive however, which accounts for their contemporary ubiquity. Finally, apart from practical matters relating to cost, complexity, and destructive capacity, cyber-based activities are unlikely to work as terrorism precisely for the reasons they are touted in other realms: stealth and deniability; attention-getting and credit-claiming are at the core of terrorism. Arguments such as the latter have been eclipsed by arguments based on modern societies' technological vulnerabilities on the one hand and potential terrorists' capabilities on the other. The capacity to launch a cyberterrorism attack, which is itself challenged herein, bears very little relationship to the actual likelihood of attack however. "Many threats are conceivable, but relatively few actually materialize" (Gartzke 2013:51). Cyberterrorism is therefore conceivable, but very unlikely. Why? Because 'real world' attacks are cheaper and less complex while also being significantly destructive of lives and property and, importantly, emotionally impactful so therefore also attention-getting to an extent that cyberterrorism will struggle to achieve.

Key Points

- The likelihood of cyberterrorism occurring needs to be contextualised against alternative options that terrorist groups will consider.
- Although events such as Stuxnet might demonstrate the technological credibility of cyberterrorism it is crucial that we do not forget its terrorism aspect.
- More conventional attacks such as via VBIED are cheaper, simpler, more readily destructive and possess greater symbolic power than cyberterrorism.

Further Reading

'Squirrel Power!' This 2013 *New York Times* article is perhaps my favourite shut-down-the-power-grid-scenario detailing as it does the very real threat posed by Kamikaze squirrels! http://www.nytimes.com/2013/09/01/opinion/Sunday/squirrel-power.html?pagewanted=all&_r=0

Dr. Thomas Rid of King's College London's Department of War Studies explains the concept of cyberterrorism and explores the risks associated with militants conducting attacks through the Internet (7 mins). http://www.youtube.com/watch?v=cPTPpb8Ldz8

Video (2 h 10 min) of UK House of Commons Science and Technology Committee hearing on cyber attacks on 17 November, 2010 with contributions from, amongst others, Prof. Ross Anderson, University of Cambridge; Professor Bernard Silverman, Chief Scientific Adviser, UK Home Office; Dr Steve Marsh, Deputy Director, Office of Cyber Security, UK Cabinet Office; Professor Mark Welland, Chief Scientific Adviser, UK Ministry of Defence. http://www.parliamentlive.tv/Main/Player.aspx?meetingId=7009

Video (2 h 11 min) of UK Public Accounts Committee hearing on cyber security on 13 March, 2013 with contributions from, amongst others, Prof. Sadie Creese, Professor of Cybersecurity, Oxford University; Dr. Thomas Rid, Kings College London; Mark Hughes, Managing Director of Security for British Telecom; Oliver Robbins, Deputy National Security Adviser, UK Cabinet Office. http://www.bbc.co.uk/democracylive/house-of-commons-21784442

References

Aasland Ravndal J (2012) A post-trial profile of Anders Behring Breivik. CTC Sentinel 5(10):16–20

Ackerman S (2011) $265 bomb, $300 billion war: the economics of the 9/11 era's signature weapon. Wired 8 September 2011. http://www.wired.com/dangerroom/2011/09/ied-cost/

Agence France Presse (2007) EU should class cyber attacks as terrorism: Estonia. Agence France Presse

Al-Arabiya (2013) Car bombs kill at least 54 people in Baghdad area. Al-Arabiya. http://english.alarabiya.net/en/News/middle-east/2013/10/27/Car-bombs-explode-across-Baghdad-killing-at-least-16-people.html

Baltic News Service (2007) Cyber terrorism is not only Estonia's problem—Russian Senator. Baltic News Service 25 June 2007

Brenner SW, Goodman MD (2002) In defense of cyberterrorism: an argument for anticipating cyber-attacks. Univ Illinois J Law Tech Pol 1:1–58.

Bucktin C (2013) Boston bombers on a budget: "shoestring" terrorist brothers' bombs cost less than £120 to make. The Mirror (UK) 24 April 2013. http://www.mirror.co.uk/news/world-news/boston-bombers-budget-shoestring-terrorist-1852203

Collins S, McCombie S (2012) Stuxnet: the emergence of a new cyber weapon and its implications. J Pol Intell Counter Terrorism 7(1):80–91

Conway M (2002a) Reality bytes: cyberterrorism and terrorist 'use' of the Internet. First Monday 7(11)

Conway M (2002b) Cyberterrorism. Curr His 101(659):436–444

Conway M (2003a) Cyberterrorism: the story so far. J Inf Warfare 2(2):33–42

Conway M (2003b) Hackers as terrorists? Why it doesn't compute. Comput Fraud Secur (12):1–13

Conway M (2007) Cyberterrorism: hype and reality. In: Armistead EL (ed) Information warfare: separating hype from reality. Potomac Books, Washington, DC

Conway M (2012) What is cyberterrorism and how real is the threat? A review of the academic literature, 1996–2009. In: Reich P, Gelbstein E (eds) Law, policy, and technology: cyberterrorism, information warfare, and internet immobilization. IGI Global, Hershey

Davis M (2008) Buda's wagon: a brief history of the car bomb. Verso, London

Dedman B, Schoen J (2013) Adding up the financial costs of the Boston bombings. NBC News 30 April 2013. http://usnews.nbcnews.com/_news/2013/04/30/17975443-adding-up-the-financial-costs-of-the-boston-bombings?lite

Deibert RJ (2010) Circuits of power: security in the internet environment. In: Rosenau JN, Singh JP (eds) Information technology and global politics. SUNY Press, Albany

Denning D (2007) A view of cyberterrorism five years later. In: Himma K (ed) Internet security: hacking, counterhacking, and society. Jones and Bartlett, Sudbury

Denning D (2012) Stuxnet: what has changed? Future Internet 4(3):672–687

Dorgan B (2013) Cyber terror is the new language of war. The Huffington Post 18 July 2013

Dunn-Cavelty M (2011) Cyberwar: a more realistic threat assessment. International Relations and Security Network (ISN) http://www.isn.ethz.ch/Digital-Library/Articles/Detail/?id=129764&lng=en

Gallagher S (2013) Security pros predict "major" cyber terror attack this year. Ars Technica 4 January 2013. http://arstechnica.com/security/2013/01/security-pros-predict-major-cyberterror-attack-this-year/

Gambetta D, Hertog S (2007) Engineers of Jihad. Sociology working papers, no. 2007–10, Department of Sociology, University of Oxford. http://www.nuff.ox.ac.uk/users/gambetta/Engineers%20of%20Jihad.pdf

Gartzke E (2013) The myth of cyberwar: bringing war in cyberspace back down to Earth. Int Security 38(2):41–73

Giacomello G (2004) Bangs for the buck: a cost-benefit analysis of cyberterrorism. Stud Conflict Terrorism 27(5):387–408

Gordon S, Ford R (2002) Cyberterrorism? Comput Secur 21(7):636–647

Gross MJ (2011) Stuxnet worm: a declaration of cyber-war. Vanity Fair. http://www.vanityfair.com/culture/features/2011/04/stuxnet-201104

Halliday J (2010) Stuxnet worm is the "Work of a National Government Agency." The Guardian (UK) 24 September 2010. http://www.theguardian.com/technology/2010/sep/24/stuxnet-worm-national-agency

Hardy K, Williams G (2014) What is 'cyberterrorism'? Computer and internet technology in legal definitions of terrorism. In: Chen T, Jarvis L, Macdonald S (eds) Cyberterrorism: understanding, assessment, and response. Springer, New York

Hicks H-R, Madelyn HD, Bagnall PM, Spagat M, Sloboda JA (2011) Casualties in civilians and coalition soldiers from suicide bombings in Iraq, 2003–10: a descriptive study. Lancet 378(9794):906–914

Hoffman B (2006) Inside terrorism (Revised and Expanded Edition). Columbia Press, New York

Hoffman B (2010) The evolving nature of terrorism: nine years after the 9/11 attacks. Written testimony submitted to Committee on Homeland Security, U.S. House of Representatives, 15 September. http://bipartisanpolicy.org/sites/default/files/Hoffman%20Testimony%20091510.pdf

Jarvis L, Nouri L, Whiting A (2014) Understanding, locating and constructing 'cyberterrorism'. In: Chen T, Jarvis L, Macdonald S (eds) Cyberterrorism: understanding, assessment, and response. Springer, New York

Kenney M (2010) Beyond the Internet: Mētis, Techne, and the limitations of online artifacts for Islamist terrorists. Terrorism Polit Violence 22(2)

Langner R (2013) To kill a centrifuge: a technical analysis of what Stuxnet's creators tried to achieve. Arlington, VA: The Langner Group. http://www.langner.com/en/wp-content/uploads/2013/11/To-kill-a-centrifuge.pdf

Leonard A (2013) Homemade bombs made easier. Salon 26 April 2013. http://www.salon.com/2013/04/26/homemade_bombs_made_easier/

Lloyds (2014) Cyberterrorism. http://www.lloyds.com/news-and-insight/news-and-features/market-news/industry-news-2013/cyber-terrorism

Long D (1990) The anatomy of terrorism. Maxwell Macmillian International, New York

Macdonald S, Jarvis L, Chen T, Lavis S (2013) Cyberterrorism: a survey of researchers. Cyberterrorism Project Research Report (No. 1), Swansea University. http://www.cyberterrorism-project.org/wp-content/uploads/2013/03/Cyberterrorism-Report-2013.pdf

Michel L, Herbeck D (2001) American terrorist: Timothy McVeigh and the Oklahoma city bombing. Harper, New York

Oklahoma City Police Department (1995) Alfred P. Murrah building after action report. Oklahoma City Police Department, Oklahoma City. http://web.archive.org/web/20070703233435/http://www.terrorisminfo.mipt.org/pdf/okcfr_App_C.pdf

Police Ombudsman for Northern Ireland (2001) Statement by the police ombudsman for Northern Ireland on her investigation of matters relating to the Omagh bombing on August 15 1998.' Police Ombudsman for Northern Ireland, Belfast. http://www.policeombudsman.org/Publicationsuploads/omaghreport.pdf

Pollitt M (1998) Cyberterrorism: fact or fancy? Comput Fraud Secur 2:8–10

Rid T (2013) Cyber war will not take place. Hurst & Co., London

Riley (ed) (2011) Cyber spies terror war; MoD and treasury targeted. Daily Star (UK) 13 June 2011

Rollins J, Wilson C (2007) Terrorist capabilities for cyberattack: overview and policy issues. Congressional Research Service, Washington, DC

Sandelson M, Smith L (2013) Oslo government headquarters building fate due for new review. The Foreigner 20 September 2013. http://theforeigner.no/pages/news/oslo-government-headquarters-building-fate-due-for-new-review/

Schmid AP, De Graaf J (1982) Violence as communication: insurgent terrorism and the western news media. Sage, London

Schmitt MN (ed) (2013) Tallinn manual on the International Law Applicable to Cyber Warfare. Cambridge University Press, Cambridge. https://www.ccdcoe.org/249.html

Sengupta K (2010) Terrorists 'gaining upper hand in cyber war'. The Independent (UK) 6 February 2010. http://www.independent.co.uk/news/uk/home-news/terrorists-gaining-upper-hand-in-cyber-war-1890913.html

Singer P, Friedman A (2014) Cybersecurity and cyberwar: what everybody needs to know. Oxford University Press, Oxford

US Department of Justice (1997) Report on the availability of bombmaking information, the extent to which its dissemination is controlled by federal law, and the extent to which such dissemination may be subject to regulation consistent with the First Amendment to the United States Constitution. US Department of Justice, Washington, DC. http://cryptome.org/abi.htm

US Senate Committee on the Judiciary (2004) Virtual threat, real terror: cyberterrorism in the 21st century. Hearing before the subcommittee on terrorism, technology, and homeland security, 108th Congress, second session, February 24 (Serial No. J-108-58). http://www.gpo.gov/fdsys/pkg/CHRG-108shrg94639/pdf/CHRG-108shrg94639.pdf

US Senate (2010) Securing critical infrastructure in the age of Stuxnet. US Senate Committee on Homeland Security and Government Affairs, Washington, DC. http://www.hsgac.senate.gov/hearings/securing-critical-infrastructure-in-the-age-of-stuxnet

Wallack T, Healy B (2013) Tsarnaev brothers appeared to have scant finances. The Boston Globe 24 April 2013

Whitlock C, Gellman B (2013) U.S. documents detail al-Qaeda's efforts to fight back against drones. The Washington Post 4 September 2013. http://www.washingtonpost.com/world/national-security/us-documents-detail-al-qaedas-efforts-to-fight-back-against-drones/2013/09/03/b83e7654-11c0-11e3-b630-36617ca6640f_story_2.html

Wilson C (2014) Cyber threats to critical information infrastructure. In: Chen T, Jarvis L, Macdonald S (eds) Cyberterrorism: understanding, assessment, and response. Springer, New York

Zetter K (2010) Blockbuster worm aimed for infrastructure, but no proof Iran nukes were target. Wired 23 September 2010. http://www.wired.com/threatlevel/2010/09/stuxnet/

Chapter 7
Cyber Threats to Critical Information Infrastructure

Clay Wilson

7.1 Finding a Definition for Cyberterrorism

Many are concerned about cyberterrorism and how to prevent it, but it is difficult to get observers to agree on an exact definition. Distinctions between crime, terrorism, and war tend to blur when attempting to describe a computer network attack in ways that parallel the physical world (Rollins J, Wilson C 2007). For example, a cyber attack attributed to a terrorist group could be considered cyberterrorism if damage reached a certain threshold level. That same cyber attack, if attributed to a nation-state, might appropriately be called cyberwarfare. However, terrorists are not mono-lithic, and an individual extremist may take action that is outside the control of governments or traditional terrorist groups. If the same cyber attack were launched by a rogue individual acting independently, would that be called cyberterrorism or cyberwarfare? Does the definition for cyberterrorism depend on the intent of the attacker, on the group or national affiliation of the attacker, or on the level of dam-age inflicted? Perhaps a more useful definition of cyberterrorism will depend on some combination of all these – but what is the appropriate balance of characteris-tics that most can agree on? Finally, the Internet also enables an attacker to operate with a high degree of anonymity. So, while a cyber attack may appear to inflict damage in an instant, the characteristics that can help determine whether it is an act of cyberterrorism may not be fully understood until several days after the cyberat-tack has taken place. Refer to the chapter by Jarvis, Nouri and Whiting for a discus-sion of cyberterrorism as a social construct, and the chapter by Hardy and Williams for a legal definition for cyberterrorism.

C. Wilson (✉)
The American Public University System, Charles Towne, WV, USA
e-mail: cwilson8040@gmail.com

T.M. Chen et al. (eds.), *Cyberterrorism: Understanding, Assessment, and Response*,
DOI 10.1007/978-1-4939-0962-9_7, © Springer Science+Business Media New York 2014

7.2 Unique Vulnerabilities Increase Risk for High Value Critical Infrastructure Systems

Critical information infrastructure (CII) is a term that describes assets that support normal functions of modern society and the economy. These include essential services and utilities such as the electrical power grid, telecommunications, transportation, financial systems and other essential services. The computerized control systems that help operate and regulate these services have various common names, including distributed control systems (DCS), programmable logic controllers (PLC), and human machine interfaces (HMI). The most commonly used terms for CII facility equipment are industrial control systems (ICS) and supervisory control and data acquisition (SCADA) systems. These computer controls make continuous and minute adjustments to the operation of industrial processes, and the facility machines and equipment are usually built sturdy enough to last years before needing maintenance or replacement. Refer to the chapter by Yannakogeorgos for a more thorough description of control devices found in a CII facility.

The scale of services provided to large populations by CII facilities can make them potential targets of high value to terrorists or extremists. If coordinated cyber attacks were successfully directed against critical infrastructures, the disruptions could cause hardship to many citizens, and could lead the population to doubt the future resilience of essential industries. In addition, the service interruptions that originally affect only one CII utility could possibly lead to a cascade of failures that might also affect other CII facilities. For example, the recent storm named "Sandy" that destroyed much property along the U.S. eastern coast in 2012 also caused flood water to rise above unexpected levels, submerging and stopping turbine generator equipment at the local power utility. Hospitals immediately switched over to their emergency power generators, but the reserve supply of generator fuel was exhausted because the outage lasted beyond the 3-day emergency plan. Automobiles could not find gas stations with working pumps. Grocery stores began to run low on food supplies because delivery trucks could not find operating fuel stations. Eventually, homes began to run low on heating oil because of the same problem with resupply trucks.

The telecommunications critical infrastructure has expanded beyond traditional SCADA and ICS facilities to now include wireless consumer equipment such as radios and cell phones. These consumer devices are now becoming targets for cyber attack, and the malicious code technologies and attack procedures are shared among hackers in online chat rooms. For example, in 2010, a cell phone virus reportedly affected over 1 million mobile users in China. The so-called "zombie virus" was built into a fake anti-virus application that many users were lured into downloading onto their mobile devices as they searched for security and protection. Instead of protection, the fake application launched a malicious virus which transmitted non-stop text messages to everyone in the victim's list of contacts, creating huge phone bills and clogging other useful mobile services (Richardson 2010). Terrorists can also access these online hacker chat rooms to gather information about malicious code for use in later plans. For example, a possible cyberattack to block cell phones from accessing 911 emergency services could greatly amplify the chaos and confusion seen during a simultaneous traditional violent terrorist attack.

7.2.1   Software Updates for Critical Information Infrastructures Can Be Expensive and Infrequent

The reason why so many cyber attacks are successful is often due to weak designs for software products, inadequate testing for those products, and the increasing complexity now found in most software products. The disclaimer agreement that users must accept before using a new software product allows designers to avoid being held liable for their mistakes, so there is little incentive to build products with stronger security features. As a result, software vendors must create and distribute updates and security patches to gradually fix problems that are uncovered by consumers and hackers. Traditional office IT systems receive software updates from vendors regularly, because improvements are published to modify operations, to add new features, and to fix newly discovered security problems. However, operating system software for some computers in CII facilities may be proprietary and non-standard, or dated, and the system vendor may eventually decide to no longer support the older model equipment and software with security patch updates.

Standard organizational policy for managing cybersecurity requires that security patch updates should be installed as quickly as possible after they are released by the vendor. However, because CII hardware and controller equipment often were originally designed to operate non-stop and remain in service over long durations, ICS and SCADA software systems are not always quickly updated with security patches. Also, because some ICS and SCADA equipment models use altered, non-standard versions of Windows, software updates and patches which are standard for regular office Windows systems must first receive special modifications by the vendor of the specific ICS and SCADA systems involved. Installations can be different at different CII facilities, with security vulnerabilities that are specific and unique for each installation. Equipment can also be configured differently for different physical locations that provide utility services to different population areas. All of these factors combine to make software updates difficult to manage, even though multiple facilities can be parts of the same critical infrastructure.

7.2.2   Real Time Equipment Commands Can Be Slowed or Intercepted

Industrial control systems are increasingly becoming real-time control systems, meaning that multiple computers controlling a critical infrastructure facility must work together and inter-operate at the millisecond level, with little or no time for delayed reactions between computers. This sometimes means that intrusion detection systems that also may operate in real-time cannot monitor and protect with maximum effectiveness. The required additional processing load would add unacceptable delays to operations between CII controllers. In addition, as CII facility management increasingly move ICS and SCADA systems towards cloud services for increased economic advantage, new security vulnerabilities are created. Sensitive data that is stored in the cloud may be at risk of theft or alteration. Measurement data or commands that travel in near real-time from the ICS and SCADA systems through the cloud can be intercepted or spoofed while beyond internally managed security controls.

7.2.3 Other Factors Contribute to Higher Risk for Critical Infrastructures

Other factors may also increase the possibility of a CII facility experiencing cyber-attack by terrorists. Because ICS and SCADA systems collect lots of data useful for generating management reports, many critical infrastructure systems are now managed through remotely-controlled networks that are increasingly connected to head-quarters office systems. For economic advantages, this connection usually involves the Internet, which means the CII facility equipment can be reached through external network connections. Connection to the headquarters office network also means that malicious virus or espionage code that has infected headquarters systems can eventually enter the connected ICS and SCADA equipment. Any unpatched software vulnerabilities in CII facility equipment may become visible to terrorists or extremists through using special search tools also available on the Internet. SHODAN is the name of a popular Internet search engine well known to hackers, and it is used to scan for computer systems with unprotected vulnerabilities. ICS and SCADA systems often fall into this vulnerable category for the reasons stated above, and they can easily be found through a SHODAN search. The relative ease of locating vulnerable critical infrastructure systems, along with possible resulting widespread effects due to disruption, and anonymity easily available to Internet users may help make a cyber attack attractive to terrorists.

In addition, when management decides that a special security patch should be installed for CII facility equipment, the entire process can be complex, lengthy, and very expensive. For example, to install a software patch for a turbine generator on a regional power grid, the selected equipment must be stopped and taken out of service before the patch is installed. Stopping a power generator requires temporary redistribution of the electrical load throughout the grid, so that customer service remains uninterrupted as it is shifted over to substitute or backup turbine generators. Once the selected generator has been stopped, it must be allowed to cool down for several hours before it can be restarted with its new software security update installed. The process for shut-down, re-routing the electrical service load, and the final cool-down and turbine restart can potentially cost hundreds of thousands of dollars. In addition, the software security update must undergo a thorough set of testing to assure absolute reliability after installation and restart. CII facility managers and engineers will not accept a software update that may possibly malfunction, causing a service interruption for customers. The expense, planning and coordination required to avoid a service interruption can make it difficult and complex for some CII facilities to install frequent software security updates.

Critical Infrastructure Information systems can also be reached by other means that do not rely on a connection to the Internet. Malicious code can be embedded in a flash drive which can then be inserted, purposely or accidentally, into a laptop computer that resides behind the CII facility firewall protecting ICS and SCADA equipment, thus possibly bypassing strong network protections. Or, an insider with sufficient access rights can also bypass network security through misuse of their authorized access.

Key Points

- The scale of services provided to large populations by CII facilities can make them potential targets of high value to terrorists or extremists.
- Software updates difficult to manage and apply to CII facilities.
- Critical infrastructure have additional risks due to special search tools and means to install malware even when facilities are not accessible by the Internet.

7.3   Examples of Cyberattacks Against Critical Infrastructure Systems

The ICS-CERT reported that they had received nine reports of cyber incidents directed against critical infrastructure systems in 2009; 41 reports in 2010; and 198 in 2011. General Alexander, the top American military official responsible for defending the United States against cyberattacks, has also stated there has been a 17-fold increase in computer attacks on American infrastructure systems between 2009 and 2011, which were initiated by criminal gangs, hackers and other nations (Schmitt 2012).

> There is an ongoing classic pattern of debate over critical infrastructures and their vulnerability to cyberattacks. Most of the process control systems designed to manage critical infrastructures, such as electric grids, oil pipelines, and water utilities, use specialized hardware and proprietary protocols. However, since the 1990s, the managers of these infrastructures have been integrating their control systems with computer networks built from commercial off-the-shelf operating systems, such as Windows and UNIX. This has simplified the task of managing facilities remotely, but it has also made process control systems vulnerable to attack over the Internet. Alarmists point to these connections as vulnerabilities that pose almost epic threats; skeptics immediately dismiss such fears, claiming that the necessary measures to prevent a catastrophic cyberattack have already been implemented. History suggests the truth lies somewhere in between (Kesler 2011).

Over the past 3 years, according to a report issued by the Department of Homeland Security, the critical infrastructure companies in the United States are reporting higher numbers of cyber attacks directed against their systems (ICS-CERT 2012).

The April 2012 report of the Industrial Control Systems Cyber Emergency Response Team (ICS-CERT) stated it has detected "an active series of cyber intrusions targeting natural gas pipeline sector companies." The report indicated that the cyberattacks were ongoing and massive, targeting the American gas-pipeline industry. Analysis has shown that the attacker was gathering sensitive information by stealing data from business systems, and could possibly also disrupt the industrial control systems of the targeted sector organizations. The ICS-CERT made this situation public in its monthly report in order to raise awareness of a possibly dangerous situation (ICS-CERT 2012). However, despite this public announcement, ICS-CERT has not received any reports of unauthorized access into the ICS and SCADA environment. The intent of the attackers remains unknown (Downing 2012).

The Industrial Control Systems Cyber Emergency Response Team (ICS-CERT) stated that attackers have been targeting other companies with access to the country's power grid, water filtration facilities and, recently, a nuclear facility. According to the ICS-CERT report, there were 198 incidents reported to DHS in 2011, up from nine incidents in 2009. Cyber emergency response teams visited the locations to investigate and further analyze the threats in 17 of the 198 cases in 2011. Eleven of the 17 incidents to which the emergency response teams physically responded were attacks that had been launched by "sophisticated actors," according to the report. The government has made a point of not identifying companies by name due to fear that such public exposure would deter other companies who are the victims of similar attacks from coming forward and sharing information about the threats.

Below are other examples of cyberattacks directed against U.S. critical infrastructure systems:

- In 2011, an unknown group reportedly succeeded in breaking into the computer network of at Diablo Canyon nuclear plant, which is located next to the Hosgri fault north of Santa Barbara. Hackers stole a contact list for subscribers to a nuclear management newsletter, and then sent them forged e-mails containing spyware. Later in August, an anonymous Internet post identified web domains that suggested a possible connection between the Diablo nuclear plant and a Chinese hacking group (Lawrence 2012) (ITC).
- In April 2009, *The Wall Street Journal* reported that that cyber spies had infiltrated the U.S. electric grid and left behind software that could be used to disrupt the system. The hackers reportedly were based in China, Russia and other nations and were apparently mapping each infrastructure system.
- In October 2006, a foreign hacker invaded the Harrisburg, Pa., water filtration system and planted malware.

To date, there have been no public reports of widespread cyberattacks against U.S. CII facilities that are directly attributed to specific extremist groups. However, the cyberattacks described above, if expanded in scope and intensity, may suit the goals of terrorists. Also, if terrorists groups and extremists do not yet have within their ranks the personnel with the technical skills needed to create sophisticated cyberattacks, those skills can be purchased from criminal organizations with highly technical individuals whose services are available for hire (Shelly 2004).

In addition, some criminal organizations may agree to exchange their technical services for permission to grow and transport illegal drugs through geographic areas under the control of extremists. Alliances and agreements between criminal organizations and extremist groups have existed in the recent past (Taylor 2002). In 2013, a report released by Kaspersky Lab describes the monitoring and analysis of the actions over time of a hacker group they now call "IceFog". Accordingly, this hacker group has been characterized by Kaspersky Lab as "cyber mercenaries" because of the "hit-and-run" style of numerous cyberattacks they have launched against defense contractors, supply chain vendors, telecommunications companies, ship builders, and government agencies (Rapoza 2013). Alliances may occur between hackers and criminals that result in a series of cyberattacks that have obscure reasons. Alliances between hackers, criminals, and terrorists may also occur because those nations that are targeted for illegal distribution of drugs are often the same nations that are targeted for attack by terrorists and extremists.

Key Points

- ICS-CERT has received increasing numbers of cyber incident reports.
- To date, there have been no public reports of widespread cyber attacks against U.S. CII facilities that are attributable to specific extremist groups.
- Terrorists might hire criminals or hackers to carry out cyber attacks.

7.4 Cyber Espionage Lays the Groundwork for Future Cyberterrorism

Cyber espionage can be used for reconnaissance, to uncover vulnerabilities in critical infrastructure computer systems, and to create precise programming instructions for future cyber terrorism attacks. Cyber espionage involves secretly gaining access to targeted computer systems in order to gather sensitive information. This is usually done through stealth technology, but may also be done through actions of an insider who secretly installs malicious cyber espionage code into a protected computer system. The information collected is necessary to help a terrorist group identify weaknesses in a targeted system. Information gathered may include uncovering a CII network configuration, or identifying the exact CII facility equipment models in operation, or copying the contents of a file containing valid user passwords. Terrorists may use the collected information to increase the effectiveness of a future cyberattack. Once installed, the malicious code may send sensitive information back to a central remote collection point. Later, a command may be sent to instruct the malicious code to begin a cyber terrorism attack. The collected details might give the malicious code the capability to shut off specific control valves at a CII facility, or issue the precisely incorrect instructions that might lead to destruction of specific equipment (Simonite 2012) at a sensitive site.

7.5 Models for Future Cyberterrorism Against Critical Infrastructures

Terrorists may already have in their possession two powerful examples of malicious code that can be redesigned for a cyber terrorism attack. The problem with malicious code that is released over the Internet is that it can be copied and reverse-engineered. Once discovered, numerous copies of malicious code are shared for analysis and become available to researchers and hackers located in all parts of the world. It is possible for these copies to be re-designed and possibly sent back to attack CII facility equipment in the U.S. (Simonite 2012).

Flame and Stuxnet are two examples of malicious code which were launched against Iran's nuclear CII facility, then later discovered on the Internet, and which were distributed globally to various researchers to help with analysis of the complex functions.

> **FLAME**: This malicious code quietly spied on targeted Iranian workers in their offices, and perhaps on the shop floor of the nuclear facility. "Flame secretly mapped and monitored Iran's computer networks, sending back a steady stream of intelligence to prepare for a cyberwarfare campaign…. Flame could activate computer microphones and cameras, log keyboard strokes, take screen shots, extract geolocation data from images, and send and receive commands and data through Bluetooth wireless technology….it evaded detection for several years by using a sophisticated program to crack an encryption algorithm" (Tate 2012).

> **STUXNET**: This malicious code targeted a specific type of controller equipment at Iran's uranium-enrichment CII facility in Natanz, causing almost 1,000 special centrifuges to spin out of control. The damage occurred gradually, over a period months, and Iranian officials were deliberately misled, through false instrument readings, to initially think the problems were the result of staff incompetence.

These cyberattacks quietly entered and then disrupted critical nuclear industrial facilities in Iran. Both cyberattacks apparently operated successfully while each remained undetected by Iran's nuclear facility systems administrators for several years (Wilson 2012). Researchers with Kaspersky Lab, a Russian security firm that researched both Flame and Stuxnet, reported their conclusion that Flame—a name they came up with—was created by the same group or groups that built Stuxnet. "We are now 100 percent sure that the Stuxnet and Flame groups worked together," said Roel Schouwenberg, a Boston-based senior researcher with Kaspersky Lab (Tate 2012).

Since the discovery and subsequent shared analysis of Flame and Stuxnet by many different research organizations, there is a good chance that many countries and organization now have their own copies and are in a position to make their own modifications for possible re-use (Zetter 2011). Extremist groups and terrorists may also be among those who now have access to their own copies (Barth 2011).

Key Point

Terrorists might have copies of Flame and Stuxnet to modify for possible re-use.

7.6   Zero-Day Exploits and Malicious Code

Both Flame and Stuxnet reportedly contain multiple zero-day exploits (ZDEs) which enabled them to bypass the cybersecurity controls for the top-secret computer systems in Iran's nuclear facility. A ZDE is special code that takes advantage of a previously unknown vulnerability in computer software. There is no technical defense against a ZDE until after it has been discovered and its stealthy methods have been analyzed by researchers.

Traditional antivirus and intrusion detection security products have difficulty in detecting or blocking the actions of a ZDE. If ZDE stealth is added onto malicious code, it can enable that code to be secretly inserted and installed on a targeted computer system. Because of increasingly sophisticated stealth features, sometimes months or years can pass until a systems administrator notices something suspicious is going on inside their computer system. Stealth capability and international tensions linked to cyber espionage have together created a growing demand for ZDEs.

Highly-skilled cyber experts who design and develop ZDEs have discovered that governments and industries will pay them handsomely (Miller 2007), and they can also offer ZDEs for sale to other organizations for use with cyberattacks (Greenberg 2012a). Sales of zero-day exploits are reportedly made to government customers in the U.S., Russia and China, plus European agencies and their supporting contractors, including for example, Northrop Grumman and Raytheon (Timm 2012). The Western governments and customers are the ones who pay the highest prices for ZDEs. Reportedly, markets in the Middle East cannot yet match the higher prices offered by Western governments (Greenberg 2012b).

Cyber experts involved in the design and sale of ZDEs include scientists, researchers, national military warfighters, students, and individual criminals. Individuals with sophisticated programming skills are actively recruited as workers by a variety of organizations, including law enforcement agencies, criminal organizations, and also possibly some extremist groups (Paganini 2012). Government agencies may explain to the sellers that the malware is intended for use to monitor communications of criminal suspects, or temporarily disable the computers and phones of suspects and targets as part of intelligence gathering programs. However, the growing body of ZDEs and malicious code are contributing to a cyber arms race, along with the familiar questions and concerns about containment and non-proliferation normally associated with CBRN weapons. ZDEs that are designed and purchased for use by the military and law enforcement may eventually come to threaten civilian critical infrastructure systems if they should find their way into the hands of terrorists and extremist groups. Reports have started to emerge that this gradual leakage of malicious ZDE code originally intended for use by law enforcement is already starting to take place.

Key Points
- There is a thriving market for zero-day exploits.
- Zero-day exploits might fall into the hands of terrorists.

7.7   Future Threats to Critical Information Infrastructures

The U.S. federal government has enacted a new policy called, Enhanced Cybersecurity Services program (ECS), to protect vulnerable CII facilities and systems. ECS is a voluntary information sharing program that helps critical infrastructure owners and operators improve their existing cybersecurity planning by providing, through a special secure environment, additional cyber threat information collected in advance by the government about a possible future cyberattacks. The ECS policy may be considered a response to observers who ask if pre-emptive cyber attacks, such as the Flame and Stuxnet attacks, launched by Western nations against the Iranian nuclear critical infrastructure will invite similar retaliatory cyberattacks against the U.S. critical information infrastructure. Some fear that the emphasis on pre-emptive cyber strikes by Western nations may accelerate the production and deployment of even more ZDEs. U.S. CII facilities and systems are vulnerable to ZDEs and to possible future cyber espionage and cyberattacks where malicious code employs ZDE stealth.

A corollary to the Western pre-emptive cyber strike strategy is what some observers call the "active cyber defense" model. Under the active defense model, extremist groups or suspected cyberterrorism groups would be actively monitored to detect planning for a terrorist attack. If a future attack is suspected, or if a cyber capability is seen to grow to a threatening level, the U.S. would require local law enforcement or military forces of the other country housing the terrorist group to arrest and block the suspected attempt. Or, if an extremist group of known cyber experts is being deliberately harbored within a country, and that country refuses to use its law enforcement to stop malicious cyber activity attributed to that group, then other nations may feel justified in taking aggressive (including military) action to stop the extremist group from continuing cyberattacks against critical infrastructures in the future (Sklerov 2012).

Other methods exist beyond the use of malicious code that terrorists may someday use to attack and disrupt computers. One technology often overlooked until recently in conversations about attacks against computer vulnerabilities is use of high-energy devices. Electromagnetic pulse (EMP) and directed high-power microwave energy are phenomena that can produce similar and damaging, energy pulse effects, and both can be used as weapons to disrupt and degrade circuitry in computers. Devices that produce these high energy effects, when powered and focused properly, can instantaneously overheat and permanently destroy electronic circuitry at a distance, sometimes without adding the attention-getting news headlines due to an accompanying explosion. "Directed energy weapons" now appears as a category on the United States Munitions List, and devices that employ directed energy are subject to export restrictions based on national security concerns.

However, despite the "munitions" category, some battery-powered directed energy microwave devices are now offered for sale on the Internet for commercial use. A terrorist group could possibly purchase an affordable directed-energy device, explore ways to dramatically boost the battery power, and fit the resulting device with a beam-focusing antenna. Many industrial microwave models are powered by battery, but other models can be re-engineered to be powered by a small or medium-size explosive charge, where the explosive energy is transformed into a high-energy pulse through use of a concentrating device called a vircator. As an example, a small, but powerful explosives-powered device the size of a suitcase could be placed in a small truck, with the focusing antenna aimed at a nearby critical infrastructure computer facility. When detonated, the explosion could be relatively minor compared to traditional explosions touched off by terrorists, but the sudden microwave energy spike could disrupt or degrade many computers within several blocks down range of the beam-focusing antenna. Normal circuit breakers and lightning surge protection devices could not clamp quickly enough to prevent damage to the computer circuitry. The primary objective of the attack could be to disrupt the targeted critical infrastructure computers, however, because of the accompanying explosion, first responders and newspapers would react primarily to the alarms created by the smoke and physical destruction of the explosives. Time would pass before a clear connection was made to show that the directed energy pulse also disrupted computers inside the nearby critical infrastructure facility. A directed energy device powered by a small explosives detonation can easily suit the purposes of a terrorist group. The commercial microwave device can be purchased and modified inexpensively, and the smoke and flames from the small explosive driver can direct attention away from the primary terrorist attack - the critical infrastructure computers. Such a violent event would create the sensational headlines that terrorist groups seem to prefer, and also produce some confusing and untraceable computer disruptions.

Other newer technologies are also relatively inexpensive, and can be used creatively to enable a cyber terrorist attack. During the war in Bosnia, U.S. military planes draped long carbon fibers across electric transmission lines that brought power to radar stations and other military computer facilities. The carbon fibers immediately shorted out the electrical supply to the targeted facilities which made them inoperable while the carbon fibers remained in place. Unmanned flying drones now come in large and smaller models, and some commercial models can even be purchased at the local corner hobby shop. Drones can also be easily and inexpensively outfitted with the same long carbon fibers and sent by terrorists on a similar set of missions to instantly disrupt the power lines going out of large power stations, or into computers operating critical infrastructure facilities in Western countries. This type of attack against computer systems could also disrupt the electrical power going to medical facilities and transportation systems such as subways, and otherwise greatly amplify the effects created from a simultaneous, violent traditional terrorist attack. Such an attack, or a string of many simultaneous drone attacks, would likely fit within the budget and planning capabilities of a terrorist cell.

Key Point

- CII might be threatened by new weapons in the future such as "directed energy weapons."

7.8   Conclusion

Because modern society relies heavily on the important functions of critical infra-structures, they are high-value targets for cyberattack. However, unique and well-known vulnerabilities that characterize many CII facilities and systems can give them the appearance of low-hanging fruit that is ripe for attack by cyber terrorists. The lack of software updates for older systems, and the difficulties and expenses associated with installing regular security software patches together leave critical infrastructure systems open to cyberattacks that could otherwise be avoided. Further, many critical infrastructure systems with software vulnerabilities can be easily found on the Internet using special search engines such as Shodan.

While there have been cyberattacks directed against critical infrastructures, to date there have been no publicly reported widespread cyberattacks directly attrib-uted to extremists or terrorists. However, it is possible to speculate about the cyber capabilities of terrorist groups. The technical skills needed for a cyber terrorist attack may be growing along with easier access to sophisticated technology tools and high-level technical skills available through the Internet. While many observers say that terrorists do not yet have the personnel with skills needed to create and launch a sophisticated cyberattack, there are programmer experts available for hire through the Internet as part of some criminal organizations, who could easily sell their technical skills for a cyberattack.

Cyber espionage has also been paired with the launching of subsequent cyberat-tacks. This has been demonstrated by Flame and Stuxnet, which researchers report were both designed by the same team, apparently as a program for espionage and sabotage cyberattacks directed against Iran's top secret nuclear facilities. Now these malicious programs have been analyzed and shared among many research organiza-tions, and it is likely that copies now exist in different parts of the world. Those with access to copies may include governments and hackers, who may choose to rede-sign them for subsequent use. Extremists and terrorists may also have access to copies of the malicious code to use as models for future cyber terrorist attacks.

New stealthy Zero-Day exploits enable cyber espionage attacks to be implanted and operate inside high-secure computer systems, often residing and performing malicious functions while undetected by systems administrators for months or years. A growing number of ZDEs and malicious code designs are now available for purchase on the open Internet market by individuals, governments, and possibly also by terrorists.

All of the above combine to reduce the effort needed by terrorists to identify critical infrastructures that have specific cyber weaknesses, and reduce the effort needed for terrorists to access to models for malicious code for cyber espionage and sabotage. Even though a cyberattack may not always produce the headlines with the equivalent sensationalism that goes with a traditional violent terrorist attack with explosives, cyber technology has advanced so that new, more sophisticated cyber weapons may someday have the capability to cause widespread physical damage and disruption. Terrorist groups, perhaps through financial association, or through other agreements for cooperation with criminal organizations, can possibly purchase zero-day exploits that can help them secretly implant cyber weapons into our critical infrastructures for cyber espionage, or for a later cyberattack.

For security in cyberspace, the offense always has the advantage over defense. It is unclear if the first-strike use of Flame and Stuxnet in cyberattacks directed against Iran's nuclear facilities will result in eventual retaliation by extremist groups that want to return the cyberattacks by targeting Western critical infrastructures. However, when terrorist observe the new Western government emphasis on preemptive cyber strikes, and when terrorists also have possible access to models for malicious code, have access to stealthy ZDEs, and have access to high-level technical skills, the likelihood of a future cyberattack by terrorists against critical infrastructures in the West does not put too much strain the imagination.

Further Reading

Goetz E, Shenoi S (2008) Critical infrastructure protection. Springer, New York

Krutz R (2006) Securing SCADA systems. Wiley Publishing, Indianapolis

Nickolov E (2005) Critical information infrastructure protection: analysis, evaluation and expectations. Int J Inform Secur 17:105–119

Shea D (2004) Critical infrastructure: control systems and the terrorist threat. Congressional Research Service, Washington

U.S. General Accounting Office (2004) Cybersecurity for critical infrastructure protection. Washington: GAO-04-321

Wiles J et al (2008) Techno security's guide to securing SCADA. Syngress Publishing, Burlington

Wilson C (2005) Computer attack and cyberterrorism: vulnerabilities and policy issues for congress. Congressional Research Service, Washington

References

Barth C (2011) Anonymous claims possession of insidious Stuxnet virus. Available from Forbes: http://www.forbes.com/sites/chrisbarth/2011/02/11/anonymous-claims-possession-of-insidious-stuxnet-virus/. Accessed 20 Sep 2013

DHS (2012) Enhanced cybersecurity services. Available from DHS: http://www.dhs.gov/enhanced-cybersecurity-services. Accessed 20 Sep 2013

Downing B (2012) Report: natural gas companies under cyber attacks. Available from Akron Beacon Journal Online: http://www.ohio.com/blogs/drilling/ohio-utica-shale-1.291290/report-natural-gas-companies-under-cyber-attacks-1.305907. Accessed 5 Sep 2012

Greenberg A (2012) Meet the hackers who sell spies the tools to crack your PC [and get paid six-figure fees]. Available from Forbes: http://www.forbes.com/sites/andygreenberg/2012/03/21/meet-the-hackers-who-sell-spies-the-tools-to-crack-your-pc-and-get-paid-six-figure-fees/print/. Accessed 3 Sep 2012

Greenberg A (2012) Shopping for zero-days: a price list for hackers' secret software exploits. Available from Forbes: http://www.forbes.com/sites/andygreenberg/2012/03/23/shopping-for-zero-days-an-price-list-for-hackers-secret-software-exploits/. Accessed 2 Sep 2012

ICS-CERT (2012) ICS-CERT monthly monitor. Available from Incident Response Activity: http://
    www.us-cert.gov/control_systems/pdf/ICS-CERT_Monthly_Monitor_June-July2012.pdf.
    Accessed 5 Sep 2012
Kesler B (2011) The vulnerability of nuclear facilities to cyber attack. Available from Strategic
    Insights—Naval   Postgraduate   School: http://www.nps.edu/Academics/Centers/CCC/
    Research-Publications/StrategicInsights/2011/Apr/SI-v10-i1_Kesler.pdf. Accessed 5 Sep 2012
Lawrence MR (2012) Hackers linked to China's army seen from EU to D.C. Available from
    Bloomberg News: http://www.bloomberg.com/news/2012-07-26/china-hackers-hit-eu-point-
    man-and-d-c-with-byzantine-candor.html. Accessed 20 Aug 2012
Miller C (2007) The legitimate vulnerability market: the secretive world of 0-day exploit sales.
    Available from Independent Security Evaluators: http://securityevaluators.com/files/papers/
    0daymarket.pdf. Accessed 3 Sep 2012
Nakashima E (2012) Senate ready to take up cybersecurity bill that critics say is too weak.
    Washington Post 25 July 2012, p A2
Paganini P (2012) Reflections on the zero-day exploits market. Available from Infosec Island:
    http://www.infosecisland.com/blogview/20819-Reflections-on-the-Zero-Day-Exploits-
    Market.html. Accessed 3 Sep 2012
Rapoza K (2013) Kaspersky lab uncovers new cyber hit-n-run op called 'Icefog'. Available from
    Forbes: http://www.forbes.com/sites/kenrapoza/2013/09/25/kaspersky-lab-uncovers-new-
    cyber-hit-n-run-op-called-icefog/. Accessed 25 Sep 2013
Richardson C (2010) Cell phone virus attacks 1 million cell phone users. Available from Christian
    ScienceMonitor:http://www.csmonitor.com/Innovation/Horizons/2010/1111/Cell-phone-virus-
    attacks-1-million-cell-phone-users
Rollins J, Wilson C (2007) Terrorist capabilities for cyberattack: overview and policy issues.
    Congressional Research Service, Washington
Schmitt DE (2012) Rise is seen in cyberattacks targeting U.S. infrastructure. New York Times 27
    July 2012, p 8
Shelly L (2004) Organized crime, terrorism and cybercrime. Available from Computer Crime
    Research Center: http://www.crime-research.org/articles/terrorism_cybercrime. Accessed 20
    Sep 2013
Simonite T (2012) Stuxnet tricks copied by computer criminals. http://www.technologyreview.
    com/news/429173/stuxnet-tricks-copied-by-computer-criminals/. Accessed 20 Sep 2013
Sklerov M (2012) Responding to international cyber attacks as acts of war. In: Carr J (ed) Inside
    cyber warfare. O'Reilly, Sebastopol, pp 45–76
Tate EN (2012) U.S., Israel developed Flame computer virus to slow Iranian nuclear efforts,
    officials say. Available from Washington Post: http://www.washingtonpost.com/world/
    national-security/us-israel-developed-computer-virus-to-slow-iranian-nuclear-efforts-offi-
    cials-say/2012/06/19/gJQA6xBPoV_story.html. Accessed 2 Sep 2012
Taylor RB (2002) Narco-terror: the worldwide connection between drugs and terror. Testimony
    before the U.S. Senate Judiciary Committee, Subcommittee on Technology, Terrorism, and
    Government Information. U.S. State Department, Washington, DC
Timm MH (2012) "Zero-day" exploit sales should be key point in cybersecurity debate. Available
    from Electronic Frontier Foundation: https://www.eff.org/deeplinks/2012/03/zero-day-exploit-
    sales-should-be-key-point-cybersecurity-debate. Accessed 3 Sep 2012
Wilson C (2012) Science collaboration and security: emerging cbrncy challenges and threat reduc-
    tion programs beyond 2012. (C. Wilson, Performer) International Working Group—Landau
    Network Centro Volta, Como, Italy
Zetter K (2011) DHS fears a modified Stuxnet could attack U.S. infrastructure. Available
    from Wired: http://www.wired.com/threatlevel/2011/07/dhs-fears-stuxnet-attacks/. Accessed
    20 Sep 2013

Chapter 8
The Citadel and Its Sentinels: State Strategies for Contesting Cyberterrorism in the UK

Tim Legrand

8.1 Introduction

The virtual and physical dimensions of society are tied in an ever-growing and ever-tightening Gordian knot. In the pre-cyber era Heidegger observed 'Everywhere we remain unfree and chained to technology whether we passionately affirm or deny it' (1977:4). Where once relatively independent, the arenas of civil society, commerce, politics, finance, manufacturing, media, and culture are increasingly integrating into fragile interdependency. Threats to these digital interdependencies have captured the public's imagination in the form of cyberterrorism. The framing of the 'cyber-terror' terminology derives power from the marriage of two entities that are uncertain in different ways: the digital cyber realms provide anonymous refuge for a host of criminal actors; while terrorism is uncertain by virtue of the unpredictable malevolence it is often ascribed. Together these uncertainties compound as the sum of two fears. The fear that terrorists will one day triumphantly exploit society's dependence on cyberspace to catastrophic effect has been widely reprised in the popular media. In recent films—such as the latest in the James Bond franchise, Skyfall (2012), or Bruce Willis' blockbuster Live Free or Die Hard (2007)—visions abound of cyber-based attackers causing trains to derail, stock markets to plummet, road traffic control systems to fail, power networks to shut down, and so on. Meanwhile, in The Daily Mail, a headline warns: 'Our No.1 threat: Cyber terrorists who can knock a jet out of the sky' (2010). In the Mirror, another headline speculates 'Could a terrorist cyber attack set off World War 3?' (2013). And there is no doubt that there are individuals and groups around the world who would, if it were possible, wish it so. For the moment, it seems that the reason any entity of malevolent purpose has not yet done so is a function of capability, not will. As Giacomello argues in his analysis of the costs and benefits of

T. Legrand (✉)
ARC Centre of Excellence in Policing and Security, Griffith University,
Brisbane, QLD, Australia
e-mail: t.legrand@griffith.edu.au

T.M. Chen et al. (eds.), *Cyberterrorism: Understanding, Assessment, and Response*,
DOI 10.1007/978-1-4939-0962-9_8, © Springer Science+Business Media New York 2014

cyberterrorism, 'for the time being, investing resources in cyberterrorism alone would entail high actual as well as opportunity costs and meager returns' (2004:401). Yet the perhaps justifiable fear remains that the falling costs of the necessary technology will bring the possibility within reach of terrorists and so to protect the public interest government must act preemptively to secure the digital landscape.

This chapter engages with the evolution of the UK's political response to concerns around cyber threats generally and cyberterrorism specifically. It begins with an overview of the significance of a digitised society and sets out the principal claims made by government in constructions of the cyber-agents that threaten it. I then turn to the detail of UK government policy and practice in tackling the postulated threat, drawing careful attention to the tensions between the government's duty to protect the public interest and the interests of the largely private owners and operators of critical infrastructure lacking any such duty.

Put simply, my argument in this chapter is that government policy towards cyber security generally, and cyber terrorism specifically, has been fundamentally constrained by privatization: the transfer of the ownership of utilities, services and property from the public to the private sector. I contend that private sector owners and operators of essential public services are caught in a bind, stretched between serving the shareholder interest and the public interest. This tension, I suggest, constitutes an overarching challenge to the UK's public policy officials.

It is worth foregrounding this chapter with some brief though important remarks. First, as far as is known in the public domain, there have been no known instances of cyberterrorism per se.[1] The UK Independent Reviewer of Terrorism Legislation, David Anderson, observed that 'The emergence of significant nuclear, chemical, biological and cyberterrorism, though long predicted, has not yet come to pass' (Anderson 2012:2.12). Second, despite the lack of existing examples, the crippling impact of the now-infamous Stuxnet virus on an Iranian nuclear facility does demonstrate that it is possible to disrupt and even destroy critical infrastructures, though it is not clear whether this has resulted in physical harm to individuals. Third, it is thereby far from clear exactly how large a gap there is between the intentions and capabilities in cyberspace of designated terrorist organisations (albeit there are obvious conceptual difficulties in separating state from non-state actors). Fourth, throughout the policy discourse of the UK government, cyberterrorism receives little direct attention in terms of potential capability to disrupt, even while thought is given to the dimensions of cyber-space as a new territory to promote the aims of extremist groups (whether bent on violence or otherwise). As a consequence, as detailed below, government policy nests cyber-terror alongside a host of potential threats without differentiating its specific vector of threat.

These are important points to make at the outset, because a running theme of cyberterrorism is ambiguity: both in defining cyber threats and in policy responses to

---

[1] Though some analysts point to an incident of cyber-sabotage to a waste management system in Maroochy Shire, Queensland in 2000, most agree that cyberterrorism -as understood as political violence- has not yet transpired.

such threats (see Hardy and Williams 2014; Yannakogeorgos 2014; Jarvis et al. 2014). On top of this, there are additional constraints of methodology involved in depicting any state-based counter-terrorism effort. In the nascent cyber world, in which the technical possibilities are only just becoming apparent, specific government operations to counter threats are quite simply rarely announced to the public. This chapter is thus confined to strategic policies, announcements and initiatives that are publicly available.

> **Key Points**
>
> - Many of the systems and processes that underpin society, politics and the economy are becoming increasingly interdependent and enmeshed in the cyber world.
> - Despite no known instances of cyberterrorism occurring, it has nevertheless caught the imaginations of the media and politicians.

8.2   The UK and Its Cyber Landscape

> Today, information and cyber security threats are becoming increasingly complex and are evolving at a rapid pace. At the same time, traditional risk management regimes used by government are no longer adequate to mitigate against this threat. (Cabinet Office 2011a:53)

We might pity the public official charged with gaining a foothold on the threat of cyberterrorism and related threats. The UK government, with many others around the world, has struggled to form a cogent position on, first, whether and how cyberterrorism can enact a catastrophe worthy of its name and, second, how to prevent this from happening. For some, it is merely an old threat in new clothes. For example, Nick Harvey, the UK Armed Forces Minister between 2010 and 2012, argued that 'cyber crime, cyber terrorism, cyber espionage or cyber war are simply crime, terrorism, espionage or war by other means' (2011 see also McGuire 2014; Stohl 2014). It is indeed increasingly apparent that the changing dimensions of threats in the cyber realm have such a fleeting half-life that the adoption of a 'fixed' taxonomy of cyber threats within policy is almost a futile task. Many will have been extinguished or become extinct by the time policy takes hold, with other, undoubtedly more sophisticated, threats taking their place. Such is the rapidity of evolution in the ruthless ecology of cyberspace. Nevertheless, there is little doubt that the internet-based economy is growing in value and that this is growth is matched by a surge in a diverse range of cyber-related crime and state-based cyber-threats. Such threats are often of ambiguous provenance and purpose; some seek financial gain, others political advantage, while others disruption or destruction. In this section, I explore the dynamics of 'cyber threats' and draw attention to the economic and strategic risks posed by the ambiguous, yet no less real, agents of the cyber realm.

8.2.1 The UK's Digital Landscape

The economic value of the cyber realm to the UK economy is steadily rising. In 2010, 717 million card payments were made online in the UK, at a total of £47.2 billion spent.[2] According to National Audit Office estimates, the UK's internet-based economy was worth £121 billion in 2010 (National Audit Office 2013). The Internet economy represents 8.3 % of the UK's overall GDP, the highest proportion of all G20 countries, and future growth is estimated at 11 % per annum. By 2016, 23 % of all retail is expected to occur online in the UK (Boston Consulting Group 2012). This growth is predicated on the increasing convergence of the UK's social, economic and political fabric with the cyber realm. Some have characterised the current cyber-scape as an 'Internet of Things', clothing evermore physical objects and processes in digital vestments: from wireless tracking and control of modern cars, to internet-enabled refrigerators (Bradley et al. 2013). Challenging these potential gains is a buoyant online criminal economy and a swathe of state and non-state groups taking advantage of the anonymity of cyberspace; what Cornish et al call 'the heterogeneous nature of cyber threats' (2011:9). The UK government cites a growing list of diverse threats including serious organised crime involved in data and identity theft, money laundering, fraud and intellectual property theft; belligerent overseas espionage agencies intruding into government and private ICT systems to attack critical infrastructure or glean government and corporate intelligence; and, politically motivated groups hacking into the systems of corporations and government agencies to 'steal information or damage computer systems to serve political agendas' (National Audit Office 2013:6). The mainstream media frequently conjures up legions of 'hackers' as freelance, lone-wolf, keyboard maestros. As the US Assistant Secretary of Defense, William Lynn, put it: 'a couple dozen talented programmers wearing flip-flops and drinking Red Bull can do a lot of damage' (Lynn 2011). Yet some of the most prolific actors are in fact organised, state-sponsored groups operating within a quasi-legal framework. Indeed, removing the mask of a good number of cyber belligerents reveals the somewhat mundane face of a government bureaucracy. The internet security firm Mandiant (2013) found that the pattern of cyber-attacks on US government and corporate systems corresponded to a Monday to Friday, 9 am to 5 pm working week in Shanghai, China. Mandiant identified the 2nd Bureau of the People's Liberation Army General Staff Department's 3rd Department or Unit 61398 as the main protagonist, working from a drab office building in an unfashionable district of the city. In addition to organised crime and state-based groups, a variety of other actors make up a 'rogues gallery' of cyber belligerents: activist groups, nationalist groups, industrial espionage agents and political extremists are all active in the cyber-world in one form or another. Some commentators, such as the former director of the US National Security Agency, Michael Hayden, have been contemptuous of cyber activists, describing a group of 'nihilists, anarchists, activists, Lulzsec, Anonymous, twenty somethings who haven't talked to the opposite sex in 5 or 6 years' (Hayden 2013).

---

[2] Figures taken: http://www.theukcardsassociation.org.uk/2010-facts-figures/Internet_card_use_2010. asp, accessed 13th August 2013.

The diversifying cyber threat has had a considerable impact on government, society and businesses. For the public, cyber-crime is an ever-present part of digitised lifestyles: from malicious emails seeking to entice individuals to divulge personal or financial data to computer viruses and malware designed to corrupt home computers. The government fares little better. The former Minister for Political and Constitutional Reform, Chloe Smith, recently claimed that the UK government faces an estimated 33,000 cyber attacks a month from criminals and state-sponsored groups (Smith 2013). According to a UK government report in 2011, online crime costs the UK an estimated £27 billion a year (Cabinet Office and DETICA 2011). The report found systemic problems in tackling cyber crime, suggesting that 'efforts to tackle it seem to be more tactical than strategic' (2011:3). Significantly, the report's authors suggest: 'The problem is compounded by the lack of a clear reporting mechanism and the perception that, even if crimes were reported, little can be done' (2011:3).

Meanwhile, the spectre of cyberterrorism remains conspicuous by its absence. As earlier foreshadowed, while cyberterrorism per se features in both the popular imagination and government policy, we are yet to experience anything worthy of the label. This is affirmed by the UK Home Secretary Theresa May, who stated: 'We continue to see little evidence of systematic cyber terrorism' (May 2011). Yet this has not prevented a discourse of cyberterrorism taking hold against a backdrop of continued cyber intrusions in the systems running critical infrastructures. According to McAfee, an internet security firm, 'nearly two-thirds of critical infrastructure companies report regularly finding malware designed to sabotage their systems' (McAfee and Center for Strategic and International Studies 2011:6). In a survey by Ixia of the Information Systems Security Association's membership,[3] security professionals expressed their fears of a cyber-terror attack on critical infrastructure. The survey found that 79 % expected a major cyber terror attack within 2013. Ixia reported that 35 % of the security professionals surveyed expected power systems to be the main target, 23 % the financial system, with 13 % believing the oil and gas industry would be targeted. However, signifying the ambiguity of this threat, the definition of cyberterrorism was not articulated in this survey. Herein lies a pressing issue: often, 'cyberterrorism' is frequently used as shorthand for any attack - by any actor, with any motive, to whatever consequence—on critical infrastructure (see Hardy and Williams 2014; Yannakogeorgos 2014; Jarvis et al. 2014).

8.2.2   The Cyber Threat and Critical Infrastructure

The agency charged with coordinating the protection of critical infrastructures in the UK is the Centre for the Protection of National Infrastructure (hereafter CPNI). Its goal is to provide 'advice that aims to reduce the vulnerability of organisations in the national infrastructure to terrorism and other threats such as espionage, including those of cyber space' (Centre for the Protection of National Infrastructure n.d.).

---

[3] Survey findings reported at http://blogs.ixiacom.com/ixia-blog/cyber-terrorism-going-happen-whoe28099s-responsible-protecting-us-part-1/, accessed 13th August 2013.

'Critical infrastructure' is so nominated for its centrality to the health of society and the UK government defines critical national infrastructure (hereafter CNI) as 'those facilities, systems, sites and networks necessary for the functioning of the country and the delivery of the essential services upon which daily life in the UK depends' (CPNI n.d.). According to the CPNI it comprises nine sectors: communications, emergency services, energy, financial services, food, government, health, transport and water. The CPNI was established in part to coordinate ongoing efforts by government agencies over the past decade to improve the capacity of CNI to withstand disruption. These efforts have been galvanised by governmental efforts to enhance infrastructure resilience, defined as 'the ability of assets, networks and systems to anticipate, absorb, adapt to and/or rapidly recover from a disruptive events' (CPNI n.d.). While this rationale has been informed primarily by the risks posed by the natural environment—indeed, the CPNI was established in the aftermath of widespread flooding in 2007—the government's response to threats to critical infrastructure from the evolving cyber environment is bounded by two significant historical constraints. First, the transfer of critical infrastructure from state to private ownership. And, second, the fragmentation of operating standards for secure information systems.

On the first of these constraints, the institutions of the British government now largely conform to the patterns of the style of government known as New Public Management (NPM), which was established some 30 years ago (see Minogue et al. 1998). During the 1980s and 1990s, as the walled garden of state delivery of public services was brought down, the private sector stepped in to take root in a competitive market for provision of public services. Few sectors were immune and, crucially, the majority of sectors that constitute critical infrastructure were transferred from public to private ownership. In less than a decade, the operation and/or ownership of telecommunications, water supply, energy provision and transport (aviation, rail and road) by the private sector was almost ubiquitous. Christopher Hood finds that NPM was a phenomenon that spread across the Anglophone world, noting the 'high degree of emphasis placed on NPM in South Africa, Hong Kong, Australia and New Zealand'(1995:99–100). The gradual transfer of critical infrastructure into private operation and ownership has reached significant proportions across the UK, where an estimated 80 % of critical infrastructure is owned and operated by private enterprise (Parliamentary Office of Science and Technology 2011). In the US, the figure is an estimated 85 % (Department of Homeland Security n.d., p. para 2); and in Australia, it is 90 % (The Western Australian Government 2011:19).

On the second constraint, the diversification of the ownership and operation of critical infrastructures is compounded by the fragmentation of cyber security standards. The 2011 UK Cyber Security Strategy states: 'The digital architecture on which we now rely was built to be efficient and interoperable. When the internet first started to grow, security was less of a consideration' (Cabinet Office 2011b:15). In the cyber world's precocious days of the 1980s, the chief concern of its architects was to maximise the efficiency of data exchange. Once the common standards and operating protocols of the 'world wide web' of interconnected networks were established, the proof-of-concept had been achieved: i.e. network terminals could remotely exchange data with one another. The next task was to increase the amount of data that could be transferred, and the speed at which it was so. This early objective to improve the efficiency and integrity of remote data exchange trumped security considerations. This has had repercussions for the UK's digital architecture, which is characterised by fragmentation of system (and security) standards across government and the private sector.

These two developments have significant repercussions for the management of cyber threats to critical infrastructures, which are increasingly dependent on information technology systems to control and administer services and processes. Now that public services are almost entirely delivered by the private sector, all cyber threats to the infrastructures upon which such services depend must primarily be addressed by the private sector irrespective of the fragmentation of security protocols.

Key Points

- The range of actors who use cyberspace for crime, espionage or other purposes is growing although frequently anonymous and difficult to detect.
- The prospects of any actor, whether a terrorist or state-sponsored agency, disrupting critical infrastructure has caught the attention of UK policy officials.
- In an era of privatization, the threats to critical infrastructure must be tackled in large part by the private sector and not government.

8.3 Describing Cyberterrorism

In UK policy, cyberterrorism is understood primarily in terms of its indirect elements (the use of cyber space to generate ideational and material support for extremist groups and to facilitate direct acts of violence) and the direct use of the cyber realm (i.e. undertaken from the cyber realm to disrupt the UK's cyber commons or critical physical processes). This is illustrated in the recent Cyber Security Strategy:

> Cyberspace is already used by terrorists to spread propaganda, radicalise potential supporters, raise funds, communicate and plan. While terrorists can be expected to continue to favour high-profile physical attacks, the threat that they might also use cyberspace to facilitate or to mount attacks against the UK is growing. We judge that it will continue to do so, especially if terrorists believe that our national infrastructure may be vulnerable (Cabinet Office 2011b:15).

While acknowledging that it is yet to come to pass, in September 2011, the UK Home Secretary Theresa May depicted cyberterrorism as an anarchic threat, deriving strength from isolation and disorganisation:

> We continue to see little evidence of systematic cyber terrorism. But this is now part of the language of Al Qa'ida. As a tactic, and as a weapon, cyber terrorism is perfectly suited to the world of the lone terrorist, operating outside a hierarchy and without traditional command and control (May 2011).

In this sense, cyberterrorism might be regarded as an atomised, insidious and ever-present threat. Theresa May embedded this sentiment with the observation that, 'technology can give much more lethal power to fewer people'. This regard for the cyber-terror threat is markedly different from the combative rhetoric deployed against defeating the identified foes of, say, Al Qa'ida.

Whereas tangible digital intrusions from state-based actors are increasing—and cyber crime continues apace—cyberterrorism remains an unrealised, speculative threat. The epistemological question, even if it is not articulated as such, courses through the policy debate: How can we calculate the nature of the cyber-threat? For the moment, the UK's cyber strategy has developed incrementally and evolved toward a broad elision of the threats of crime, terrorism and belligerent state agencies through a risk-based approach:

> In a globalised world where all networked systems are potentially vulnerable and where cyber attacks are difficult to detect, there can be no such thing as absolute security. We will therefore apply a risk-based approach to prioritising our response (Cabinet Office 2011b:22)

The risk-based approach is premised on the calculation of threat using information gathered from state and private bodies: 'Much of the infrastructure we need to protect is owned and operated by the private sector. The expertise and innovation required to keep pace with the threat will be business-driven' (Cabinet Office 2011b:22). This approach blurs the lines of responsibility between the public and private sector and possibly confounds the 'old' Cold War security paradigm in which government was unambiguously responsible for identifying and tackling threats. Amoore and de Goode argue that 'the application of risk techniques in the war on terror fosters complex new spaces of governing in which public and private authorities, knowledges and datasets cooperate closely, and sometimes become practically indistinguishable' (2008:7). This approach, they claim, does not seek to reduce risk, acquire control or diminish threats to safety, but instead is concerned to ensure that 'the appearance of securability and manageability is maintained' (2008:9). The 'newness' of cyberterrorism specifically, and cyber threats broadly, challenge the capacity of government security agencies to guard against the changing cyber environment:

> Today, information and cyber security threats are becoming increasingly complex and are evolving at a rapid pace. At the same time, traditional risk management regimes used by government are no longer adequate to mitigate against this threat (Cabinet Office 2011a:53)

The blurring of responsibility for identifying and mitigating the risks of cyber threat has led to cyberterrorism becoming subsumed within a framework of threat lacking a subject. Of course, the cyber-terror bracket serves a useful secondary purpose as a catch-all term for unspecified threat. The ambiguous antagonist, as the 'cyber-terrorist' is constructed as simultaneously the unknown individual, organisation, agency, institution or, indeed, the state. This perspective is borne out in one of the earliest Cabinet Office observations on the subject:

> Hacking or 'cyber-terrorism' can also be done for political reasons by terrorist groups, agencies of foreign states or activist groups (Cabinet Office 2004:7)

While later iterations of government policy abandoned the elision of 'hackers', activism, foreign states and terrorism, this 2004 depiction of cyberterrorism is illustrative of how government has struggled to develop a coherent description of the threats of the cyber world. Invariably, government publications side-step any nuanced discussion of cyberterrorism and instead align it with online crime and belligerent foreign agencies. That this is so is a product of the uncertainty of the magnitude and nature of the cyber-terror risk and the newness of cyber security as a UK policy area.

In short, the manner in which cyber-terror has been construed by government can therefore be characterised by three related vectors that view cyberterrorism as (i) a diffuse, atomised collection of terrorists, operating outside of the command-and-control hierarchy; (ii) an unquantified and ambiguous threat that can only be addressed within a risk-based strategy, and (iii) aligned with other societal 'threats' such as financial crime, and intellectual property theft.

Key Points

- UK policy officials have struggled to develop a coherent notion of cyber-terrorism: it is regarded as an atomised threat that can operate without explicit links to a hierarchy or organisation.
- The uncertain threat posed by cyberterrorism is managed by the UK government through a risk-based framework. This gives the appearance that the risk is being addressed.
- Because of the uncertainty of cyberterrorism, the UK government has aligned it with a range of cyber 'threats' to be addressed under the same policy rubric.

8.4 Guarding Against Britain's Cyber Foes

The first concerted move by the UK government to generate a whole-of-government strategy to protect government digital data systems occurred after the government agency responsible for the provision of information assurance advice to government and industry, the Communications-Electronics Security Group (CESG), recommended that government create a central sponsor for the security of government data systems from data loss or penetration in 2001(National Audit Office 2013). This recommendation resulted in the 2003 Information Assurance (IA) strategy, which represented the overarching framework for securing government and public data systems. The coordination of this strategy, updated in 2007 to become the National Information Assurance Strategy (NIAS), came under the responsibility of the Central Sponsor for Information Assurance (CSIA) in the Cabinet Office. The role of the CSIA was to provide assurance to government that 'risks to the information systems underpinning key public interests are appropriately managed' (Cabinet Office 2004:3). The NIAS was substantially updated in 2009 with publication of the first national Cyber Security Strategy. The Strategy set out the historical antecedents of government's responsibility to secure the country's territories:

> Just as in the 19th century we had to secure the seas for our national safety and prosperity, and in the 20th century we had to secure the air, in the 21st century we also have to secure our advantage in cyber space (Cabinet Office 2009:5).

The Strategy firmly established a rationale of cyber-security that, under the auspices of 'securing the UK's advantage in cyber space', looked to exploit the opportunities it presented. This entailed recognition of the uncertainty associated with the new environment:

> The low cost and largely anonymous nature of cyber space makes it an attractive domain for use by those who seek to use cyber space for malicious purposes. These include criminals, terrorists, and states, whether for reasons of espionage, influence or even warfare (Cabinet Office 2009:12).

The 2009 Cyber Security Strategy put in place new structures to address the existing and emerging cyber threats. Out of the revamped strategy the government established the Cyber Security Operations Centre (CSOC) and the Office of Cyber Security (now the Office of Cyber Security and Information Assurance (OCSIA)). The former, CSOC, is a multi-agency unit intended to 'monitor developments in cyberspace…, analyse trends and to improve technical response coordination to cyber incidents' (Cabinet Office 2009:17). The latter, OSCIA, manages the Cyber Security Strategy and its constituent cross-government programmes from within the UK Cabinet Office. Government efforts to understand and counter cyber threats were bolstered by the 2010 Strategic Defence and Security Review which allocated £650 million to a cross-government National Cyber Security Programme (NCSP) over four years to secure and enhance the resilience of the UK's digital architecture. Together, the 2010 National Security Strategy (NSS) and the 2010 Strategic Defence and Security Review (SDSR), underlined the significance of cyber threats as a 'Tier 1' threat to the UK.

The most recent strategy developed by the UK government is the 2011 UK Cyber Security Strategy. The National Cyber Security Programme is led by OCSIA within the Cabinet Office and administers the £650 m budget of the NCSP. Responsibility for the delivery of elements of the NSS are spread across six central departments and nine further government organisations. The 2011 CSS recognises that 'much of the UK's critical infrastructure is not in Government hands but is owned and managed by the private sector' (Cabinet Office 2011b:28). As a consequence, two parallel approaches have been developed by government to address the risks of cyber threats. These can be characterised as: (i) a walled 'citadel' of protection for core government services, (ii) and a 'sentinel' programme to provide protective advice to UK private enterprises that operate beyond.

8.4.1   The Citadel...

While the CSS stipulates the specific strategies to meeting and mitigating the diverse threats of the cyber realm, it is underpinned by the government's broader ambition to digitise core government services. The Government Digital Service (GDS) leads the whole-of-government effort to provide digital public services under the aegis of the Digital by Default strategy (see Cabinet 2012). This commitment is complemented by an ICT Strategy (ICTS) which seeks to redesign all core government systems to align with a common ICT architecture over the next few years. The architecture will be extended to all central government agencies and their attendant agencies or bodies. The ICTS has four key objectives: 'reducing waste and project failure, and stimulating economic growth; creating a common ICT infrastructure; using ICT to enable and deliver change; and strengthening governance' (Cabinet Office 2011a:6). In addition to the projected efficiency savings of £460 million in 2014/15, the standardisation of core government services directly contributes to the 'the creation of an environment for a common and secure ICT infrastructure, underpinned by a suite of mandated standards' (p. 10). Where diversity and fragmentation typify the range of ICT systems operating in private sector critical infrastructures, the deployment of a common operating environment allows government to construct a single digital citadel:

> Complete implementation of security model and cyber defence regime across government which ensures that the boundaries of the environment are suitably protected, that users are appropriately authenticated and trusted and that key capabilities are always available to key personnel, even in disaster or terror situations. (Cabinet Office 2011a:41).

The walled-off digital space is overseen by the CESG, which acts as the government's National Technical Authority for Information Assurance. CESG is the information assurance arm of Government Communications Headquarters (GCHQ) and provides cyber protection to core government services.

8.4.2   ...and the Sentinels

In recognition of the diverse and fragmented array of CNI that are owned and/or operated by private providers, there is little prospect of bringing these digital systems within the citadel of protected government digital systems. Thus the government has pursued a strategy to establish a programme of technical advisory 'sentinels'. Coordinated by the peak body charged with managing threats to critical infrastructure owners and operators, the CPNI aims to provide, 'advice on protective security measures and direct technical support to organisations within the national infrastructure' (CPNI n.d.).

The CPNI manages its responsibilities in two key ways. First, since 2003 it has administered the Information Exchange Mechanism, which facilitates the sharing of threat information (including, but not exclusive to cyber) between government and private owners of critical infrastructure. The IEM currently hosts 14 information exchanges arranged by sector: aerospace and defence manufacturers, communications industry personnel security, civil nuclear sector SCADA, financial services, managed service providers, Northern Ireland, network security, pharmaceutical industries, SCADA and control systems, space industries, security researchers, transport sector, vendor security and water security. Through the IEMs, the CPNI provides both general advice to the business sector on security and resilience as well as specific advice on emerging threats. Second, the CPNI in partnership with the CESG, announced in August 2013 a Cyber Incident Response Scheme. The scheme involves (i) the development of industry-wide cyber-security standards, managed by the Council of Registered Ethical Security Testers, and (ii) the deployment of a team dedicated to 'responding to sophisticated, targeted attacks against networks of national significance' (GCHQ 2013).

State strategies for the protection of the UK's critical infrastructures have progressed, as suggested by the title of this chapter, along two parallel lines: first, with the construction of virtual citadels, within which core government networks are nested; and second, within a governance framework the deployment of government 'sentinels' with responsibility to provide ongoing security advice about the threat environment and to provide ad hoc security management in the event of specific attacks. The analogy is crude but illustrates the binary nature of the public/private divide in the guardianship of critical infrastructure.

Key Points

- The transfer of the ownership and operation of critical infrastructures to (a fragmented) private sector has created a fundamental division between the management of threats to government and to the private sector.
- The UK government has opted to address cyberterrorism, and associated cyber threats, by constructing (i) a virtual citadel of government services which can be managed centrally, and (ii) a programme of 'sentinels'; government agencies mandated to advise the private sector on cyber protection measures.

8.5 Cyber Protection and Privatised Critical Infrastructure: Towards Cyber-Governance

Reading across the various state strategies enacted thus far, there are two latent challenges to government which, here, merit further attention. There are, of course, a wider range of issues at stake, but for our current purposes I draw attention to those that relate to the threat to critical infrastructure in an era of privatisation.

8.5.1   Challenge 1: The Threats Are Diverse and Ambiguous

All these different groups—criminals, terrorists, foreign intelligence services and militaries—are active today against the UK's interests in cyberspace. But with the borderless and anonymous nature of the internet, precise attribution is often difficult and the distinction between adversaries is increasingly blurred (Cabinet Office 2011b:16).

There is little doubt that the cyber landscape has deepened the age-old problem of accurately identifying threat. Historically, ambiguity of threat has played a useful role in terms of provocation. For instance, the cassus beli for the war in Iraq was, of course, constructed via the ambiguity of the threat posed by Saddam Hussein, irrespective of the private assessments of UK and US intelligence agencies. Perhaps in recognition of the futility of offering a rigid definition of the cyber threat, authors of UK government policy have fallen back on associating terrorism with other known social ills: creating a relation of equivalence between quite diverse threats. This is a useful way of managing uncertainty, irrespective of its coherence. For example, speaking in support of proposed internet surveillance measures contained in the Draft Communications Data Bill in December 2012, Theresa May stated: 'Criminals, terrorists and paedophiles will want MPs to vote against this bill. Victims of crime, police and the public will want them to vote for it. It's a question of whose side you're on' (May 2012).

8.5.2   Challenge 2: The Threat of Cyberterrorism Must Be Managed in Conjunction with the Private Sector

The 2011 Cyber Security Strategy states that 'government capacity...is not sufficient or sufficiently scaled to meet the growing security challenges of the digital age' (emphasis in original, Cabinet Office 2011b:18). This recognition is embedded in over a decade of structural reforms to the public sector and amplified by a cyber-realm that has been constructed largely in the private and civil arenas. The challenge for government is to manage risk and threat at arms-length by encouraging greater information-sharing by private owners and operators of critical infrastructure. The mandate of the CPNI is to set up a framework to manage the sharing of threat intelligence amongst private owners and operators of critical infrastructure. Yet in the absence of legal powers to force such information-sharing, there remains a substantial risk that the balance between the business and public interest is weighted in favour of corporate profitability.

8.5.3   Cyberterrorism, Threat and Critical Infrastructure

The challenges outlined above are problematised by the relationship between government and the private owners and operators of critical infrastructure. The privatisation patterns associated with the New Public Management set in place in the 1980s and 1990s constrain the available options for policy officials today in what the public policy literature terms a 'path dependency'. That is, past decisions often determine future policy options, forcing officials to continue a policy 'path' whether or not they wish to do so (see Peters et al. 2005). The transfer of critical infrastructure ownership to the private sector is an example of path dependency and has had several key consequent challenges. These include, first, a lack of common ICT architecture; second, differential understanding of a problem (in this case cyberterrorism) that is not a traditional challenge to each sector, thus creating a reliance on government know-how; third, and related to this, dispute over who is responsible for meeting the costs of cyber-security that increase business costs (Clemente 2013); and, fourth, a desire of businesses to maximise their competitive advantage, while implementing security measures hinder efficiency. As NATO's Special Rapporteur noted, 'there is little financial incentive for private firms to invest in a socially desirable level of security, as the true cost of an attack to society is much larger than the damage this attack would cause to a private firm' (Lord Jopling 2009:9).

It is indicative of the scale of the tension between the public and private interest that the CPNI must facilitate the exchange of knowledge and experience with private sector actors via Information Exchanges, which operate only on a voluntary basis to dampen fears of competitive advantage loss. Delegating the responsibility for addressing cyber threats to the private sector is ridden with risks: the Managing Director of BAE Systems Detica Martin Sutherland has stated that, 'The question is whether they will do this voluntarily, or whether the Government finds, in addition, that it needs to provide some incentive for this to happen'(Sutherland 2012). Presently, as noted above, there is no legal obligation on critical infrastructure owners to report cyber attacks. The National Audit Office found that: 'Many incidents go unreported, as news of them could damage corporate reputation and customers could lose confidence in using online services' (National Audit Office 2013:25).

Using the private sector to deliver public interests in cyber space can confer considerable benefits. The instinct of the private sector is to deliver better outcomes for a lower costs to the public purse, or so the reasoning goes. In so doing, a private sector entity's profit-maximising behaviour is leveraged by the public sector: that is, the public interest is served as an anticipated side-effect of corporate motivations. Yet the protection of the public interest remains incidental to, not constitutive of, the private entity's action, whose core objective is profitability. The relationship between the state and private sector in this respect is fundamentally instrumental and represents a significant weakness in the protection of the public interest. The behaviour of corporate enterprise is fundamentally the same: businesses act in the interests of their shareholders.

This is not a particularly novel observation; examples abound of corporations privileging the company interest, often with deleterious consequences to the public interest. For example, the electricity shortages (known as 'brown-outs') that afflicted California's power grid in 2000 were induced deliberately by corporate energy traders, of the now infamous company Enron, manipulating market supply and demand to maximise the unit price of electricity provision. It is sufficient for the moment to recognise this essential difference between the public and private interest. The two excerpts below, taken from the OECD and NATO's Special Rapporteur respectively, highlight this tension:

> The reluctance of some private owners of critical infrastructure to disclose information beyond what is required by industry regulations presents a challenge to country risk managers who are tasked with taking accurate account of the capabilities of critical infrastructure systems to withstand disasters (Organisation for Economic Co-operation and Development 2009:21)

> Most critical infrastructures are today owned and operated by private sector businesses, which therefore bear the primary responsibility for protecting their infrastructure. This situation raises difficult questions regarding the relative roles of governments and private sector stakeholders in the CIP architecture, and the compatibility of national security objectives with business interests (Lord Jopling 2009:1).

It is the intrinsic nature of corporate entities to act in their self-interest, and not in the public interest, except where acting in the public interest furthers the corporate interest. This represents an ongoing dilemma for government insofar as privatisation is largely irreversible. The core imperative for government in the pursuit of protecting the public interest is therefore in ensuring that public services that are delivered by private providers; that is, ensuring that as far as possible the interests of the company are made synonymous with the public interest.

Key Points

- There are two key challenges to the government's capacity to address cyberterrorism specifically and cyber threats generally: (i) the ambiguity and diversity of cyber threats; and (ii) threats to critical infrastructure can only be addressed in collaboration with the private sector
- It is not clear whether private sector owners and operators of critical infrastructure can serve both their business interests and the public interest.

8.6   Conclusion: Framing Cyberterrorism in an Era of Cyber-Governance

The diminished capacity of the state to directly deliver or control outcomes for the public interest is clearly reflected in current approaches to tackling cyber-threats and cyberterrorism. With much of the national critical infrastructure now firmly held in private hands, government's power to manage external threats to the resilience of these systems carrying significant public interest has been diminished, with two worrying repercussions.

First, government is reliant on voluntary compliance: there is no legal obligation for corporate owners to disclose cyber-security vulnerabilities or even security breaches. Though the UK government has sought to manage this relationship by providing secure threat information-sharing channels, it is far from clear whether these will become effective. Second, research by Chatham House on how cyber risks are managed by owners and operators of national critical infrastructure shows extant tensions between security, accountability and profitability: 'these same organizations were willing, for a variety of resource and other reasons, to accept an unexpectedly high level of cyber security-related risk. There was even a tendency, as noted earlier, to distance the handling of this risk from the authority and responsibility of the board or senior management' (Cornish et al. 2011:13).

The UK government's approach to addressing the threat of cyberterrorism remains in nascent form. There is an epistemological ambiguity at the heart of managing a risk that, thus far, has been threatened more than it has been experienced. 'Terrorism' in the cyber domain has been transformed from a specific, identifiable foe -such as the organised extremism of Al Qaeda- to a nebulous, disordered yet nonetheless powerful agency. Overlaying this ambiguity is an on-going tension between the state and private owners and operators of critical infrastructure. It is far from clear how, in an era of fragmented delivery of public services via the private sector, government is able to resolve the risk-sharing and information-sharing challenges that are crucial to the public interest. There is a reliance on the resources of private sector and their willingness, or goodwill perhaps, to be transparent about risks and threats to critical infrastructure. While protecting the public interest is the government's mandate in cyber space, it is far from clear whether it has the capacity to do so.

Key Points

- Because of the fragmented nature of critical infrastructure, the government has a diminished capacity to address cyberterror threats.
- The tension between pursing corporate interests and adequately protecting public services from cyber threats is unresolved and represents a vulnerability in the critical infrastructure sector.

Further Reading and Resources

Amoore L, de Goede M (eds) (2008) Risk and the war on terror. Routledge, Oxford

Clemente D (2013) Cyber security and global interdependence: what is critical? The Royal Institute of International Affairs: Chatham House, London

Giacomello G (2004) Bangs for the buck: a cost-benefit analysis of cyberterrorism. Stud Conflict Terrorism 27(5):387–408

References

Amoore L, de Goede M (eds) (2008) Risk and the war on terror. Routledge, Oxford

Anderson DQC (2012) The terrorism acts in 2011: report of the independent reviewer on the operation of the terrorism act 2000 and part 1 of the terrorism act 2006. The Stationary Office, London

Black C (2013) Could a terrorist cyber attack set off World War 3? Mirror 10 July 2013http://www.mirror.co.uk/news/world-news/could-terrorist-cyber-attack-set-2041439. Accessed 9 Aug 2013

Boston Consulting Group (2012) The Internet economy in the G20: the $4.2 trillion growth opportunity. The Boston Consulting Group, Boston. https://publicaffairs.linx.net/news/wp-content/uploads/2012/03/bcg_4trillion_opportunity.pdf. Accessed 5 Jan 2013

Bradley J, Barbier J, Handler D (2013) White paper: embracing the Internet of everything to capture your share of $14.4 trillion. http://www.cisco.com/web/about/ac79/docs/innov/IoE_Economy.pdf. Accessed 2 Feb 2013

Cabinet Office (2004) Protecting our information systems: working in partnership for a secure and resilient UK information infrastructure. Cabinet Office, London

Cabinet Office (2009) Cyber security strategy of the United Kingdom: safety, security and resilience in cyber space. Cabinet Office, London

Cabinet Office (2011a) Government ICT strategy—strategic implementation plan: moving from the 'what' to the 'how'. Cabinet Office, London

Cabinet Office (2011b) The UK cyber security strategy: protecting and promoting the UK in a digital world. Cabinet Office, London

Cabinet Office (2012) Government digital strategy

Cabinet Office & DETICA (2011) The cost of cyber crime. Cabinet Office, London

Cabinet Office (2012) Government Digital Strategy. Cabinet Office, London

Centre for the Protection of National Infrastructure (n.d) Retrieved 10 September 2013, from http://www.cpni.gov.uk/about/cni/. Accessed 20 Feb 2013

Clemente D (2013) Cyber security and global interdependence: what is critical? The Royal Institute of International Affairs: Chatham House, London

Cornish P, Livingstone D, Clemente D, Yorke C (2011) Cyber security and the UK's critical national infrastructure. The Royal Institute of International Affairs: Chatham House, London

Department of Homeland Security (n.d) Critical infrastructure sector partnerships. Available at http://www.dhs.gov/critical-infrastructure-sector-partnerships. Accessed 23 Apr 2013

Drury I, Shipman T (2010) Our No.1 threat: cyber terrorists who can knock a jet out of the sky. The Daily Mail 19 October 2010. http://www.dailymail.co.uk/news/article-1321554/Our-No-1-threat-Cyber-terrorists-knock-jet-sky.html#ixzz2fh7ffTVF. Accessed 18 Aug 2013

Giacomello G (2004) Bangs for the buck: a cost-benefit analysis of cyberterrorism. Stud Conflict Terrorism 27(5):387–408

Government Communications Headquarters (2013) Cyber incident response scheme launched. GCHQ Press Release 13 August 2013. http://www.gchq.gov.uk/Press/Pages/CIR_Scheme_Launched.aspx. Accessed 20 Aug 2013

Hardy K, Williams G (2014) What is 'cyberterrorism'? Computer and internet technology in legal definitions of terrorism. In: Chen T, Jarvis L, Macdonald S (eds) Cyberterrorism: understanding, assessment, and response. Springer, New York

Harvey N (2011) Forget a cyber Maginot line. The Guardian 30 May 2011. http://www.theguardian.com/commentisfree/2011/may/30/forget-cyber-maginot-line?guni = Article:in%20body%20link. Accessed 7 Aug 2013

Hayden M (2013) Speech to the Bipartisan Policy Center. The Guardian 6 August 2013. http://www.theguardian.com/technology/2013/aug/06/nsa-director-cyber-terrorism-snowden. Accessed 8 Aug 2013

Heidegger M (1977) The question concerning technology and other essays. Translated and with an introduction by William Lovitt. Harper & Row, London

Hood C (1995) The "New Public Management" in the 1980s: variations on a theme. Account Organ Soc 20(2):93–109

Jarvis L, Nouri L, Whiting A (2014) Understanding, locating and constructing 'Cyberterrorism'. In: Chen T, Jarvis L, Macdonald S (eds) Cyberterrorism: understanding, assessment, and response. Springer, New York

Live Free or Die Hard. (2007). Twentieth Century Fox Film Corporation. Los Angeles, USA

Lord Jopling SR (2009) The protection of critical infrastructures: draft special report, 162 CDS 07 E. NATO Parliamentary Assembly. http://www.europarl.europa.eu/meetdocs/2004_2009/documents/dv/270/270907/270907jopling_en.pdf

Lynn WJ (2011) Remarks on cyber at the RSA conference. RSA conference 15 February 2011. http://www.defense.gov/speeches/speech.aspx?speechid=1535. Accessed 12 Sep 2013

Mandiant (2013) Apt1: exposing one of China's cyber espionage units. http://intelreport.mandiant. com/Mandiant_APT1_Report.pdf. Accessed 20 Sep 2013

May T (2011) Terrorism: Home Secretary's speech to the Council on Foreign Relations. http:// www.homeoffice.gov.uk/media-centre/speeches/HS-US. Accessed 17 Apr 2013

May T (2012) Interview. The Sun 3 December 2012. http://www.thesun.co.uk/sol/homepage/ news/politics/article4678082.ece. Accessed 20 Sep 2013

McAfee & Center for Strategic and International Studies (2011) In the dark: crucial industries confront cyberattacks. http://www.mcafee.com/us/resources/reports/rp-critical-infrastructure-protection.pdf. Accessed 12 Aug 2013

McGuire M (2014) Putting the 'cyber' into cyberterrorism: re-reading technological risk in a hyperconnected world. In: Chen T, Jarvis L, Macdonald S (eds) Cyberterrorism: understanding, assessment, and response. Springer, New York

Minogue M, Polidano C, Hulme D (1998) Beyond the new public management: changing ideas and practices in governance. Edward Elgar, Cheltenham

National Audit Office (2013) The UK cyber security strategy: landscape review. Report by the comptroller and auditor general (HC 890). The Stationary Office, London

Organisation for Economic Co-operation and Development (2009) Innovation in country risk management. http://www.oecd.org/futures/Innovation%20in%20Country%20Risk%20Management%20 2009.pdf. Accessed 23 Sep 2013

Parliamentary Office of Science and Technology (2011) Cyber security in the UK. Houses of Parliament, London

Peters BG, Pierre J, King DS (2005) The politics of path dependency: political conflict in historical institutionalism. J Polit 67(4):1275–1300

Skyfall (2012) Eon Productions. London, United Kingdom

Smith C (2013) Reported in the independent. http://www.independent.co.uk/news/uk/politics/ government-faces-around-33000-cyber-attacks-a-month-reveals-cabinet-office-minister-chloe-smith-8584636.html. Accessed 12 May 2013

Stohl M (2014) Dr. Strangeweb: or how they stopped worrying and learned to love cyber war. In: Chen T, Jarvis L, Macdonald S (eds) Cyberterrorism: understanding, assessment, and response. Springer, New York

Sutherland M (2012) Interview, in focus. http://www.employeepublications-baesystems.com/ infocus/infocus_3/1. Accessed 12 May 2013

The Western Australian Government (2011) Western Australian Government submission to the Australian Defence Force Posture. http://www.defence.gov.au/oscdf/adf-posture-review/ submissions/WA%20Government%20Submission.pdf. Accessed 12 May 2013

Yannakogeorgos P (2014) Rethinking the threat of cyberterrorism. In: Chen T, Jarvis L, Macdonald S (eds) Cyberterrorism: understanding, assessment, and response. Springer, New York

Chapter 9
The Criminalisation of Terrorists' Online Preparatory Acts

Lord Carlile QC and Stuart Macdonald

9.1 Introduction

Our focus in this chapter is the use of the criminal law to prevent terrorist attacks by prohibiting online preparatory activities. Just as the use of the Internet for terrorist purposes has increased in recent years, so too has the number of terrorism-related criminal offences which target different forms of (online and offline) preparatory activities. This expanding use of the criminal sanction has received much attention from criminal law theorists (see, for example, Duff et al. 2010; Simester and von Hirsch 2011; Ashworth and Zedner 2012; Sullivan and Dennis 2012). Their central concern is whether, in an attempt to increase security against terrorism by facilitating early intervention, rule of law values and human rights have been unjustifiably sacrificed.

In this chapter we examine this tension. We begin by explaining the difference between acts of cyberterrorism and online acts of preparation, by outlining the ways in which terrorists use the Internet in preparation for both cyber and non-cyber attacks and by explaining why it has been deemed necessary to supplement existing criminal offences with special terrorism-related offences. The chapter then examines suggestions that these new offences should be circumscribed in two ways: by requiring proof that the individual has some normative involvement in future terrorist attacks; and by only penalising conduct that is inherently wrongful or morally ambiguous. We express our doubts about the second of these proposals, and emphasise the importance of having regard to the context in which prosecutorial decisions are made when critiquing criminal laws.

L. Carlile QC
House of Lords, London SW1A 0PW, UK

S. Macdonald (✉)
College of Law, Swansea University, Singleton Park, Swansea SA2 8PP, UK
e-mail: S.Macdonald@swansea.ac.uk

T.M. Chen et al. (eds.), *Cyberterrorism: Understanding, Assessment, and Response*,
DOI 10.1007/978-1-4939-0962-9_9, © Springer Science+Business Media New York 2014

9.2   The Distinction Between Acts of Cyberterrorism and Acts of Preparation

It is important to begin by distinguishing acts of cyberterrorism from acts which are preparatory. To do this, it is necessary to define the term cyberterrorism itself. This section accordingly sets out our position on the two major definitional issues which divide researchers working in this area: to what does, or should, the term cyberterrorism refer?; and, how is cyberterrorism similar to, and different from, other forms of terrorism? (Jarvis and Macdonald 2014)

9.2.1   Narrow and Broad Conceptions of Cyberterrorism

The first definitional issue concerns the scope of the term cyberterrorism. Some have adopted a broad conception which not only encompasses terrorist attacks conducted via or against computer networks and information infrastructures, but also a diverse range of other online activities such as fundraising, reconnaissance, communication and propagandising. For example, Gordon and Ford have warned that a narrow focus on attacks against computers, networks and the information stored therein has the potential to obscure the role the Internet plays in all aspects of the 'terrorism matrix' (Gordon and Ford 2002:642). In their view a broad understanding of cyberterrorism is needed in order to understand the 'true impact' of the convergence of terrorism and cyberspace (p. 637). This may be contrasted with narrow conceptions of cyberterrorism, which remain far more prevalent (see, for example, Pollitt 1998; Denning 2000; Conway 2002; Weimann 2005; Hua and Bapna 2012). Whilst there are differences in the details of these narrow conceptions, what they share is a focus on computers as the means and/or the target of cyberterrorist attacks.

Any discussion of the appropriate breadth of the term cyberterrorism should be informed by the purpose the definition will serve. As in other jurisdictions, in the UK the statutory definition of cyberterrorism—and terrorism in general—has several important applications. As well as delineating the boundaries of the terrorism precursor offences that we examine later in this chapter, it also specifies when a range of other investigative, sentencing and other special terrorism-related powers and procedures are available. Many of these involve significant departures from the powers and procedures available for non-terrorist offences. For example, a police officer may arrest a person whom he reasonably suspects is or has been involved in the commission, preparation or instigation of acts of terrorism, even if the arresting officer has no specific offence in mind.[1] Similarly, a police officer may stop and search any person whom he reasonably suspects to be a terrorist in order to discover whether he has anything which may constitute evidence that he is a terrorist, and to seize and retain anything which he reasonably suspects may

---

[1] Terrorism Act 2000, s. 40-41.

constitute such evidence.[2] In cases involving suspected terrorists the maximum period of **pre-charge detention** is 14 days, as opposed to the normal maximum of 4 days.[3] A person who is reasonably believed to be involved in terrorism-related activity may also be issued with a **Terrorism Prevention and Investigation Measures** (TPIMs) notice if this is necessary to protect the public from a risk of terrorism.[4] A TPIMs notice may impose a range of measures, including a curfew and restrictions on where the individual may go, who they may associate with and their use of telephones and computers.

These special terrorism-related powers and procedures are available not only in cases involving acts of terrorism, but also cases involving acts which are preparatory to an act of terrorism. So they would not only be available in a case which involved terrorists launching a cyber-attack. They could also be used in cases involving other forms of online terrorist activity—such as recruitment and radicalisation, planning an attack, training and fund-raising—since these activities are all forms of preparation. If these other online activities were instead classified as substantive acts of cyberterrorism, as suggested by advocates of broad conceptions of the term, the scope of the special terrorism-related powers and procedures would expand dramatically. They would then be available in any case involving acts which are preparatory to online recruitment, planning, training or fund-raising—all activities which are themselves forms of preparation for subsequent acts of terrorism. To permit the special terrorism-related powers and procedures to be used against conduct which is so remote from a terrorist attack would show insufficient respect for the **rule of law** and human rights, both of which require that the powers of the state be tightly circumscribed.

9.2.2 The Relationship Between Cyberterrorism and Terrorism

The second divisive definitional issue concerns the relationship between cyberterrorism and terrorism. For some, cyberterrorism is simply a subset of the broader category terrorism. On this approach, an attack only qualifies as cyberterrorist if all components of the definition of terrorism have been satisfied. Michael Stohl, for example, has argued that we should 'restrict cyber terrorism to activities which in addition to their cyber component have the commonly agreed upon components of terrorism' (Stohl 2006:229). From this, it follows that a definition of cyberterrorism is not strictly necessary. Cyberterrorist attacks already fall within the definition of terrorism, and the cyber prefix denotes nothing more than the means employed.

By contrast, others have argued that cyberterrorism is qualitatively distinct from other forms of terrorism and therefore requiring of its own definition. Thomas J. Holt, for example, has argued that cyberterrorism must encompass a wider range of

---

[2] Terrorism Act 2000, s. 43.

[3] Terrorism Act 2000, s. 41(7) & schedule 8.

[4] Terrorism Prevention and Investigation Measures Act 2011, s. 3.

behaviours than terrorism 'due to the dichotomous nature of cyberspace as a vehicle for communications as well as a medium for attacks' (Holt 2012:341). He accordingly argues that an act should qualify as cyberterrorist even if it does not cause any physical harm and there was no intention to generate fear, as long as the attack was intended to interfere with the political, social or economic functioning of a group, organization or country or induce either physical violence or the unjust use of power. This, he argues, provides 'a much more comprehensive framework for exploring the ways that extremist groups utilize technology in support of their various agendas' (p. 341).

The correct approach, we believe, is an amalgam of these two approaches. Cyberterrorism should be conceived narrowly and treated as a subset of terrorism in order to ensure the authorities have access to the full panoply of terrorism-related powers and procedures and to ensure that these are tightly circumscribed. At the same time, however, it is important to recognise that cyberterrorism is qualitatively distinct from other forms of terrorism. Consider the following two examples:

1. An extremist group interferes with an air traffic control system, causing two passenger aircraft to collide in mid-air.
2. An extremist group targets the computer system of the nation's stock exchange, sending the national economy into chaos and causing significant economic damage.

Traditionally, definitions of terrorism have required some form of serious physical violence. Indeed, Schmid and Jongman's review of definitions of terrorism identified 'violence, force' as the most prevalent of word categories, appearing in 83.5 % of the definitions examined (Schmid and Jongman 2008:5). But if cyberterrorism is conceived simply as "hacking with a body count" (Collin, quoted in Ballard et al. 2002:992), the raft of terrorism-related powers and procedures would be unavailable in the second of our two examples. This would be unacceptable. Although it does not involve physical violence, such a large scale attack on a country's economy could affect millions of people, cause significant loss and hardship and generate widespread anxiety and fear about the attackers' future targets. For this reason, we endorse the proposal advanced by Hardy and Williams earlier in this volume, which encompassed computer-based attacks which intentionally cause serious interference with an essential service, facility or system if such interference is likely to endanger life *or* cause significant economic or environmental damage.

Key Points

- There are different views of the scope of the term cyberterrorism and how it relates to terrorism in general.
- It is important that statutory definitions of cyberterrorism construe the term narrowly in order to limit the scope of special terrorism-related powers and procedures.
- Whilst cyberterrorism should be regarded as a subset of terrorism, it is also important to recognise that it is qualitatively different to traditional forms of terrorism.

9.3 Terrorists' Online Preparatory Acts

The use of the Internet for terrorist purposes is a rapidly growing phenomenon (UNODC 2012). Terrorists may use the Internet in a number of ways in preparation for both cyber and non-cyber based attacks (see generally Conway 2006; Hoffman 2006; Libicki 2007; Denning 2010). This section outlines this variety of online preparatory activities.

9.3.1 Recruitment

The worldwide reach of the Internet provides terrorist organisations with a global pool of potential recruits. So it is unsurprising that numerous studies have argued that recruitment and radicalisation are amongst the top priorities for terrorist organisations online (Weimann 2004; Goodman et al. 2007; Denning 2010; Keller et al. 2010). Technological advances have also increased the efficiency of terrorists' recruitment efforts (Cronin 2003). For example, terrorist organisations capture information about users who browse their websites, identify those that seem most interested or suited to carrying out their work, and then contact them. Recruiters may also use electronic bulletin boards and roam chat rooms and cybercafés looking for receptive members of the public. Video games such *Special Force* and *Special Force 2* (developed by Hezbollah) have even been used as recruitment tools, by promoting the use of violence against a state or particular political figures (Homeland Security Institute 2009).

9.3.2 Propaganda

The Internet gives terrorists direct control over the content of their message, allowing them the opportunity to shape how they and their adversaries are perceived by different target audiences (Tsfati and Weimann 2002). It has been estimated that in 2007 there were approximately 50,000 websites with extremist or terrorist content (Chen and Larson 2007). Terrorist organisations also use social media, including Facebook, Twitter, YouTube and Rapidshare (UNODC 2012). A variety of multimedia formats have been used, including literature, videos, songs, images, comics and video games (Piper 2008). Cartoons and stories have even been employed in some cases in order to target children (Weimann 2006).

9.3.3 Planning

Terrorists are almost certain to use the Internet when planning and preparing an attack. Much of the information needed for a physical attack is publicly available online, including information on transport, critical infrastructure, shipping lanes, maps, building blueprints, flight paths and counterterrorism strategies (Best 2008). An al Qaeda training manual recovered in Afghanistan, for example, stated that public sources can be used to "gather at least 80 percent of all information required about the enemy" (Weimann 2004). Numerous tools are available to facilitate data collection and online searching capabilities allow terrorists to capture information anonymously and with little effort or expense, while mitigating the risk involved in offline reconnaissance operations.

9.3.4   Communication

The Internet also has benefits as a mode of communication. Email allows for asynchronous communication. Many email accounts are also free, so terrorists can own several accounts simultaneously (Conway 2002). If synchronous communication is required Internet Relay Chat can be used, such as Skype. This is fast, largely unsupervised and most importantly digital, so publicly available encryption programmes can be used. Anonymising software is also available to mask the IP address, reroute Internet communications to other jurisdictions or encrypt traffic data on websites accessed.

9.3.5   Training

The range of resources which are available online mean that the Internet has the potential to operate as a virtual training camp (Stenersen 2008). Extremist websites contain resources ranging from step-by-step instructions on how to build and detonate weapons, conduct surveillance and target acquisition to tools to facilitate counterintelligence and hacking activities and improve the security of illicit communications and online activity through the use of encryption tools and anonymising techniques. In 2003 al Qaeda created an online digital library which provided free access to numerous manuals on subjects ranging from bomb-making and marksmanship to outdoor survival skills (Weimann 2004).

9.3.6   Fund-Raising

A number of terrorist organisations have made extensive use of the Internet to raise and transfer funds to support their activities, including al Qaeda, Hamas, Lashkar e-Taiba, and Hezbollah (Jacobson 2010). Various methods have been used, including: direct solicitation; selling CDs, DVDs, badges, flags and books; diverting funds intended for seemingly legitimate organisations like charities; and, cybercrime such as identity theft (Conway 2002; Weimann 2004; UNODC 2012). In fact, cybercrime has now surpassed international drug trafficking as a terrorist financing enterprise (Theohary and Rollins 2011).

> **Key Points**
>
> - There are a variety of ways in which terrorists might use the Internet in preparation for both cyber and non-cyber based attacks.
> - These include: recruitment; propaganda; planning; communication; training; and, fund-raising.

9.4 Criminalising Preparatory Acts: Terrorism Precursor Offences

In the years since 9/11 a number of jurisdictions have enacted new criminal offences which target the kinds of activities outlined in the previous section (McSherry 2009). This section begins by explaining why it has been deemed necessary to expand the scope of the criminal law in this way. The section then focuses on two specific offences, introduced by the UK's Terrorism Acts of 2000 and 2006, in order to illustrate how important it is that the criminal law does not overreach.

9.4.1 The Limited Scope of Full and Inchoate Offences

The **harm principle** forms an important part of liberal accounts of the criminal law. Implicitly rejecting the claim that immorality alone is a sufficient basis for criminalisation, the harm principle insists that conduct may only justifiably be criminalised if it wrongfully causes harm to others. This is obviously the case for many offences of general application which might be used in cases involving terrorists, such as murder, causing grievous bodily harm with intent, hostage-taking, kidnap, hijacking and explosives offences. The difficulty, however, is that for one of these 'full' offences to apply the harm in question must have occurred. The victims must have suffered death or injury, or been kidnapped or taken hostage. The vehicle must have been hijacked. Or the substance must have exploded. For this reason, the criminal law also contains the **inchoate offences** of attempt, conspiracy and encouraging crime. These offences recognise that the criminal law also has a preventive role (Horder 2012). As Ashworth and Zedner have observed, 'If a certain form of harmful wrongdoing is judged serious enough to criminalize, it follows that the state should assume responsibility for taking steps to protect people from it' (Ashworth and Zedner 2012:543). Indeed, 'a law that condemned and punished actually harm-causing conduct as wrong, but was utterly silent on attempts to cause such harms, and on reckless risk-taking with respect to such harms, would speak with a strange moral voice' (Duff 1996:134).

Whilst there have been some high profile convictions for inchoate offences in terrorist cases—including Abu Hamza's conviction for soliciting to commit murder and the convictions of seven men on conspiracy charges in the airline liquid bomb plot case[5]—there are significant practical difficulties. The offences of conspiracy and encouraging crime are notoriously difficult to prove. Obtaining admissible evidence of an agreement or words of encouragement within secretive organisations is difficult, particularly given the UK's ban on the use of intercept as evidence. Moreover, even if admissible evidence is obtained it may lack evidential value (many members of terrorist organisations observe good communications security and disguise the content of their communications) or there may be public interest reasons for not disclosing it (perhaps because it would expose other on-going investigations or reveal sensitive techniques or capabilities) (Privy Council Review of Intercept as Evidence 2008).

The law governing criminal attempts, meanwhile, has a limited scope. A person only commits the offence of attempt once they have performed an act that is 'more than merely preparatory' to the commission of the full offence.[6] So, for example, in the case of *R v Campbell*,[7] the Court of Appeal quashed the defendant's conviction for attempted robbery—notwithstanding the fact that he was stopped by police outside a post office wearing sunglasses and in possession of an imitation firearm and threatening note—because he had not yet embarked on the crime. Views differ on whether the law governing criminal attempts is unduly restrictive (see, for example, Clarkson 2009; Simester et al. 2013:339–59). But in the specific context of terrorism, the level of risk and severity of the potential harm provide strong reasons to penalise conduct at an earlier stage. In the words of the Independent Reviewer of Terrorism Legislation, it is necessary to 'defend further up the field' (Anderson 2013:237). This is the function of precursor—or pre-inchoate—offences. Whilst the law of attempts criminalises acts which are more than merely preparatory, precursor crimes focus on various forms of preparatory conduct.

9.4.2   The Principle of Normative Involvement

There is a wide range of terrorism precursor offences, found predominantly in the Terrorism Acts 2000 and 2006. The following indicative list contains offences which could potentially be deployed in cases involving one of the forms of online preparatory acts outlined above:

- Support for a proscribed organisation (Terrorism Act 2000, section 12)
- Fund-raising for terrorist purposes (Terrorism Act 2000, section 15)

---

[5] Three of the men (the ringleader, his right hand man and the explosives expert) were convicted of conspiracy to murder aircraft passengers using explosives. The other four (the would-be suicide bombers) were convicted of conspiracy to murder. See *R v Ali* (*Ahmed*) & *others* [2011] EWCA Crim 1260.

[6] Criminal Attempts Act 1981, s. 1(1).

[7] (1990) 93 Cr App R 350.

- Use or possession of money or other property for terrorist purposes (Terrorism Act 2000, section 16)
- Possession of an article for terrorist purposes (Terrorism Act 2000, section 57)
- Collecting information or possessing a document likely to be useful to a terrorist (Terrorism Act 2000, section 58)
- Inciting terrorism overseas (Terrorism Act 2000, section 59)
- Encouragement of terrorism (Terrorism Act 2006, section 1)
- Dissemination of terrorist publications (Terrorism Act 2006, section 2)
- Preparation of terrorist acts (Terrorism Act 2006, section 5)
- Training for terrorism (Terrorism Act 2006, section 6)

Terrorism precursor offences significantly expand the boundaries of the criminal law (Macdonald 2014). First, they apply to actions that are more remote from a terrorist attack than the inchoate offences. Second, they encompass a wider range of actors, penalising those not directly involved but with an associative or facilitative role. The dangers of this expansion have been highlighted by the Independent Reviewer of Terrorism Legislation who, whilst urging the need to defend further up the field, has also warned:

> [T]he *potential* for abuse is rarely absent … By seeking to extend the reach of the criminal law to people who are more and more on the margins, and to activities taking place earlier and earlier in the story, their shadow begins to loom over all manner of previously innocent interactions. The effects can, at worst, be horrifying for individuals and demoralising to communities (Anderson 2013:240, emphasis original)

In order to keep the realm of precursor offences within justifiable bounds, Simester and von Hirsch have advanced the principle of normative involvement. Many of the kinds of actions penalized by the precursor offences—such as collecting information, possessing items, or raising funds—will not themselves directly cause harm to others. Harm will only result if some other person or the defendant himself subsequently chooses to behave in a particular way. According to the principle of normative involvement, if the defendant 'in some sense affirms or underwrites' this subsequent choice he may justifiably be penalized for his preparatory acts (Simester and von Hirsch 2011:81). He has endorsed the potential future harmful actions of either himself or another, and so responsibility for the feared future harm may fairly be imputed to him.

If normative involvement provides a principled constraint on the scope of the precursor offences, some of the existing offences overreach. An example is the offence of collecting information or possessing a document likely to be useful to a terrorist. An individual may be convicted of this offence notwithstanding the absence of any normative involvement in a terrorist plot. This is illustrated by *R v G*.[8] The defendant in this case was a paranoid schizophrenic. He had been detained for a number of non-terrorism offences. While in custody he collected information on explosives and bomb-making, and also drew a map of the Territorial Army centre in Chesterfield and wrote down plans to attack the centre. The items were discovered

---

[8] [2009] UKHL 13.

during a search of his cell. He was charged with collecting information of a kind that was likely to be useful to a terrorist under section 58 of the Terrorism Act 2000. His explanation for collecting the information was that he wanted to wind up the prison staff because he believed they had been whispering about him. He said 'I wanted to wind them up and I know how this terrorism stuff … really gets on their nerves'. The prosecution accepted expert evidence that he had collected the information as a direct consequence of his illness.

Section 58 of the Terrorism Act 2000 simply says that a person commits an offence if, without reasonable excuse, he collects information of a kind likely to be useful to a person committing or preparing an act of terrorism. At trial the judge held that G had no defence of reasonable excuse and granted leave to appeal. On appeal, the Court of Appeal followed its earlier decision in *R v K*[9] that a reasonable excuse is 'simply an explanation that the document or record is possessed for a purpose other than to assist in the commission or preparation of an act of terrorism'. It therefore held that G's excuse—winding up the prison guards—was a reasonable one and allowed his appeal. The prosecution appealed against this ruling to the House of Lords.

The House of Lords examined the section 58 offence in its entirety. On the face of it, the scope of the offence is enormously broad. There is a vast array of information that might be useful to a terrorist, including a London Underground map, train timetable, telephone directory and street map, as well as numerous biographies, works of fiction and newspaper reports. The House of Lords accordingly stated that, whilst the information need not only be useful to a terrorist, it must by its very nature call for an explanation. So information on explosives would qualify (even though it might also be useful to a bank robber), but a train timetable would not.

The House of Lords then turned to the mental elements of the offence. Since section 58 itself does not specify any mental elements at all—instead leaving all the exculpatory work to the defence of reasonable excuse—their Lordships read two mental elements into the legislation: first, the defendant must have known that he had possession or control of the document; and, second, he must have been aware of the nature of the information contained therein. On their own, however, these requirements are insufficient to establish any normative involvement in terrorist activity. A defendant may satisfy them even though he has no terrorist intentions whatsoever. The key question was thus whether the Court of Appeal's interpretation of the reasonable excuse defence was correct. The House of Lords held that it was not. To have a defence, the defendant must have had an objectively reasonable excuse for collecting the information. It is not reasonable to antagonise prison guards, and G's illness could not render his actions *objectively* reasonable. Therefore the defence was unavailable to him. His illness would be considered when sentencing. So G was guilty of a serious terrorism offence, carrying a maximum sentence of 10 years' imprisonment, even though no terrorist connections had been established. The effect was to 'make a terrorist out of nothing' (Hodgson and Tadros 2009).

---

[9] [2008] EWCA Crim 185.

Broader human rights and rule of law considerations also support close adherence to the principle of normative involvement. This is illustrated by our second example: the encouragement of terrorism offence created by section 1 of the Terrorism Act 2006. This offence—which was introduced following the 7/7 bombings in London—implements the requirement set out in Article 5 of the Council of Europe Convention on the Prevention of Terrorism (CECPT) to criminalise public provocation to commit a terrorist offence. It was targeted at extremists who spread a message of hate and seek to produce a climate in which others come to believe that unlawful violence may be justified (Marchand 2010). A defendant commits this offence if: (i) he publishes a statement (or causes another to do so); (ii) which is likely to be understood by some or all of the members of the public to whom it is published as a direct or indirect encouragement or other inducement to them to the commission, preparation or instigation of acts of terrorism[10]; and (iii) his intention was that members of the public would be directly or indirectly encouraged or otherwise induced by the statement to commit, prepare or instigate acts of terrorism or he was **reckless** as to whether members of the public would be so encouraged/induced. Where the allegation is one of reckless encouragement, a non-endorsement defence is available.[11]

Significant concerns have been expressed about the encouragement of terrorism offence. Its broad scope means that there is a discrepancy between what the offence targets and what it actually encompasses. One effect of this is to deprive the courts of the opportunity to adjudicate on the actions that the offence is targeting (Edwards 2010). Another is the possible inhibition of the right to freedom of expression. Consider the following examples, each of which could now potentially amount to a criminal offence:

1. A person tweets that terrorists are incredibly brave to give up their lives for their cause;
2. Another person, entering into the debate, re-tweets the previous statement without condemning it;
3. A third person makes an online statement indicating that terrorism is the most effective way of getting a government to listen to a point of view and praises the strategy used by the Mumbai terrorists as an example.

All of these examples could be interpreted as the use of the Internet to encourage acts of terrorism under section 1. The encouragement of terrorism offence does not contain any requirement that an actual act of terrorism was committed as a result of the act of encouragement, nor that there was even a danger that an act of terrorism might be encouraged (Joint Committee on Human Rights 2007). To establish liability it is also not necessary to prove any intention to encourage terrorism. Recklessness as to the interpretation of the statement will suffice. Moreover, the non-endorsement

---

[10] Indirect encouragement includes any statement which 'glorifies' the commission or preparation of terrorist acts (whether past, present or future) if members of the public could reasonably infer from the statement that they should emulate the conduct being glorified (Terrorism Act 2006, s. 1(3)).

[11] Terrorism Act 2006, s. 1(6).

defence is only available if: (i) the statement in question neither expressed the defendant's views nor had his endorsement; and (ii) this was clear from the circumstances of the statement's publication. The defence is therefore unlikely to apply in our three examples. The offence is thus far broader in scope than Article 5 of the CECPT, which is limited to the distribution of messages with an intention to incite the commission of a terrorist offence where such conduct causes a danger that one or more such offences may be committed.

All three of our examples could be argued as nothing more than contributions to a debate on terrorism using the Internet. An individual may therefore be guilty of the section 1 offence and yet lack any normative involvement in future acts of terrorism. Following the introduction of the offence, the **Joint Committee on Human Rights** warned that 'Such theoretical possibility of committing the serious criminal offence of encouraging terrorism can only inhibit freedom of discussion and debate on topical and contentious political issues' (Joint Committee on Human Rights 2007:16). The full impact of this chilling effect is unknowable for there is an inherent difficulty in measuring something which, by its very nature, prevents people from publishing statements they might otherwise have published (Lester 2007). However, its effects will be felt most acutely by particular communities. Members of Black, Asian and Minority Ethnic communities have expressed concern about the possible consequences of expressing legitimate views relating to foreign and other government policies, as has the Muslim Council of Britain (Joint Committee on Human Rights 2007). Lord Lester has accordingly warned that the offence may prove 'divisive as between people of different ethnic, religious and political identities' (Lester 2007:104). Such an impact would hamper the UK Government's efforts to foster community cohesion in order to make communities more resilient to radicalisation (Home Office 2011).

Key Points

- The criminal law has a preventive role as well as a punitive one.
- Terrorism precursor offences are necessary because of the limited scope of the inchoate offences of attempt, conspiracy and encouraging crime.
- The principle of normative involvement provides a justification for the creation of precursor offences and also a constraint on their scope.

9.5 Terrorism Precursor Offences and Discretionary Decision-Making

Offences which comply with the principle of normative involvement may still have a broad scope. An example is the offence of preparation of terrorist acts, created by section 5 of the Terrorism Act 2006. A person commits this offence if he 'engages in any conduct' with the intention of committing or assisting an act of terrorism. Offering the example of an individual who eats muesli for breakfast as part of a fitness programme in preparation for a terrorist act, Simester argues that the section 5 offence overreaches (Simester 2012). He argues that a distinction should be drawn between inherently wrongful conduct and morally ambiguous conduct, on the one hand, and inherently innocent conduct, on the other. The scope of the section 5 offence could be circumscribed, he suggests, by stipulating that inherently innocent conduct (such as eating muesli) should fall outside the scope of the criminal law.

In this section we evaluate Simester's proposal. The section begins by explaining that attempts to dichotomise rules and discretion are flawed. It then examines the context in which decisions whether to prosecute for terrorism precursor offences are made. Our argument is that it is necessary to examine the extra-legal constraints on how prosecutorial discretion is exercised in particular contexts and evaluate whether these are sufficient.

9.5.1   The Inevitability of Discretionary Decision-Making

The intention of legal strategies for countering terrorism is to favour legislation over administration in order to preserve rights and both democratic and legal accountability. The principles are therefore based on constitutionalism, which emphasises the desirability of the rule of law as opposed to rule by the arbitrary judgment of public officials. The overall idea is to restore normal existence without the regular invocation of special powers, preventing injustice insofar as is possible.

At the same time, it is important to recognize the inevitability of discretion in every legal system. The belief that discretionary power has no place in any system of law or government—that government, in all its actions, should be bound by rules fixed and announced beforehand—has been dubbed the extravagant version of the rule of law (Davis 1971). It ignores the stark reality that no legal system can operate without significant discretionary power. As Bradley and Ewing observe, 'If it is contrary to the rule of law that discretionary authority should be given to government departments or public officers, then the rule of law applies to no modern constitution' (Bradley and Ewing 2003:94).

Given the inevitability of discretion in every legal system, proponents of the extravagant version of the rule of law seek to eliminate as much discretion as possible from the legal sphere. Beyond this they urge the need to 'bring such discretion as is reluctantly determined to be necessary within the "legal umbrella" by regulating it by means of general rules and standards and by subjecting its exercise to legal scrutiny' (Lacey 1992:372). But this is also problematic, for three reasons. For a start, it overlooks the fact that discretionary decision-making can be beneficial. Discretion may be necessary to enable a decision-maker to do justice. In areas which are especially complex it also enables difficult issues to be addressed on a case-by-case basis (Schneider 1992). Second, whilst there are a number of dangers associated with discretionary decision-making—such as the possible use of illegitimate criteria, the risk of inconsistencies of outcome, and the potential for arrogant, careless decision-making—these dangers can only be expressed in general terms and so their application in a particular context should not be accepted as 'unproblematic truth' (Lacey 1992:371). It is necessary to investigate the extent to which these concerns apply in a particular context. Finally, it is mistaken to assume that there is a neat dichotomy between rules and discretion. In fact, the distinction between the two is far more uncertain (Galligan 1986; Hawkins 1992). Discretion is heavily implicated in the interpretation and application of rules, and rules enter the exercise of discretion. As Hawkins explains, it 'does not make sense from a social scientific point of view to speak of "absolute" or "unfettered" discretion, since to do so is to imply that discretion in the real world may be constrained only by legal rules' (Hawkins 1992:38). In fact, 'much of what is often thought to be the free and flexible application of discretion by legal actors is … guided and constrained by rules to a considerable extent. These rules, however, tend not to be legal, but social and organizational in character' (Hawkins 1992:13). Turpin and Tomkins thus conclude that, 'The administrative process cannot, in any event, be understood as involving a simple choice between rules and discretion. They can work in combination, and procedures of decision-making should be constructed which are appropriate to the objectives sought' (Turpin and Tomkins 2011:118).

9.5.2 Terrorism Precursor Offences and Prosecutorial Discretion

Some of the terrorism precursor offences have been criticised for being both too broad and too vague. For example, the two offences examined in the previous section—collecting information or possessing a document likely to be useful to a terrorist and encouragement of terrorism—have not only been criticised for overreaching but also for being unclear (Hodgson and Tadros 2009; Joint Committee on Human Rights 2007). But over-breadth and vagueness do not always go hand-in-hand. Broad definitions may sometimes be clear, just as vague definitions may sometimes be narrowly drawn. Indeed, criticism of the preparation of terrorist acts offence has focussed on its breadth, not its clarity. Whilst the offence may have a wide scope, its wording is clear and comprehensible.

Simester's proposal to exclude inherently innocent conduct from the ambit of the section 5 offence is intended to narrow its scope. It is worth noting, therefore, that the proposal would involve some sacrifice of clarity. It would require a distinction to be drawn between inherently innocent conduct and morally ambiguous conduct—a distinction which is far from certain. This is evident in Simester's discussion of the Australian offence of connecting to the Internet with intention to commit a serious offence. He concludes that connecting to the Internet is like eating cereal, 'It is the kind of everyday activity that should be regarded as inherently innocent' (Simester 2012:74). But, given the wide range of illegal activities perpetrated online every day, it is possible to construct an equally strong case for saying that connecting to the Internet cannot be described as inherently innocent. The same would apply to numerous other forms of everyday conduct, leaving the boundaries of the section 5 offence uncertain.

There is also a more fundamental problem with Simester's proposal: many would say that it is impossible to ever describe any conduct that is carried out with an intention to commit or assist a terrorist act as inherently innocent. On this view, the need to establish a terrorist intention renders the inherently innocent category redundant. Admittedly, Simester addresses this point—arguing that some forms of conduct (such as picking up an item in a shop or eating cereal) cannot be made wrongful by the intentions with which they are performed.[12] But there is no guarantee that judges (nor juries or prosecutors) would accept this reasoning. As we have seen, discretion is heavily implicated in the interpretation of rules. The criminal law has seen many examples of the courts placing an interpretation on a statute that was different to the one that was originally intended.[13] Simester's proposal would thus complicate the wording of section 5 with no guarantee that the section's scope would be reduced.

So—if a general catch-all offence like section 5 is deemed necessary, notwithstanding the existing raft of other terrorism precursor offences—it is more fruitful to consider the extra-legal constraints on its practical operation and evaluate whether these are sufficient. The key constraint on the use of the offence is the decision of the **Crown Prosecution Service** (CPS) whether to prosecute. In order to understand the political, social and organisational forces which influence the CPS's prosecutorial discretion, it is helpful to use the framework advanced by Hawkins. This seeks to understand decisions by reference to their surround (broad setting in which decision-making activity takes places), decision field (defined setting in which decisions are made) and frame (the interpretative behaviour involved in decision-making about a specific matter) (Hawkins 2003).

In terms of surround, the CPS is accountable to politicians, the media and the public for its decisions in terrorism cases. This is reinforced by the publication each year of the details of all concluded terrorism cases[14] and by the intense scrutiny that terrorism cases attract. In terms of decision field, the CPS has a specialist Counter-Terrorism Division consisting of a specialist group of lawyers who are experts in counterterrorism prosecutions. Furthermore, for most terrorism offences (including the ones examined in this chapter) prosecutions may only be brought with the consent of the Director of Public Prosecutions.[15] An independent review has found that the Director exercises this discretion responsibly (Carlile 2007). The Director also has the

---

[12] Simester's proposal is based on the reasoning of the House of Lords in the indecent assault case *R v Court* [1989] AC 28.

[13] One well-known example is the House of Lords' judgment in *DPP v Gomez* [1993] AC 442 on the meaning of the word 'appropriates' in the offence of theft. Whilst Lord Lowry's dissenting judgment emphasised the meaning the Criminal Law Revision Committee intended the word to have, Lord Keith in his majority judgment stated that to look at the Committee's intention would serve 'no useful purpose'.

[14] The reports are available on the CPS website (www.cps.gov.uk).

[15] Terrorism Act 2000, s. 117; Terrorism Act 2006, s. 19.

benefit of an expert legal advisor, and decisions to prosecute and not to prosecute are both open to judicial review. In terms of frame, the CPS's Code for Crown Prosecutors sets outs two tests for determining whether a prosecution should be brought: there must be sufficient evidence to provide a realistic prospect of conviction (the evidential test); and, the prosecution must be required in the public interest (the public interest test) (Crown Prosecution Service 2013). There are also further guidance documents on a number of specific issues, including domestic violence, sexual offences and racially and religiously aggravated offences. A failure to follow settled policy in a particular case may provide grounds for judicial review. The discretion whether to prosecute in terrorism cases is clearly far from unfettered.

Whilst the CPS has published a number of other specific guidance documents, it does not currently have one on the terrorism precursor offences. Such a document would be welcome. Amongst other things, it could, first, explain whether there are any circumstances in which a prosecution should not be brought under section 5 of the Terrorism Act 2006. If sufficient evidence was available to prove that Simester's hypothetical would-be terrorist ate his bowl of muesli with an intention to commit an act of terrorism in the future, should he be prosecuted? Second, a guidance document could address the relationship between the section 5 offence and the numerous other terrorism precursor offences. In *R v Iqbal*[16] the Court of Appeal confirmed that section 5 overlaps with the other precursor crimes; so, in that particular case, the fact that the defendant's conduct might also have fallen under the section 6 offence (training for terrorism) did not preclude him from being convicted of the section 5 offence. This is significant not only for labelling purposes, but also for sentencing. The maximum sentence for the section 5 offence (life imprisonment) is more severe than for many of the other specific precursor crimes (the maximum sentence for the section 6 offence, for example, is 10 years' imprisonment). Where a choice has to be made between different precursor offences, what considerations should influence this decision? Whilst previous examples of successful convictions may offer some help, it would be useful to have more general guiding principles.

Key Points

- Discretionary decision-making is inevitable in any legal system.
- It is mistaken to contrast rules with discretion and to assume that by creating legal rules we will drive out unfettered discretion.
- There are numerous political, social and organisational constraints on the exercise of prosecutorial discretion in terrorism cases.
- A specific guidance document on the terrorism precursor offences would be welcome.

---

[16] [2010] EWCA Crim 3215.

9.6   Conclusion

In this chapter we have argued that the criminal law does have a preventive role and that the limitations of the inchoate offences of attempt, conspiracy and encouraging crime mean that terrorism precursor offences are justified. We have examined two suggestions for how to limit the scope of terrorism precursor offences. We have argued that the proposed distinction between inherently innocent and morally ambiguous conduct would generate uncertainty without necessarily imposing any meaningful limits. On the other hand, the notion of normative involvement not only offers a principled basis on which to justify the criminalisation of preparatory activities, but also a yardstick for evaluating whether these offences overreach.

Further Reading and Resources

Hodgson J, Tadros V (2009) How to make a terrorist out of nothing. Mod Law Rev 72:984–998

Macdonald S (2014) Prosecuting suspected terrorists: precursor crimes, intercept evidence and the priority of security. In: Jarvis L, Lister M (eds) Critical perspectives on counter-terrorism. Routledge, Abingdon

Marchand SA (2010) An ambiguous response to a real threat: criminalizing the glorification of terrorism in Britain. George Wash Int Law Rev 42:123–157

United Nations Office on Drugs and Crime (2012) The use of the Internet for terrorist purposes. United Nations, New York

Weimann G (2004) How modern terrorism uses the Internet. United States Institute of Peace special report 116

Weimann G (2006) Terror on the Internet: the new arena, the new challenges. United States Institute of Peace Press, Washington, DC

References

Anderson D (2013) Shielding the compass: how to fight terrorism without defeating the law. Eur Hum Right Law Rev 233–246

Ashworth A, Zedner L (2012) Prevention and criminalization: justifications and limits. New Crim Law Rev 15:542–571

Ballard JD, Hornik JG, McKenzie D (2002) Technological facilitation of terrorism: definitional, legal and policy issues. Am Behav Sci 45:989–1016

Best C (2008) Open source intelligence. In: Fogelman-Souie F, Perrotta D, Piskorski J, Steinberger R (eds) Mining massive data sets for security: advances in data mining, search, social networks and text mining and their applications for security. IOS Press, Amsterdam, pp 331–344

Bradley A, Ewing K (2003) Constitutional and administrative law, 13th edn. Longman, Harlow

Carlile A (2007) The definition of terrorism, Cm 7052. The Stationery Office, London

Chen H, Larson C (2007) Dark web terrorism research. http://ai.arizona.edu/research/terror/. Accessed 16 Oct 2013

Clarkson C (2009) Attempt: the conduct requirement. Oxf J Leg Stud 29:25–41

Conway M (2002) Reality bytes: cyberterrorism and terrorist 'use' of the Internet. First Monday 7. http://firstmonday.org/ojs/index.php/fm/article/view/1001/922. Accessed 4 Oct 2013

Conway M (2006) Terrorist 'use' of the Internet and fighting back. Inform Secur 19:9–30

Cronin AK (2003) Behind the curve: globalisation and international terrorism. Int Secur 27:30–58

Crown Prosecution Service (2013) The code for Crown prosecutors. CPS Communication Division, London

Davis KC (1971) Discretionary justice: a preliminary inquiry. University of Illinois Press, Urbana

Denning D (2000) Cyberterrorism. Testimony before the Special Oversight Panel on Terrorism Committee on Armed Services U.S. House of Representatives. http://www.cs.georgetown. edu/~denning/infosec/cyberterror.html. Accessed 4 Oct 2013

Denning D (2010) Terror's web: how the internet is transforming terrorism. In: Jewkes Y, Yar M (eds) Handbook of Internet crime. Willan Publishing, Devon, pp 194–213

Duff A (1996) Criminal attempts. Clarendon, Oxford

Duff AR, Farmer L, Marshall SE, Renzo M, Tadros V (eds) (2010) The boundaries of the criminal law. Oxford University Press, Oxford

Edwards J (2010) Justice denied: the criminal law and the ouster of the courts. Oxf J Leg Stud 30:725–748

Galligan D (1986) Discretionary powers. Clarendon, Oxford

Goodman S, Kirk J, Kirk M (2007) Cyberspace as a medium for terrorists. Technol Forecast Soc Change 74:193–210

Gordon S, Ford R (2002) Cyberterrorism? Comput Secur 21:636–647

Hawkins K (1992) The use of legal discretion: perspectives from law and social science. In: Hawkins K (ed) The uses of discretion. Clarendon, Oxford

Hawkins K (2003) Order, rationality and silence: some reflections on criminal justice decision-making. In: Gelsthorpe L, Padfield N (eds) Exercising discretion: decision-making in the criminal justice system and beyond. Willan Publishing, Cullompton

Hodgson J, Tadros V (2009) How to make a terrorist out of nothing. Mod Law Rev 72:984–998

Hoffman B (2006) Inside terrorism. Columbia University Press, Chichester

Holt TJ (2012) Exploring the intersections of technology, crime, and terror. Terrorism Polit Violence 24:337–354

Home Office (2011) CONTEST: the United Kingdom's strategy for countering terrorism, Cm 8123. The Stationery Office, London

Homeland Security Institute (2009) The Internet as a terrorist tool for recruitment and radicalization of youth. Homeland Security Institute, Arlington

Horder J (2012) Harmless wrongdoing and the anticipatory perspective on criminalisation. In: Sullivan GR, Dennis I (eds) Seeking security: pre-empting the commission of criminal harms. Hart Publishing, Oxford, pp 79–102

Hua J, Bapna S (2012) How can we deter cyberterrorism? Info Secur J Global Perspect 21:102–114

Jacobson M (2010) Terrorist financing and the Internet. Stud Conflict Terrorism 33:353–363

Jarvis L, Macdonald S (2014) What is cyberterrorism? Findings from a survey of researchers. Terrorism Polit Violence. Forthcoming

Joint Committee on Human Rights (2007) The Council of Europe Convention on the Prevention of Terrorism. First report of session 2006–07, HC 247

Keller J, DeSouza K, Lin Y (2010) Dismantling terrorist networks: evaluating strategic options using agent-based modelling. Technol Forecast Soc Change 77:1014–1036

Lacey N (1992) The jurisprudence of discretion: escaping the legal paradigm. In: Hawkins K (ed) The uses of discretion. Clarendon, Oxford

Lester A (2007) Redefining terror. Index Censorship 36:103–107

Libicki MC (2007) Conquest in cyberspace: National Security and Information Warfare. Cambridge University Press, Cambridge

Macdonald S (2014) Prosecuting suspected terrorists: precursor crimes, intercept evidence and the priority of security. In: Jarvis L, Lister M (eds) Critical perspectives on counter-terrorism. Routledge, Abingdon

Marchand SA (2010) An ambiguous response to a real threat: criminalizing the glorification of terrorism in Britain. George Wash Int Law Rev 42:123–157

McSherry B (2009) Expanding the boundaries of inchoate crimes: the growing reliance on preparatory offences. In: McSherry B, Norrie A, Bronitt S (eds) Regulating deviance: the redirection of criminalisation and the futures of criminal law. Hart Publishing, Oxford

Piper P (2008) Nets of terror: terrorist activity on the internet. Searcher 16:28–38

Pollitt MM (1998) Cyberterrorism: fact or fancy. Comput Fraud Secur 2:8–10

Privy Council Review of Intercept as Evidence (2008) Report to the Prime Minister and the Home Secretary, Cm 7324. The Stationery Office, London

Schmid AP, Jongman AJ (2008) Political terrorism: a new guide to actors, authors, concepts, data bases, theories, & literature (updated edn.). Transaction, New Burnswick

Schneider CE (1992) Discretion and rules: a lawyer's view. In: Hawkins K (ed) The uses of discretion. Clarendon, Oxford

Simester AP (2012) Prophylactic crimes. In: Sullivan GR, Dennis I (eds) Seeking security: pre-empting the commission of criminal harms. Hart Publishing, Oxford

Simester AP, von Hirsch A (2011) Crimes, harms, and wrongs: on the principles of criminalisation. Hart Publishing, Oxford

Simester AP, Spencer JR, Sullivan GR, Virgo GJ (2013) Simester and Sullivan's criminal law: theory and doctrine, 5th edn. Hart Publishing, Oxford

Stenersen A (2008) The Internet: a virtual training camp? Terrorism Polit Violence 20:215–233

Stohl M (2006) Cyber terrorism: a clear and present danger, the sum of all fears, breaking point or patriot games? Crime Law Soc Change 46:223–238

Sullivan GR, Dennis I (eds) (2012) Seeking security: pre-empting the commission of criminal harms. Hart Publishing, Oxford

Theohary CA, Rollins J (2011) Terrorist use of the Internet: information operations in cyberspace. Congressional Research Service report for congress 7-5700

Tsfati Y, Weimann G (2002) www. Terrorism.com: terror on the Internet. Stud Conflict Terrorism 25:317–332

Turpin C, Tomkins A (2011) British Government and the constitution. Cambridge University Press, Cambridge

United Nations Office on Drugs and Crime (2012) The use of the Internet for terrorist purposes. United Nations, New York

Weimann G (2004) How modern terrorism uses the Internet. United States Institute of Peace special report 116

Weimann G (2005) Cyberterrorism: the sum of all fears? Stud Conflict Terrorism 28:129–149

Weimann G (2006) Terror on the Internet: the new arena, the new challenges. United States Institute of Peace Press, Washington, DC

Chapter 10
Adaptive Responses to Cyberterrorism

Gil Ad Ariely

10.1 Introduction

Cyberterrorism is a controversial term that is still not situated comfortably as a paradigm in either academic or practitioners' communities. This is partially due to definitions of its components—the definition of terrorism is disputed (Ganor 2001), and cyber is yet a social construction. Also, the nature of terrorists' usage of the Internet, cyberspace, and information technology (IT), is not clearly delineated. While definitions vary, the basic construct of "convergence of cyber space and terrorism" covers not just terrorism targeting IT and cyberspace but also usage of cyberspace and IT for terrorist activities. "Cyberspace is a habitat for knowledge and information, and terrorists are knowledge-workers proficient in it" (Ariely 2008). IT and cyberspace are an equalizer for small groups, networks or individuals to large organizations (even nation states) which supports asymmetrical effects and low entry barriers. Terrorists have been using cyberspace widely for a variety of purposes ranging from secure encrypted communications to radicalization and recruitment, fundraising, or planning (Thomas 2003) of physical attacks (e.g., Lashkar-e-Taiba used Google Earth for the 2008 Mumbai attack). It is the same societal power shift predicted by Toffler (Toffler 1990).

Cyberspace is changing society profoundly, and the dynamic nature of terrorist involvement in cyberspace requires agile capabilities for a spectrum of responses. Taking lessons from past incidents is insufficient preparation for unknown future threats. Hence the central theme of this chapter is the conceptual foundations to support agility and adaptiveness in responses to cyberterrorism, as well as organizational mechanisms and methods to adapt quickly in the face of attacks and threats. We aim to connect conceptual and practical responses in a "layered" approach, first

G. Ad Ariely (✉)
Interdisciplinary Center (IDC), Herzliya, Israel
e-mail: GilAd.Ariely@gmail.com

T.M. Chen et al. (eds.), *Cyberterrorism: Understanding, Assessment, and Response*,
DOI 10.1007/978-1-4939-0962-9_10, © Springer Science+Business Media New York 2014

promoting synergy of national policy to counter cyber terrorism with other national security policy, then connecting the national to organizational and individual levels.

This chapter builds on earlier discussions of definitions (Jarvis et al. 2014) and taxonomies of threats to elaborate the need for high-level conceptual discussions of responses. We build upon the argument made by Jarvis, Nouri and Whiting to approach cyberterrorism as a social construction and highlight the usefulness of such efforts for responses. From a high-level conceptual analysis, the chapter moves to cover the spectrum of responses with two emerging dimensions as "aligning ideas": aligning responses on a timeline, and aligning by type of response.

Finally, the chapter covers possible futures of ubiquitous IT and how developments in cyberspace create more vulnerabilities, which further argues for adaptive responses. It proposes methodologies from the field of futures-studies (such as scenario planning or Delphi methods).

10.2 Why Definitions Matter for Responses

Cyberterrorism is interdisciplinary and crosses boundaries (national borders and knowledge domains). When covering the spectrum of responses to cyberterrorism, we must not ignore cyber activities that are not a direct attack on IT assets or critical infrastructure, or that may not directly endanger human life. This chapter aims to be more holistic and bypass the divide in the literature, one side maximizing cyberterrorism's devastating potential and the other side seeing cyberterrorism as hype (Singer 2012). For the sake of developing a "toolkit" of responses, such a divide and discussion is futile. Furthermore, these cyber activities may well be merely phases in the rapid evolution in cyberterrorism. As the convergence of IT and society is accelerated, society faces more inherent risk due to its dependence on IT. Cyberspace is becoming more entangled with the physical world, first through programmable logic controllers (PLCs) and supervisory control and data acquisition (SCADA) systems, and then with embedded IT envisioned in the "Internet of things" (Ashton 2009). It is more relevant to analyze the conceptual, technical and practical bounds of responses to cyberterrorism, than the actual direct response to a specific threat (which is arguably non-existent so far).

In relating responses to threats, a taxonomical classification is an important vehicle to support a social construction of a common understanding within professional communities. It can also support the pragmatic discussions of definitions in the context of responses (as base for international cooperation, legislation, etc.). A high level taxonomy of responses would need to set a different path from familiar taxonomies of attacks and threats, by taking a proactive and longer time-span dimension. Reactive responses derived from "lessons learned" of attacks are focused on specific threats. Yet cyber security as defense starts from prevention, and may even escalate in the spectrum of responses to preemptive attacks. While this chapter does not presume to fully cover such a taxonomy, it exemplifies elements and possible methodology towards it, demonstrating the need and "return on investment" on such an effort. This serves as a foundation for the need for an ongoing adaptive mechanism for responses in cyberspace, which is not unconnected but independent of emerging threats and attacks.

10.2.1 Taxonomies and Definitions

Taxonomies and definitions support countermeasures as foundations for discussion and cooperation, yet they may act as paradigms. Organizationally, the inherited industrial age tendency for division of labor and task specialization tends to limit organizations to what is defined within the boundaries of their expertise and authority. If, for example, a police service is focused on crime, then definition of something as cyber crime, and a classification scheme as a tool for clearly positioning it, points to an organizationally familiar range of responses. However, the complexity of the post-industrial information age is challenging organizational boundaries, for example, when criminal and terrorist networks operate together, or used as state-proxy, in cyberspace.

Taxonomies of attacks and threats in the literature are relevant to some elements in analyzing responses, as some responses are derived from and directly focused on, specific threats or type of attacks. This is a point of departure for a more holistic, longer term approach to prevention and responses. An extensive coverage of taxonomies of attacks and adversaries can be found in a report commissioned by the U.S. (Meyers et al. 2009).

An early CERT (computer emergency response team) taxonomy by Howard and Longstaff (1998) was extended by Kiltz et al. (2008) by modifications in categories of attacker, vulnerability and objective. The taxonomy classified: attackers, tool, vulnerability, type of action, target, result, and objective (Kiltz 2008). These type of categories are crucial for a responding CERT exactly because they can be connected in response to a specific incident or attack using standard operating procedures (SOP) prepared in advance, and implementing best practices. Other taxonomies of cyber crime (Alkaabi et al. 2010) refer also to cyberterror (included within cyber crime) with a similar high-level differentiation used here earlier: attacking IT infrastructure (type I), or using IT and cyberspace to target physical or any other target (type II). However, the fact they intertwine cyberterror with cyber crime might be confusing to readers, which is the reason for relating definitions to responses: internationally agreed upon definitions are a tool and "weapon" to confront terrorism and cyberterrorism. The notion of "one man's terrorist is another man's freedom fighter" is an obstacle to international legislation and cooperation. This is only extrapolated in cyberspace where no physical boundaries exist. Who would define an attack as hacktivism or cyber terrorism? To quote Albert Einstein, "Ethical axioms are found and tested not very differently from the axioms of science. Truth is what stands the test of experience."

Pragmatism for the sake of discussions of responses requires subscribing to definitions. So cyberspace is "a global domain within the information environment whose distinctive and unique character is framed by the use of electronics and the electromagnetic spectrum to create, store, modify, exchange, and exploit information via interdependent and interconnected networks using information-communication technologies" (Kuehl 2009). Cyberspace depends on the electromagnetic spectrum and on physical ICT objects that maintain it, thus there are artifacts and physical locations to attack and thus to defend.

10.2.2 Grounded Theory Methodology for Social Construction of Cyberterrorism

Accepting that social construction of cyberterrorism is required in order to develop a practical taxonomy of responses, we require a methodological approach to accelerate it. A possible approach is to employ grounded theory (Glaser and Strauss 1967) on cyberterrorism literature and studies. Grounded theory is not hypothetico–deductive but rather allows the theory to emerge from the data. Through an extensive coding process—for which many methodological variations exist (Strauss and Corbin 1990; Locke 2001; Goulding 2002)—it allocates categories and identifies emerging patterns. When the data is the actual literature reviewed (reflecting the state of the art), the theory is thus grounded in the data and reality which is socially constructed in an emerging paradigm (Kuhn 1962).

For example, in a recent study by a national academic working group (forthcoming, Institute for Counter Terrorism (ICT) at IDC Herzliya), this grounded theory approach was implemented to aim for a working definition of cyberterrorism. It used extensive literature review as data, coding and grouping the elements into emerging categories to identify recurring elements and their patterns. While not the aim of this chapter, it is interesting to mention the emerging categories, as they relate specifically to cyberterrorism:

- Origin of attack—entity (identity of attacker)
- Origin of attack—system (type of IT and systems)
- Motivation for attack
- Target of attack—entity (population, organization, identity)
- Target of attack—type (cyber security context/IT, systems, critical infrastructure)
- Desired outcome (including impacts and perceived effects)
- Results and actual outcome (what were the achievements and impact in reality?).

Most of the categories can be corroborated in other unrelated studies implementing grounded theory (Ahmad and Yunos 2012). Another example is a study mentioned later (in connecting cyber terrorism policy and national counter terrorism policies) implementing grounded theory to analyze categories of responses to terrorism. Taxonomies emerging through grounded theory are useful as a point of departure for a catalog of responses. Some responses are focused and directly connected to specific categories, while others such as policy and governance or education are more holistic and cover varied threats.

Key Points

- A taxonomical classification serves as a foundation for an ongoing adaptive mechanism for responses in cyberspace.
- A possible approach is to employ grounded theory.

10.3   Two Proposed Dimensions to Align Responses on a Spectrum

Two "aligning ideas" are proposed for a spectrum of responses: responses can be aligned by "type" of response and aligned on a "time span." The type of response refers to the nature of the response and the domains of knowledge relevant to it. Types of responses are either reactive or proactive, and can be conceptual, educational, or technological (with subcategories elaborated later). Reactive responses can be also punitive (e.g., prosecution) or framework enhancements (e.g., changes in legislation). Conceptual responses include formulation of cyber security strategy and policies. The outcome must be corporate governance or national regulations, and the vehicles and authority to monitor compliance (many nations designate national authorities to produce national cyber policy, e.g., Israel's National Cyber Bureau—INCB).

Time-span refers to attacks as the "point of reference." It starts long before incidents with prevention, education, preparations, etc. and includes intrusion detection or information assurance efforts. Then a different set of responses is relevant during attacks which may include similar tools but focused differently towards real-time crisis management, such as public education campaigns through rapid knowledge permeation mechanisms, or even modular and dynamic staffing of cyber security helpdesks. It continues to recovery and seamless operation, a discipline of "business continuity." The third phase relates to the aftermath of attacks, which differ in short or long term responses. In the immediate term, evaluation and damage control is required. In the long term, analysis, learning lessons, and sharing knowledge are necessary for core improvements.

A holistic and long term approach is not limited to dealing with attacks but also addresses other terrorist activities in cyberspace. Since some of the activities are not attacks (such as online radicalization), they should be first understood and then confronted. Efforts of terrorists to recruit start from nurturing radicalization online. While there is a clear line between a radicalized youngster and a recruited terrorist in the physical world, this distinction is more blurred online. Radicalization converged with hacktivism ethos allow for seamless and immediate operational participation in cyberterror attacks.

Cyber security policy is the first step to create governance and protect cyberspace and IT infrastructure. Even the very basics of securing physical locations of servers, or physical access to privileged computers connected to more secure environment, is dependent on smart policy and its strict application. Many organizations that use clouds for storage do not know where their data is kept as it could be physically anywhere. Similarly, the concept of insider threats or threats of "social engineering" require agile and applicable policy. The meaning of policy is lost if it not strictly applied in real life. For a good coverage of cyber security policies, see (Bayuk et al. 2012); their cyber security policy taxonomy details categories of governance, user, conflict, management and infrastructure is applicable to cyberterrorism as well.

Key Point

- Responses can be aligned by type of response and aligned on a time span.

10.4   National Level Policy on Cyberterrorism

The discussion of national strategy for responses to cyberterrorism starts from cyber security strategy. As nations started to designate agencies for cyber security, they started shaping national policy on cyber strategy, sometimes as a reactive measure to external events. For instance, Estonia published its national cyber security strategy in 2008 following the massive cyber attack on government, public sector and banks in 2007. Cyber warfare moved to center stage after the 2007 Estonia cyber attacks. In other cases, it reflected awareness at national level and internal pressures (including amongst competing agencies).

Today many nations have published a national cyber security strategy, which is part of a national cyber posture (see "deterrence by capabilities" discussed later). For example, France identified cyber security as one focal point in a whitepaper by the president in 2008, inaugurated the French Network and Information Security Agency (ANSSI) in 2009 and published a national strategy on cyber defense in 2011.

Here we focus on national cyber policy moving into the public domain (in many cases reflecting prior classified efforts). Perhaps the best example to follow the process of policy formation and the "evolution of knowledge" on policy for cyber security is the U.S. In 2008, the National Security Presidential Directive (NSPD) 54/ HSPD 23 formalized the Comprehensive National Cybersecurity Initiative (CNCI), and it was unclassified in 2010. An analysis of "evolutionary epistemology" of cyber policy in the U.S. is found in (Chen 2013).

The myriad of cyber policy papers and national strategy produced by various agencies converge nationally, but it is the emergence of frameworks for national cyber security that is a sign of a policy paradigm. For example, the U.N. agency ITU (International Telecommunication Union) published a guide for national security policy in 2011 which covers various elements in formulating strategy and responses, including legal measures, technical measures, and organizational structures, as well as education and capacity building. While it explicitly includes international cooperation in responses, such guides support cooperation by the convergence towards a policy paradigm very much like definitions and taxonomies. In 2012, both NATO and the European Union published meta-policy guides for national cyber policy. The NATO Cooperative Cyber Defence Centre of Excellence (CCDCOE) published a "Cyber Security Framework Manual," and the European Network and Information Security Agency (ENISA) published a guide for member states on creating National Cyber Security Strategies ("Practical Guide on Development and Execution").

10.5 Convergence in Evolution of Cyber Threats Mitigation

In the past, cyberterrorism was analyzed within both fields of IT security and counter terrorism. However, the theoretical gap in definitions and the fusion of actors (hackers, hacktivists, cyber criminals or terrorists) allowed for responses and other operational knowledge to develop in parallel lanes. Within the community of practice of CISOs (chief information security officers) and CERTs dealing with daily breaches and various sorts of attacks, an evolution in knowledge created a corpus of practical, hands-on knowledge. It included policy guidelines, best practices, technical responses and capabilities to prevent, detect, and recover from incidents. The emerging discipline was less concerned with the conceptual implications of a single specific type such as cyberterrorism but rather in mitigating cyber threats as a whole, and they were right as evident today.

The industrial age and specialization created separated departments, especially in the government sector, to deal with each phenomenon. In fact this led to "Parkinson's Law" (Parkinson 1957) creating new organizational structures to deal with new postmodern challenges (e.g., the Department of Homeland Security following 9/11, and U.S. Cyber Command now). Not to undermine overarching policy and operational knowledge management, any division of labor must not create a division of knowledge. Artificially, we have clarified our paradigms of domains in society within cyberspace too, in the simplest manner possible: if a domain names ends with .gov or .mil then it probably should be protected by authorities, but what about .com? "Unrestricted" warfare means that businesses become legitimate targets. Today this is understood at the national level. Of course, in cyberspace any target is "fair game" for hackers, cyber terrorists or cyber criminals. A combination of targeted attacks and opportunistic ones mean that the original practitioners' approach—mitigating cyber threats as a whole—was and still is the right one.

Now is the time that all these separated, yet not unconnected, theoretical efforts can synergize in a better understanding of how cyberspace actors interrelate and the complexities of cyberspace. The fruits of convergence are knowledge transfer across the public and government sector, businesses, and military and defense establishment. This is critical because critical infrastructure is interconnected, and mostly not under government control. Thus any policy recommendations, regulation and governance must be done in cooperation with the industry. Most of the public transportation sector in the U.S. is in private hands, and more than 85 % of the energy sector and government communications pass through privately operated infrastructure.

Part of the responses that create critical infrastructure resilience include redundancies replication and backup systems that conflict directly against the basic economic logic of maximizing profits for the specific operator as a business. This calls for a holistic national overview of policy and resource prioritization, as elaborated further in business continuity and risk management.

Key Points

- Now is the time to converge all historically separate, yet not unconnected, theoretical efforts to synergize a better understanding.
- The fruits of convergence are knowledge transfer across the public and government sector, businesses, and military and defense establishment.

10.6   Countering Cyberterror as Inherent Part of Counter-Terrorism Policy

As portrayed in the last two sections, cyberterror is usually entwined in national cyber security policy, but it must be entwined with the national counter terrorism policy. Various models developed for cyber terrorism can not "stand alone." Relevant measures for countering cyberterror must be implemented as part of counter terrorism policy, and existing frameworks for cooperation and operation in countering terror must be adapted to include cyberterror. This prevents reductionism in understanding patterns of terrorism that include usage of cyberspace as merely one element. For example, a comparative international study on counter terrorism measures and their effectiveness include the following categories of responses (Warnes 2014): diplomatic/political; legal; security—framework; intelligence; policing; military/tactical; technical/operational; economic; and civil liberties.

The overlap between the emerging policy foundations at national level on cyber security, and national counter terrorism policy doctrine must be clear and synergetic. For example, in reference to the categories above, each category should be related to cyberterrorism (where relevant) in both types of papers and cross referenced where possible. This is especially important at national level policy directives, allowing for a synergy in efforts and responses. This is how social construction can be advanced at conceptual and doctrinal level, in a dynamic field with differing communities of practice. Using the same example, all the categories could be applied to cyber terrorism aspects.

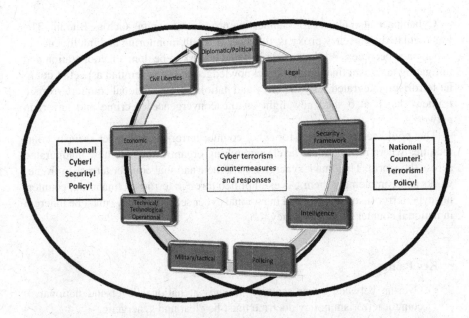

The "economic" category, for example, would relate both to using cyberspace for economic goals and financing, but also to targeting the economy and specific economic sectors using cyber terrorism attacks. Such attacks could be on specific sectors (like cyberterror attacks against the oil and gas sector in the Gulf). The effects on economy are grave and could parallel physical attacks on facilities and installations. Coupled with cyber attacks through SCADA systems, the oil Industry and energy sector could prove extremely vulnerable (Averill and Luiijf 2010).

In a more sophisticated economic approach, reality is the perception of reality (as stock exchanges and currency rate fluctuation prove) and information assurance could play an important role in mitigating cyberterrorism. So far cyberterrorists have aimed at trivial defacing of websites or DDoS attacks, but could aim to alter data on servers. The implications of presenting erroneous data on formal websites would be far more damaging than an altered homepage. This calls for continuous information assurance policies and practices for the attacks "we don't know that we don't know about."

A reference for considering integration of cyber counter terrorism policies is terrorism financing, which has taken center stage in the recent decade for countering terrorism in a global environment. The attempt to "follow the money" has led to inauguration of international communities of practice (CoP) and national organizations entrusted with creating legal frameworks and banking regulations which respond to financing terrorism from drugs, smuggling and other organized crime, or clandestine channels from states sponsoring terror, and money laundering mechanisms. Many of these operate in cyberspace (as does most of the banking system) through formal legitimate channels.

Cyberspace also allows for clandestine proxies for capital such as Bitcoin. The less regulated a currency proxy is, the more difficult monitoring and intelligence in cyberspace becomes. While there is still much work to be done on cooperation and mitigating terrorism financing, it is acknowledged today as seminal aspect of counter terrorism, integrated fully in policy and national organizational counterterrorism frameworks. It also shed new light on the convergence of crime and terrorism networks.

That could act as reference for cyber counter terrorism and cyber security communities where new national level overarching organizations are now inaugurated across the world. They must synergize with their national counter terrorism frameworks and complement them. As exemplified through terrorism financing, countering cyberterror (usually entwined in national cyber security policy) must be inherent in national counter terrorism policy too.

> **Key Points**
>
> • Overlap between cyber security policies at national level and national counter terrorism policy doctrine must be clear and synergetic.
> • Countering cyberterror, (usually entwined in national cyber security policy), must also be inherent in national counter terrorism policy.

10.7   Weapons of Mass Disruption, and Cyberspace as Global Commons

The more sophisticated a nation's infrastructure is, and the more advanced its citizens and businesses are in using the Internet, that nation becomes more vulnerable to cyberspace disruptions. This is true regardless of the cause of disruptions or the nature of the attacker, whether cyberterrorists, cyber criminals, or enemy nation state. The basic "tool kit" of responses is similar, derived from concepts of business continuity. The same concepts that allow an enterprise to run its operations without interruption even throughout natural disasters can apply to preparing, mitigating, and reducing the risks of cyberterrorism. This is a significant factor and business case for investment in cyber counter terrorism since most resources invested in preparation to mitigate cyberterrorism support business continuity in the context of other threats. For example, backup and backup sites are an example of how ICT can rapidly shift location upon incidents, in disaster recovery, and maintain business continuity.

The growing dependence of society on information technology and cyberspace (Weimann 2005) has created new forms of vulnerability nationally (Clarke and Knake 2012). Once electronic commerce, banking, and e-government become inherent in daily life, disruptions can have immediate effects on economic markets and perception of security. For example, the most common form of cyber attacks is distributed denial of service (DDoS) which is fully dependent on how people depend on the services disrupted. An example of the connection between extensive usage of cyberspace and vulnerability to disruptions is the 2007 cyber attacks on Estonia. That does not necessarily mean that the answer is to avoid progress and technological advances. However, it does bring to the table the discipline, approach, and myriad of methodologies related to risk management. Since organizations cannot protect everything at the same level of investment, allocation of limited resources to defense is required, based on risk analysis. For review and discussion of different information security risk analysis methodologies see (Vorster and Labuschagne 2005).

On the other side, some risks involve not just the use of cyberspace to attack physical critical infrastructure, but the opposite: to physically attack cyberspace infrastructure. Today, most of the global communications are carried along undersea fiber-optic cables. In 2008, four such cables were found cut (at least one due to an anchor). More recently, the Egyptian coast guard caught three divers trying to cut the SEA-ME-WE-4 cable near Alexandria (Saffo 2013). In a wild card (although feasible) scenario, cyberterror could easily become a weapon of mass disruption (WMD) to nations by deploying a ship's anchor.

What does this mean in the context of responses, and what can we do? Simply put, cyberspace must be understood in terms of a global commons: a public good that must be protected by nations and internationally. As people expect to breathe freely, and drink clean water, they have come to expect access to cyberspace, the Internet, and their information. We note that maritime security in face of piracy is tackled by international task forces; it is sufficient to leverage awareness of cyberspace as a global commons. Indeed this conceptual shift is starting to take place, as evident in the NATO 2011 report, "Assured Access to the Global Commons: Maritime, Air, Space, Cyber."

Key Points

- The growing dependence of society on information technology and cyberspace has created new forms of vulnerability.
- Cyberspace must be understood in terms of a global commons.

10.8   Projecting Cyber Power: Reality Is the Perception of Reality

This section does not elaborate the discussion of cyber power at nation state levels and its projection in cyberspace and beyond into the physical world (Nye 2010). However, some features may bear similarity and relevance, especially with future evolution in terrorist organizations' capabilities and resources. Possible convergence of efforts and players might happen by using proxy organizations or hackers' networks with the commercialization of cyber security where both tools and hackers' knowledge become commodity. Or it could be state sponsorship of terrorism which might give terrorists unconventional capabilities and definitely cyber capabilities, training, and resources.

In fact, such convergence of terrorism and strategic alliances supports cyber power projection in the physical world, employing both information instruments (e.g., to attack SCADA systems) and physical instruments for terrorist attacks on installations. Nations may relate to cyberterrorism, as historically there were cases of using terrorism as proxy in the physical world to achieve strategic goals while not attributing attacks to nation states.

However terrorism is an asymmetric threat that by its nature usually does not form an existential threat to nations. It is aimed mostly to change reality through perceptions and proxies. Public resilience was part of the responses (as well as other measures) to mitigate suicide terrorism in public transportation. The attacks were aimed to reduce both security and the feeling of security which is part of the basic treaty between citizens and democratic government.

Cyber power supports the "power shift" that Toffler predicted. This is true to all elements and aspects of society, evident in the "occupy" movements or the "Arab Spring" protestors. Power is shifting from large organizations to smaller, networked organizations and individuals. This power shift, based on knowledge as a resource, did not skip terrorism as a societal phenomena. Cyber power shifts further capabilities, and lowers the entry barriers to terrorism participation from radicalization, even blurring lines from hacktivism.

An example of perception of attacks as relevant as the attack itself is #OpIsrael (April 2013) where responses included technical preparations, a public awareness campaign, and knowledge permeation beforehand as well as CSIRTs (computer security incident response team) operating in real time. While successfully monitoring attacks, mitigating and recovering within business continuity, part of the disruption came from people avoiding the Internet on that day. Terrorism is aimed to terrorize and disrupt, and while rapid knowledge permeation campaigns are important adaptive response, the line between being aware and "beware" is a thin one.

Key Points

- Terrorism does not form an existential threat to nations but instead is aimed mostly to change reality through perceptions and proxies.
- Cyber "power shift" lowers the entry barriers to terrorism participation from radicalization.

10.9   Multi-layered Approach to Responses and Prevention

Security measures apply from the individual level to corporate, sector, national levels, and even international (e.g., legal or cooperation frameworks like the Budapest convention). First and foremost, education is both a preventive and responsive measure at all levels. Education always applies first to the individual—the weakest link is always the human in the loop.

In targeted attacks at individual level, a common technique is "ladder climbing" which means attackers would spear-phish an individual's personal computer in hopes of climbing the ladder based on data or access gained then to their work computer or mobile device. Climbing the ladder then to a corporate machine might open an ocean of cyber serendipity in connected organizations. Sometimes technological "mudus operandi" can be identified (Thonnard et al. 2012) if surveyed globally. The more tools and datasets are open and widely available to researchers, the more rapid is the IT security response.

Responses at the personal level should aim to avoid the familiar "usability versus security" trade-off. Certainly it is crucial to permeate rules and regulations. Governance should include employee training and education, however it can not suffice. Any mundane repetitive activity will encounter innovative creativity by users (e.g., passwords written on keyboards, sessions left open). "Technically increasing the security by adding strict requirements on the behavior of the users can often lead to less de-facto security since people compensate in non-secure ways" (Adams and Sasse 1999). Wherever possible, security measures should be unobtrusive on people's behaviors and workflow. This can be done through user-centered design of security technology, such as proximity-based user authentication mechanism or biometrics.

Such integration and education can have significant impact on basic security habits: choosing complicated passwords that differ across applications; updating operating systems; patching browsers; using personal security software (firewall, antivirus). "Ladder climbing" is also why corporate governance is not enough, and why CISO or IT departments can not suffice for automated updates. In a BYOD (bring your own device) era, it is best to educate for security across the board—at home and at work.

Key Points

- Security measures should be applied at all levels.
- Education is a preventive and responsive measure at all levels.
- Responses at the personal level should be unobtrusive on people's behaviors and workflow.

10.10   Technical Classifications

A technical classification of cyberterrorism countermeasures categorized six types of responses: CSIRTs and their actions; intrusion prevention; network monitoring; interception and blockage; disaster recovery; and forensics (Veerasamy and Grobler 2010).

Information and communication technologies are of immense value to terrorist organizations (Don et al. 2007). Thus, on the technical level, intelligence in cyberspace becomes critical. It includes continual monitoring of online activities (e.g., discussion threads in forums) and recognition of emerging patterns in near real time. Intelligence in cyberspace has become the most valuable approach for intelligence to counter terrorism in general. It extrapolates an ages-old operational dilemma of intelligence: once you know, do you let them know that you know? In other words, it is a trade-off between maintaining future intelligence or "burn" the source to thwart an attack, exposing your intelligence. Intelligence in cyberspace allows counter attacks, or when known in advance, it allows organizations to better prepare systems for an attack.

Monitoring must be done based on understanding adversaries' behaviors and cyber-habitats, such as the "Darknet". This layer of the Internet refers to the websites and locations not mapped by conventional search engines but instead accessed through an infrastructure called TOR "The Onion Router" (Dingledine et al. 2004) designed for online anonymity. While anonymity may be important for variety of valid reasons, TOR has become the habitat and tool of choice for cyber criminals, hackers, terrorists, and various illegal activities.

Challenges of cyberspace and terrorism go beyond the problems of anonymity and attribution. A dedicated and highly sophisticated effort is required in "cyber forensics." Re-engineering IT and software to identify anything that may support attribution is beyond corporate IT and CISO capabilities. Such efforts must be part of national efforts to support industry sectors such as security software vendors. The convergence of networks of crime and terror forms an almost impossible post modern challenge. Traditionally, the government sector operates in a division of labor, knowledge and jurisdiction. Thus, cyber "Cerberus hybrids" are confronted by domain-specific organizations in the government sector. They operate within boundaries, jurisdictions and legal frameworks that differ to each organization. That is exploited by adversaries who are usually aware of these limitations.

There are efforts to "territorialize" the Internet, which means although cyber space is borderless, there are means to restrict access to certain information (Zittrain 2006). Location is crucial in the context of legislation, but even successful cyber forensics (attributing responsibility) is not enough. It becomes irrelevant with no global governance or international law in the context of cyberterrorism.

Key Point

• On the technical level, intelligence in cyberspace is critical.

10.11 Deterrence in Cyberspace

Is deterrence relevant for cyber terror? The short answer is no, or very little. Yet, a discussion of deterrence is worthwhile because it can lead to important insights. Deterrence in cyberspace is problematic at the nation state level (Libicki 2009).

Some of the basic tenets of cyberspace such as lack of a specific physical location, anonymity, and attribution, make retaliation almost impossible. Thus, the basis for deterrence fades away. In the case of cyberterror, it might be in the interest of terrorist organizations to have cyber attacks attributed, if to achieve a political impact. For terrorist organizations, the payoff for cyberterrorism may be higher, lower, or just different than other forms of terrorism, but the risks are immensely lower. Cyberterrorism can be practiced from the comfort of a relatively safe environment, which may be beyond the immediate reach of an attacked nation. Even if anonymity is breached, the armchair terrorist may sit beyond the effective reach of any legal framework that might define his actions as illegal. Considering international legal frameworks, accountability is only an outcome of the ability to follow it through.

The terrorist risks the possibility of nations mobilizing forces to respond to threats. That is a totally different element in deterrence. Essentially it means that cyberterrorism must be perceived as part of terrorism, and countering it must be become an inherent part of counter terrorism policy (as argued earlier). According to media publications, an Iranian cyber warfare commander was killed in a shooting incident in early October 2013. Regardless of the facts, when perception of reality socially constructs the reality, then media discussions on how cyberterrorists can be targeted just as others serves deterrence of cyberterrorism by the very discussion of it. Similarly, if nations perceive cyber warfare as risky enough to be considered casus belli (e.g., relevant for article 5 in the NATO treaty), it becomes deterrence and part of their security dilemma. Alas, for that to happen in a way that forms deterrence equations for cyber terrorism, a generational shift in perception still awaits ahead of us.

10.11.1   Deterrence by Capabilities?

Technological deterrence by capabilities has more interesting implications. This is not preemptive cyber attacks nor exposing the cyber attacker in real time. This is analogous to the concept of security cameras resulting in possible legal enforcement and persecution. However, exposing hackers in real time is merely an operational tool versus cyberterrorism, which results in adaptation rather than in deterrence. In a recent example, during a cyber attack named #OpIsrael in 7th April 2013, a commercial CSIRT identified and published the picture of an Indonesian hacker. The child was sitting in front of his computer immersed in a DDoS attack as his own computer took his picture. Does this create deterrence? Such publicity only stirs hackers' pride and sense of acknowledgement. However, the concept of technological capabilities and exposing it as an approach is more interesting to consider. With the usual balancing act of trading exposure for surprise and capability in the future, the knowledge that as a cyberterrorist you become immediately a target yourself may at the very least raise the entry barrier. In other words, it may get the novice actors to think twice.

A strong cyber defense posture may have a positive effect on deterring cyberterrorists practically by hardening targets. To borrow the concept from another defense measure and response, Israel developed an anti-missile/rocket array called the "Iron Dome" to intercept rockets shot across the border into Israel. Once the system proved itself effective, certain deterrence was created through the defensive capability. There is no use in shooting rockets that are intercepted. The prestige of the attacker is harmed, as would be the cyberterrorist's, if cyber attacks are foiled.

10.11.2   The Learning Competition in Cyberspace with Terrorists

Networks are seminal in terrorist organizations (Ganor 2009). Cyberspace is the natural environment for what was defined in the 1990s as "netwar" (Arquilla and Ronfeldt 1996). Cyberspace is a swiftly evolving environment where actors are continuously innovating to penetrate or attack systems. Adaptations in responses are quickly met with new breaches. This ever-changing competition of learning and adapting lies at the core of cyberterrorism. This calls for quick and rapid adaptation mechanisms and a dynamic model for cyber counter terrorism responses that include operational knowledge management and wide, rapid knowledge permeation capabilities. The need for agile learning to create a capacity to adapt is an essential characteristic of cyberspace.

Cyberspace has become a crucial infrastructure for learning and innovation for terrorists. Terrorist networks are intuitive learning organizations (Jackson et al 2007) which act as a complex adaptive systems (Ariely 2006). There are clear patterns of conducting AARs (After Action Reviews) and learning lessons from attacks, including physical attacks (Azani et al. 2008), and much of the learning is done in cyber space (for example in Jihadist forums). This challenges the abilities of hierarchies to outlearn them. This requires government agencies and organizations to become agile and a complex adaptive system, without losing the advantages of hierarchy. That is the "learning competition" (Ariely 2008) put to practice. The U.S. Army even made the term "learning competition" doctrinal: "In counter insurgency, the side that learns faster and adapts more rapidly—the better learning organization—usually wins" (U.S. Army 2006).

> **Key Points**
>
> - Deterrence is problematic for cyberterror but is worthy of discussion.
> - A strong cyber defense posture may have a positive effect on deterring cyberterrorists.
> - The continual competition of learning and adapting at the core of cyberterrorism calls for quick and rapid adaptation mechanisms.

10.12   An Eco-System That Promotes Adaptive Responses

In NetWar, "it takes a network to beat a network" (the motto of the International Counter Terrorism Academic Community—ICTAC). We need to create an eco-system that supports networking practitioners and experts across boundaries to become a complex adaptive system capable of swarming together to respond to cyberterrorism attacks (and ideally prevent them). An eco-system of cyber security is reflected globally by cyber norms, not just legislature. The attempts and evolution of such is reflected in a detailed account by Maurer (2011).

One of the imperatives for international, rapid, operational knowledge management and information sharing on cyber terrorism is mitigating the threats and attacks that go unnoticed for long periods. "We don't know what we don't know." Examples include zero-day attacks exploiting IT vulnerabilities not disclosed publicly (Bilge and Dumitras 2012). Data is usually unavailable but once discovery is published, exploitation attempts would accelerate. Swift attention to closing security holes becomes a matter of wide and rapid knowledge permeation mechanisms.

There are various models of operational knowledge management which can act as conceptual foundation to international, interagency interoperability, to enable cooperation and knowledge sharing, learning and adapting based on other's experiences. From communities of practice (CoP) to formal statutory organizations in nations, the essence is trust and tacit knowledge transfer. There are numerous examples of global CoPs in the field of CT (especially following 9/11) but suffice it to mention examples of ICTAC (International Counter Terrorism Academic Community), a networked community of academic experts in fields related to counter terrorism founded in 2003 to create an active network amongst the academic community to share knowledge and lead research aiming to guide policy and decision makers in countering terrorism. A similar example of an academic CoP is START that was funded by the U.S. Department of Homeland Security. This is a model for nurturing a network of cyber security experts into an operational CoP. The more interrelated these CoPs become, the more serendipity and effective adaptation can be expected.

The need to shorten learning cycles and implement lessons learned is imperative to be entwined in education as part of a wider interdisciplinary approach. On one side, cyber security must continue to become a discipline with a corpus of knowledge that includes overlapping domains of knowledge—risk management, business continuity and disaster management. All of them are not directly aimed at cyber terrorism but are relevant to confront and prepare for the fluid environment of cyberspace. There needs to be more academic programs beyond the practitioners' certifications on securing cyber space and information. The ability to change and remain agile is essential in the government sector, and requires educating all echelons in organizations to constantly adapt and innovate in a changing environment like cyberspace. The model for education is layered and should include: academic programs and education for the relevant disciplines; accreditation frameworks and practitioners' certifications; security IT vendors' accreditation and training; corporate education programs; and public education campaigns.

This is a long-term approach to create and nurture a cyber security eco-system. It starts from elementary schools with education for safety in cyberspace and continues with high school finals in IT and cyber security. Israel is an example of such an educational effort including the overarching concept of "cyber eco-system." Israel acknowledges the additional economic benefits of the cyber security industry. A nation perceived as an eco-system for cyber security attracts attention as target for cyber terrorism, but also positions itself in a strong cyber security posture.

Key Points

- An eco-system is needed to support networking practitioners and experts across boundaries to become a complex adaptive system.
- There are various models of operational knowledge management which can act as conceptual foundation to international, interagency interoperability, to enable cooperation and knowledge sharing.
- A need to shorten learning cycles and implement lessons learned is imperative to be entwined in education as part of a wider interdisciplinary approach.

10.13   The Futures

Cyberspace is becoming more entangled with the physical world, first through PLCs and SCADA, then with embedded IT towards the "Internet of things" (Ashton). ICT has become ubiquitous to every aspect of life, and anything can become a target for cyberterrorists. It will be easier to inflict damage in the physical environment through cyberspace. In preparing for unknown futures, we can also borrow methodologies from the discipline of futures studies in the context of cyberterrorism.

Socio-technical aspects are seminal. People become dependent on any technology they get used to. Humans have come to build on IT and "media as extensions of man" (McLuhan 1966) as extension of senses and memory. The cyberterror threat is a physical reality due to fear. Increasing efficiency and daily quality of life requires more and more ICT embedded in daily equipment. Future scenarios of the transportation sector, for example, include autonomously driven cars and more intrusive extensions of man (e.g., Google Glass) hackable by cyberterrorists.

Although backup at local and machine level may be created for each new technology that becomes dependent on remote or cloud based data, it is the socio-technical factor which creates the greater risk. The more embedded cyberspace is in our lives, the more potential for cyber terrorism to become a weapon of mass disruption.

Virtual environments like Second Life are being used today by terrorists for training and education. The implications and potential for using virtual worlds for such purposes is not much different than the benefits of virtual worlds for the government sector for education and training (Ariely 2009). However, futures scenarios beyond the horizon would examine what disrupting "imagined communities" (to borrow Benedict Andersen's term) in cyberspace, would mean.

10.14   Conclusions

This chapter continues an earlier call for social construction of cyberterrorism but goes further to propose practical and relevant methodologies to forward it, and urges it as base for responses to cyberterrorism. This chapter developed some of the concepts of perceived reality, from perceived deterrence or threat, for security. As terrorism is a societal phenomenon that is closely entwined with trends in society, cyberterrorism must be understood as part of terrorism. This chapter promotes entwining the policy, methods and tools to confront cyberterrorism with the grounded field of counter terrorism, up to national level counter terrorism policy. This goes against the common paradigm which places sole "ownership" of cyberterrorism and responses under the umbrella of cyber security. We propose specific categories as bridging concepts for policy, policy makers and practitioners' communities. It is important to try to be one step ahead of cyber terrorists in the "cyberspace learning competition." Knowledge and methodologies can be taken from the field of futures studies to be useful now.

Further Reading

Falessi N et al (2012) National cyber security strategies: practical guide on development and execution. European Network and Information Security Agency (ENISA)

Klimburg A (2012) National cyber security framework manual. Estonia: NATO Cooperative Cyber Defence Centre of Excellence (CCDCOE)

Luiijf E, Besseling K (2013) Nineteen national cyber security strategies. Int J Crit Infrastruct 9(1/2):3–31

References

Adams A, Sasse MA (1999) Users are not the enemy. Comm ACM 12(42):40–46

Ahmad R, Yunos Z (2012) A dynamic cyber terrorism framework. Int J Comput Sci Inform Secur 10(2):149–158

Alkaabi A et al (2010) Dealing with the problem of cybercrime. In: Proceedings of 2nd international ICST conference on digital forensics & cyber crime, Abu Dhabi

Ariely G (2006) "Learning to Digest During Fighting – Real Time Knowledge Management," International Institute for Counter-Terrorism, IDC Herzliya http://www.ict.org.il/Articles/tabid/66/Articlsid/229/currentpage/10/Default.aspx

Ariely G (2008) Knowledge management, terrorism, and cyber terrorism. In: Janczewski L, Colarik A (eds) Cyber warfare and cyber terrorism. IGI Global, Hershey

Ariely G (2009) Futures of virtual spaces for higher education in the government sector: immersive learning and knowledge exchange. In: Proceedings of OECD conference on higher education spaces & places for learning innovation & knowledge exchange, Riga

Arquilla J, Ronfeldt DF (1996) The Advent of Netwar. RAND, Santa Monica

Ashton K (2009) That 'Internet of things' thing. RFID J. http://www.rfidjournal.com/articles/view?4986. Accessed 4 Aug 2013

Averill B, Luiijf EAM (2010) Canvassing the cyber security landscape: why energy companies need to pay attention. J Energ Secur. http://www.ensec.org/index.php?view=article&id=243%3Acanvass ing-the-cyber-security-landscapewhy-energy-companies-need-to-pay-attention&option=com_ content&Itemid=361. Accessed 24 Jan 2014

Azani EY et al (2008) Global jihad groups as learning organizations: overcoming outer-perimeter security obstacles. ICT's Jihadi Websites Monitoring Group- Insights, International Institute for Counter-Terrorism (ICT)

Bayuk JL et al (2012) Cyber security policy guidebook. Wiley, Hoboken

Bilge L, Dumitras T (2012) Before we knew it: an empirical study of zero-day attacks in the real world. In: Proceedings of 2012 ACM conference on computer and communications security

Chen TM (2013) An assessment of the department of defense strategy for operating in cyberspace. Strategic Studies Institute, Carlisle

Clarke RA, Knake R (2012) Cyber war. HarperCollins, New York

Dingledine R et al (2004) Tor: the second-generation onion router. In: Proceedings of 13th USENIX security symposium

Don BW et al (2007) Network technologies for networked terrorists: assessing the value of information and communication technologies to modern terrorist organizations. RAND, Santa Monica

Ganor B (2001) Defining terrorism: is one man's terrorist another man's freedom fighter? http://www.ict.org.il/ResearchPublications/tabid/64/Articlsid/432/Default.aspx. Accessed 4 Aug 2013

Ganor B (2009) Terrorism networks: it takes a network to beat a network. In: Kleindorfer R, Wind YJ, Gunther RE (eds) The network challenge: strategy, profit, and risk in an interlinked world. Wharton School, Upper Saddle River, pp 453–470

Glaser BG, Strauss AL (1967) The discovery of grounded theory: strategies for qualitative research. Aldine de Gruyter, Hawthorne

Goulding C (2002) Grounded theory: a practical guide for management, business and market researchers. Sage, London

Howard JD, Longstaff TA (1998) A Common Language for Computer Security Incidents, Livermore, CA, Sandia National Labs

ICTAC (International Counter Terrorism Academic Community) founded by Ganor, Institute for Counter Terrorism (ICT) at the Interdisciplinary Center (IDC) Herzliya

Jackson BA et al (2007) Breaching the fortress wall: understanding terrorist efforts to overcome defensive technologies. RAND, Santa Monica

Jarvis L, Nouri L, Whiting A (2014) Understanding, Locating and Constructing 'Cyberterrorism'. In: Chen T, Jarvis L, Macdonald S (eds) Cyberterrorism: understanding, assessment, and response. Springer, New York

Kiltz S et al (2008) Taxonomy for computer security incidents. In: Janczewski L, Colarik A (eds) Cyber warfare and cyber terrorism. IGI Global, Hershey

Kuehl DT (2009) Cyberspace and cyberpower. In: Kramer FD, Starr SH, Wentz LK (eds) Cyberpower and national security. National Defense University Press, Washington, DC

Kuhn TS (1962) The structure of scientific revolutions. University of Chicago Press, Chicago

Libicki MC (2009) Cyberdeterrence and cyberwar. RAND, Santa Monica

Locke K (2001) Grounded theory. Sage, London

Maurer T (2011) Cyber norm emergence at the United Nations—an analysis of the UN's activities regarding cyber-security? Belfer Center for Science and International Affairs, Harvard Kennedy School, Cambridge

McLuhan M (1966) Understanding media: the extensions of man. McGraw-Hill, London

Meyers C et al (2009) Taxonomies of cyber adversaries and attacks: a survey of incidents and approaches. Lawrence Livermore National Security, LLC, Livermore, CA

NATO (2011) Assured access to the global commons: maritime, air, space, cyber

Nye JS (2010) Cyber power. Harvard Kennedy School, Belfer Center, Cambridge

Parkinson NC (1957) Parkinson's law and other studies in administration. Houghton Mifflin, Boston

Saffo P (2013) Disrupting undersea cables: cyberspace's hidden vulnerability. http://www.acus.org/new_atlanticist/disrupting-undersea-cables-cyberspaces-hidden-vulnerability. Accessed 4 Aug 2013

Singer PW (2012) The Cyber Terror Bogeyman. Armed Forces Journal. Washington, D.C.: Brookings Institution. Retrieved from http://www.brookings.edu/research/articles/2012/11/cyber-terror-singer

Strauss AL, Corbin JM (1990) Basics of qualitative research: grounded theory procedures and techniques. Sage, Newbury Park

Thomas TL (2003) Al Qaeda and the Internet: the danger of 'cyberplanning'. Parameters Spring 33(1):112–123

Thonnard O et al (2012) Industrial espionage and targeted attacks: understanding the characteristics of an escalating threat. Research in attacks, intrusions, and defenses

Toffler A (1990) Powershift: knowledge, wealth, and violence at the edge of the 21st century. Bantam Books, New York

U.S. Army (2006) FM 3-24/MCWP 3-33.5 Counterinsurgency

Veerasamy N, Grobler M (2010) Countermeasures to consider in the combat against cyberterrorism. http://researchspace.csir.co.za/dspace/bitstream/10204/4486/3/Veerasamy3_2010.pdf. Accessed 24 Jan 2014

Vorster A, Labuschagne L (2005) A framework for comparing different information security risk analysis methodologies. In: Proceedings of South African Institute for Computer Scientists and Information Technologists (SAICSIT 2005)

Warnes R (2014) Modelling terrorism and counter-terrorism. Ph.D. dissertation (forthcoming). University of Surrey, Surrey

Weimann G (2005) Cyberterrorism: the sum of all fears? Stud Conflict Terrorism 28:129–149

Zittrain J (2006) A history of online gatekeeping. Harv J Law Tech 19(2):253

Conclusions

Thomas M. Chen, Lee Jarvis, and Stuart Macdonald

In the late twentieth century, the rate of adoption and innovation for two interrelated technologies—computers and the Internet—was remarkable. In contrast, the basic telephone had not really changed much in the previous 100 years; calling another person in 1980 was quite similar to calling someone in 1880. In about three decades however, computers and Internet connectivity have become ubiquitous, transforming the ways we live, work, and socialize. Today smart phones and tablets—handheld computing—keep much of the world's population constantly connected regardless of time and location. "Cyber" has changed crime and warfare as well. Though cybercrime is a small part of overall crime, it is a widespread and growing global problem. Modern warfare, moreover, has become completely network-centric in the sense that military operations are critically dependent on information collection and sharing facilitated by computer networks. Consider James Der Derian's (2001: 5–6) description of the US 194th Separate Armored Brigade from Kentucky who he observed on a training exercise recounted in his book *Virtuous War*:

> At the high end of the lethality spectrum there was the improved M1A2 Abrams main battle tank, carrying an IVIS (Inter-Vehicular Information System) which could collect real-time battlefield data from overhead JSTAR aircraft (Joint Surveillance and Target Attack Radar System), Pioneer unmanned aerial vehicles equipped with video cameras, and global positioning satellite systems (GPS) to display icons of friendlies and foes or a computer-generated map overlay. At the low end, there was the "21st Century Land Warrior" (also called "warfighter." but never "soldier" or "infantryman"), who came equipped with augmented day and night vision scopes mounted on his M-I6, a GPS, 8mm video camera, and one-inch ocular LED screen connected by a flexible arm to his Kevlar, and an already-dated 487 Lightweight Computer Unit in his backpack, all wired for voice or digital-burst communication to a Battlespace Command Vehicle with an All Source Analysis System that could collate the information and coordinate the attack through a customized Windows programme.

Given the dramatic and far-reaching nature of these changes, terrorism seems to stand out as an important anomaly: Certainly terrorists use the Internet routinely for the same purposes that most people use the Internet, but there is general consensus that terrorists have kept to traditional physical attacks instead of turning to cyber attacks. Yet starting in the twenty-first century, it is easy to speculate that terrorism may someday change with the times. This, after all, is what happened with previous technologies from the printing press through to dynamite and the airplane. Consider the usual MMO (motive, means, and opportunity) factors. Are terrorists motivated to carry out cyber attacks? Terrorists clearly often want to cause widespread damage and fear, and cyber attacks offer obvious advantages over physical attacks for so doing. Not least, here, is that cyber attacks can be carried out instantaneously across any distance with low risk to the attacker. Is there opportunity? Experts (including authors in this book) have pointed out that serious vulnerabilities in critical infra-structures are well known to exist. For various reasons these vulnerabilities will not be patched any time soon. Do terrorists have the means? They are familiar with computers and the Internet but currently appear to lack the capabilities for sophisti-cated cyber attacks. This is perhaps a large reason why a major cyberterrorist attack has not yet occurred, but is it only a matter of time before terrorists develop suffi-cient skills and capabilities?

If cyberterrorism is a real emerging threat, then research is needed in many inter-esting issues such as counter terrorism policies and laws. However, cyberterrorism is much like the parable of the blind men and the elephant. One man feels the trunk and believes the elephant is like a snake. Another feels a leg and believes the elephant is like a tree. A third man feels the tail and believes it is like a rope. Cyberterrorism is a complex topic evoking different viewpoints; this is evident from the diversity of the chapters in this book. In each chapter, the authors have given their unique perspective from their area of research and expertise. Our hope is that sharing the collection of viewpoints in this book will help to facilitate a dialog within and across academic, technical and policy communities, and that this dialog will connect the dots so that a more complete view of the elephant emerges. To help in this, the experts in this book spoke to three major themes: understanding, assessment, and response.

Understanding Cyberterrorism

As seen from some of the chapters, the first obstacle encountered by any treatment of cyberterrorism is the lack of a universal definition of this term. The difficulty arises because both parts of this composite whole are not well defined. Terrorism is a heavily debated subject, and "cyber" is used inconsistently. For instance, modern cars and airplanes are intrinsically computerized but no one says "cyberdriving" or "cyberflying." Academic research today depends on computer networks extensively but we do not call it "cyber research." Adding "cyber" to terrorism therefore has vague connotations that mean different things to different people.

Naturally, definitions have a practical importance in law enforcement, but laws concerning computer crimes have traditionally been somewhat vague. Perhaps it is not surprising that countries have different definitions of terrorism in relation to cyber attacks. As Hardy and Williams note, a major challenge in legal definitions is drawing the line between use of computers and networks comprising cyberterrorism threats and less serious acts. Consistency among different countries would be ideal because cyber terrorism (like cyber crime) is a global problem requiring international cooperation between law enforcement agencies. Hardy and Williams find that countries generally agree on major principles: cyberterrorism is motivated by a political, religious or ideological cause; the intention is to intimidate a government or a section of the public; and cyberterrorism seriously interferes with infrastructure. The UK and Australian definitions of terrorism go beyond the threat of serious cyber-attacks and encompass attacks against non-essential electronic systems, while Canadian and New Zealand definitions of terrorism are more restrained. After careful analysis of similarities and differences, Hardy and Williams offer a legal definition that they believe covers the essential aspects of this phenomenon. In their words:

'Cyberterrorism' means conduct involving computer or Internet technology that (1) is carried out for the purpose of advancing a political, religious or ideological cause; (2) is intended to intimidate a section of the public, or compel a government to do or abstain from doing any act; and (3) intentionally causes serious interference with an essential service, facility or system, if such interference is likely to endanger life or cause significant economic or environmental damage.

Although important, it is also useful to look beyond questions of definition. In Jarvis, Nouri and Whiting therefore argue that cyberterrorism should be approached as a social construction rather than a stable and coherent ontological entity. This involves asking *how* cyberterrorism is represented or produced through language and other social practices, rather than asking *what* cyberterrorism is. Viewed in historic context, cyberterrorism can be seen as a part of terrorism which is itself a fluid and changing phenomenon. The meaning and methods of terrorism have changed over time, and cyber attacks can be incorporated within the heading of terrorism as a contemporary method. Jarvis, Nouri and Whiting argue that a constructivist framework offers the greatest potential for engaging with the concept of cyberterrorism in spite of its challenges, not least because it already exists as a category of discourse and hence social reality.

Yannakogeorgos's contribution divides the notion of cyberterrorism into two parts: the use of cyberspace by terrorist organizations, and the ability to cause physical effects via cyber attacks. In his view, these parts are distinctly separate. There is little doubt that terrorists are using the cyberdomain to advance their tactical, operational and strategic objectives, for instance through recruitment, propaganda, and fund raising. On the other hand, terrorists have not shown a capability to carry out cyber attacks of substantial impact against critical infrastructures. News articles speculating about a "cyber 9/11" are, as such, mostly hype. However, Yannakogeorgos notes that a feasible but overlooked possibility is psyber operations where terrorists could manipulate mass public emotion to cause masses of people to spontaneously move in specific ways. In the near-term, this is the more likely use of cyber to create physical effects in his view.

Assessing the Threat

Assessments of the threat posed by cyberterrorism arguably produced the most diverse range of opinions among the authors within this book. It is admittedly difficult to know exactly what threat exists because terrorists have not carried out a major cyber attack (of which we are aware), nor are they likely to at any time soon. In a way, this is a glass half empty or half full situation. On one hand, the likelihood is evidently low, and it is tempting to see this as evidence of a non-existent threat. On the other hand, there is no doubt that vulnerabilities exist in critical infrastructure exist, and critical infrastructure is an attractive target for terrorists. The opportunity for cyberterrorism exists. Perhaps terrorists have been too busy elsewhere but might turn their attention to cyber attacks. The threat is imminent and waiting to happen.

In an approach dealing with the broader social context of modern technology, McGuire approaches the threat of cyberterrorism by introducing the notion of hyperconnection. This refers to the modern condition in which people can connect with anyone else regardless of time and location. McGuire argues that hyperconnectivity (not simply ICT) leads to a more sophisticated understanding of technology and its social importance, and ultimately a better understanding of the risks posed by cyberterrorism. Admittedly a fairly new approach, it is an open issue to determine how the concept of hyperconnection can improve threat assessment and risk management.

Stohl follows a vastly different approach drawing parallels between discussions of cyberterrorism and cyber war on the one hand, and discussions of terrorism and state terrorism on the other. He noted that cyberterrorism has been hyped for various economic and political reasons. The U.S. and other major countries have condemned cyberterrorism while building up their own cyberwar capabilities. A consequence of this inconsistency is the undermining of the norms required for international cooperation given that major powers such as the U.S. essentially shape the norms within the international system. In effect, these states dictate which behaviors are labeled as cyberwar or cyberterror, just as they also dictate which behaviours are labeled warfare or terrorism. The importance of this comparison, for Stohl, is that it sheds light on the gap between realities and rhetoric. The threat of cyberterrorism is more trumpeted yet far less material than that associated with the cyber capabilities of the world's major states.

The subsequent chapters by Conway and Wilson offer a fascinating study in contrasting viewpoints: one perhaps explicable, in part, due to their different professional roles and academic backgrounds. Conway downplays the likelihood of the cyberterrorism threat while Wilson emphasizes the potentially catastrophic consequences of a cyberterrorist attack. It is logical to say that major cyber attacks by terrorists have not happened yet, and there must be reasons behind this. Therefore, attacks are not likely tomorrow for the same reasons. Conway argues that while opportunity exists, it will be unlikely to be made manifest due to a number of plausible reasons.

Wilson seems to take the opposite view focusing on the vulnerabilities in industrial control systems and proliferation of zero-day exploits and malware code based on an analysis of Flame and Stuxnet. Wilson agrees there has been no major cyberterrorist attack but his concern is the possibility that terrorists might take advantage of the ready opportunity created by weakness. Vulnerabilities are like an open door inviting intruders. One does not worry necessarily about the likelihood of an intruder going through the door; the main worry is the fact of the open door. In the unlikely event of a successful cyberterrorist attack, the consequences could be catastrophic. Clearly, the U.S. government still vividly remembers 9/11 and would understandably go to extremes to avoid a recurrence. Even if the likelihood is admittedly low, would the government be prudent to ignore the possibility: not least given the subsequent political ramifications of such an occurrence? In daily life, people take out insurance as protection against rare but catastrophic events. Precautionary approaches to risk management play an important role, too, in debate around and efforts to counter such security challenges as global climate change. Might, then, we argue, that similar calculations may be entered in relation to (cyber)terrorism? At what point, in other words, are incremental increases in security from (cyber) terrorism insufficient to justify governmental expenditures or efforts?

Responding to the Threat

The question of response is much more open than questions of definition or assessment. This is evident by the sheer diversity of questions that are explored throughout this book, which include but are not limited to: How should cyberterrorists be identified, pursued and prosecuted? Are new laws needed? Are new ideas for response needed? Can cyberterrorism be prevented, e.g., by deterrence? Issues such as these are perhaps too large to be addressed adequately in one collection.

Legrand puts his finger on a specific important problem that can and should be fixed: the insecurity of critical infrastructure. The challenges are both technological and political. It is an enormous technical problem because the infrastructure contains complex legacy systems that are hard to replace or patch. They cannot be easily taken out of service for patching because they are carrying out critically important functions for the public. It is also a political problem because the vast majority of infrastructure is held by the private sector which is naturally driven by profit motives. Legrand details the UK government approach regarding cyberterrorism under a broader umbrella of cyber threats. The government has refrained from mandating cyber security improvements, instead depending on persuasion and cooperation. However, cyber security in the profit-driven private sector has long faced a problem of return on investment. Why should owners improve cyber security without a clear return on investment (even if the return is enhanced public safety)? It is an open issue how to devise policies that will financially motivate private owners to improve cyber protection of their infrastructures.

Speaking to the first chapter by Hardy and Williams which also addresses the criminality of cyberterrorism, Lord Carlile QC and Macdonald ask an interesting question relating to response: whether laws can and should aim to prevent terrorist acts by prohibiting online preparatory activities. There is little argument that terrorists use the Internet in a variety of ways, some for organizational support and others for attack preparation. Noting that criminal law has a preventive role as well as a punitive one, they argue that terrorism precursor offences have been deemed necessary and the notion of normative involvement offers both a justification for criminalisation of preparatory activities as well as a yardstick for evaluating whether these offences overreach. They welcome a guidance document to spell out principles for prosecutorial discretion concerning terrorism precursor offences.

The book's final chapter then brings these discussions of public policy, law and technical matters together by exploring what a comprehensive holistic response might look like. In it, Gil Ad Ariely examines a taxonomy of distinct potential responses to cyberterrorism, and recommends a combination of policy, methods, and tools within the grounded field of counter terrorism. Cyberterrorism, he suggests, is not strictly a problem of cyber security as which it is sometimes portrayed. As such, his preferred approach to its prevention and resolution emphasizes adaptiveness, intelligence sharing and education.

Final Observations and Open Issues

Cyberterrorism is a controversial subject that evokes many opinions. That said, there are a few lines of agreement running throughout this book, not least, for instance, that terrorists are using the Internet for their organizational activities, and that there have not really been any major cyber attacks by terrorists on critical infrastructures. If anything, cyberterrorism might be said to represent an emerging threat, rather than a current one. Outside of these facts, everything else is debatable. In this book, we have not tried to find definitive answers (if any exist) as it is not clear if consensus is desirable at this point. Instead we have welcomed the diversity of expertise and sharing of different opinions. To paraphrase the character Spock on the television show Star Trek, "may our differences combine to create meaning." Our hope is that the preceding chapters do this and in the process bridge disciplinary gaps without, necessarily offering any definitive resolution to the questions with which we began. In light of this, let us finish by offering three final observations that might serve as a stepping stone for subsequent studies in this area: interdisciplinary and otherwise.

First, through history new technologies do not usually replace existing ones. Television did not replace radio, and the Internet did not replace television. Airplanes have not replaced cars which have not stopped people from riding bicycles or horses. It is true that technologies have become obsolete on occasion, e.g., computers have replaced typewriters, though not pen and paper. In most cases, however, new technologies broaden the available choices. By implication, we might speculate that cyberterrorism will not replace traditional terrorism but will more likely augment it. Terrorists will not give up bombs and IEDs but may add cyber attacks to their arsenal.

Second, cyber security is a little unlike many other fields of study in that much information is publicly inaccessible. In cyber crime, for example, most cyber crimes are not reported or undetected. Known incidents are a small fraction of the totality. Likewise in cyber warfare (referring to the current cyber arms buildup by nations), the public sees only the tip of the iceberg. Much more is going on behind the scenes. Unfortunately, most of these activities are classified as secret. For instance, the U.S. government has been publicly vocal about building up defensive cyber capabilities but silent about offensive capabilities. It stands to reason that the U.S. has probably stockpiled a massive offensive capability (Stuxnet being one rare visible example) but none of this is yet publicly known.

Similarly, the publicly available information about cyberterrorism is most likely a small window into the total arena. Whether the real situation is worse or better, it is impossible to say, especially given the additional noise of sensationalized news reports and government press releases. As such, the field of cyberterrorism would benefit greatly from better availability of (reliable) data to which researchers might have access.

Finally, it is fortunate in a way that cyberterrorism is attracting attention before a real cyberterrorist attack with deadly consequences. Terrorists have not attacked but are using the Internet. It is easy to imagine terrorists acquiring new skills and adapting their methods to the modern hyper-connected world. As a social phenomenon, terrorism and terrorists—like the rest of us—are moving apace into the twenty-first century, by choice or necessity. There is, in this context, an opportunity to be proactive about the emerging cyberterrorism threat (in contrast to the usual reactive mode of cyber security), and to think through, in advance, the implications of reactions and over-reactions to this emerging threat for relations between states, civil liberties and much else besides. As the great Wayne Gretzy reportedly said, "I skate to where the puck is going to be, not where it has been." We have the advantage of being ahead of the puck and an opportunity to stay ahead by continuing the dialogue here.

Acronyms

CESG	Communications-Electronics Security Group
CNI	Critical National Infrastructure
CPNI	Centre for the Protection of National Infrastructure
CSIA	Central Sponsor for Information Assurance
CSOC	Cyber Security Operations Centre
CSS	Cyber Security Strategy
GCHQ	Government Communications Headquarters
GDS	Government Digital Service
IA	Information Assurance
ICTS	Information and Communication Technology Strategy
IEM	Information Exchange Mechanism
NAO	National Audit Office
NCSP	National Cyber Security Programme
NIAS	National Information Assurance Strategy
NPM	New Public Management
NSS	National Security Strategy
OSCIA	Office of Cyber Security and Information Assurance
SCADA	Supervisory control and data acquisition
SDSR	Strategic Defence and Security Review

T.M. Chen et al. (eds.), *Cyberterrorism: Understanding, Assessment, and Response*,
DOI 10.1007/978-1-4939-0962-9, © Springer Science+Business Media New York 2014

Glossary

Constructivism A broad theoretical framework within the social sciences that focuses on the production, challenge and transformation of meaning in social, political and other contexts.

Crown Prosecution Service The Government Department responsible for prosecuting criminal cases in England and Wales. It advises the police on cases for possible prosecution, reviews cases submitted by the police, determines any charges in more serious or complex cases and prepares and presents cases at court.

Distributed Denial of Service (DDoS) An attack on one or more networked computers that disrupts normal operations such that users can no longer access their services.

Epistemology/Epistemological Claims relating to knowledge, and what is or can be known.

Globalisation A contested term, but one that is often used to describe or explain the increasingly interconnected character of life today.

Hacktivism A combination of 'hacking' and 'activism' that refers to online protests of government policy.

Harm principle According to this principle, conduct should only be criminalised if it involves harmful wrongdoing. This is a necessary, but not necessarily sufficient, precondition for criminalisation.

Harm requirement A sub-section in a statutory definition of terrorism which stipulates that conduct will qualify as an act of terrorism only if it causes one of a list of specified harms, such as causing death, endangering life, or seriously interfering with electronic systems.

Inchoate offences These offences have a preventive rationale. They penalise conduct which is prior to the harmful wrong that the defendant plans to commit. The principal inchoate offences are attempt, conspiracy and encouraging crime.

Intention requirement A sub-section in a statutory definition of terrorism which stipulates that conduct will qualify as an act of terrorism only if the person envisages that it will have some additional effect on a government or a population (such as compelling a government to act in a particular way, or intimidating a section of the public).

T.M. Chen et al. (eds.), *Cyberterrorism: Understanding, Assessment, and Response*, DOI 10.1007/978-1-4939-0962-9, © Springer Science+Business Media New York 2014

Intertextuality A term used within discourse analysis and theory to explore how the meaning of a particular 'text' is impacted by others. A politician making reference to a Hollywood movie in a speech, for example, would be an instance of intertextuality.

Joint Committee on Human Rights A committee of the UK's Parliament. It consists of 12 members appointed from both the House of Commons and the House of Lords and is charged with considering human rights issues in the UK.

Motive requirement A sub-section in a statutory definition of terrorism which stipulates that conduct will qualify as an act of terrorism only if it is committed for the purpose of advancing a political, religious or ideological cause. The UK definition of terrorism also encompasses 'racial' causes.

Political protest exemption A sub-section in a statutory definition of terrorism which excludes acts of political protest, dissent and industrial action from the scope of criminal offences and other statutory powers, even if those acts would otherwise fit within the definition.

Pre-charge detention This is the period of time that an individual can be held and questioned by the police before being charged with an offence.

Preparatory offences A range of special terrorism offences that target conduct only remotely connected to a future act of terrorism, such as possessing terrorist documents or receiving terrorist training.

Recklessness For the purposes of the criminal law of England and Wales, a person acts recklessly with respect to a particular consequence if he is aware of a risk the consequence will occur and unjustifiably chooses to take that risk.

Rule of law The rule of law encompasses a number of principles, including the principle that the criminal law should be stated as clearly as possible and that changes to the criminal law should not be applied retrospectively. It is based on the notion that the law should act as a constraint upon actions of the state.

Statutory definition of terrorism A section in a piece of legislation which stipulates the scope and meaning of 'terrorism' wherever that word is used in other pieces of legislation within the same jurisdiction.

Terrorism Prevention and Investigation Measures (TPIMs) A TPIMs notice may impose a set of restrictions and obligations on an individual who is reasonably believed to be involved in terrorism-related activity if doing so is necessary to protect the public from a risk of terrorism.

Trojan Horse Malicious software programmes infiltrated into computer systems disguised as benign data for the purposes of stealing information or harming their host.

Index

A

Adaptive responses
  aligning ideas, 179–180
  counter-terrorism policy
    categories, 182
    clandestine proxies, 184
    economic approach, 183
  cyber power, 185–186
  cyber threats mitigation, 181–182
  description, 175–176
  deterrence, cyberspace, 189–190
  eco-system, 191–192
  grounded theory, 178
  IT and cyberspace, 175
  ladder climbing, 187
  national level policy, 180–181
  PLCs and SCADA, 176
  socio-technical aspects, 192
  taxonomies and definitions, 177
  technical classifications, 187–188
  toolkit, 176
  virtual environments, 192–193
  WMD, 184–185
Alternate domain name systems (altDNS), 50–51
Amoore, L., 144
Anderson, D., 138
Ariely, G., 175–193
Armed-attack, 43, 44, 54–55
Ashworth, A., 161
Assessment
  complexity factor, 107
  cost factors, 107
  cyber insecurity and threat, 103
  cyberspace, 105
  destruction factor, 107
  journalists and policymakers, 106

media impact factor, 107
  political motive, 104–105
  violence, 105
  vs. VBIED attacks, 105, 107–116
Australia, definition of terrorism
  The Australian Security Intelligence
    Organisation Act 1979, 13
  Criminal Code Act 1995, 10
  criminal offences, 12–13
  Division 104 of the Australian Criminal
    Code, 13
  political protest exemption, 11, 12
  Resolution 1373, 9
  Section 100.1 of the Australian Criminal
    Code, 10–11
  Security Legislation Amendment
    (Terrorism) Act 2002, 9–10
  vs. UK situation, 11–12
Australian Security Intelligence Organisation
    (ASIO), 13

B

Bamford, J., 94
Bendrath, R., 27
Bradley, A., 167

C

Canada, definition of terrorism
  amendments, 17
  Section 83.01, Canadian Criminal Code,
    14–15
  similarities with UK and Australian
    definitions, 15
  vs. UK and Australian definitions, 15–16
Car bombing, 108

Carlile QC, L., 7, 155–171
Central Sponsor for Information Assurance
        (CSIA), 145–146
CERT. *See* Computer emergency response
        team (CERT)
CESG. *See* Communications-Electronics
        Security Group (CESG)
Communications-Electronics Security
        Group (CESG), 145, 147, 148
Computer emergency response team (CERT),
        177, 181
Constructivism, 36
Conway, M., 28, 33, 89, 103–116, 200
Cornish, P., 140
Counter-terrorism policy
    categories, 182
    clandestine proxies, 184
    economic approach, 183
CPS. *See* Crown Prosecution
        Service (CPS)
Critical information infrastructure (CII)
    automobiles, 124
    computerized control systems, 124
    critical infrastructures, 126–127
    modern society and economy, 124
    real-time control systems, 125–126
    service interruptions, 124
    software updates, 125
    telecommunications, 124
    terrorists/extremists, 124
    "zombie virus," 124
Crown Prosecution Service (CPS), 169–170
CSIA. *See* Central Sponsor for Information
        Assurance (CSIA)
CSOC. *See* Cyber Security Operations Centre
        (CSOC)
Cyber enabled terrorist operations
    cyber influence, 46
    cyber planning, 46
    internet radicalization, 47–48
    planning, command, control and
        communications, 51–53
    recruitment and radicalization, 47–51
    technical realities, 46
Cyber espionage, 2, 27, 53, 96, 129,
        131–132, 134, 139
Cyber forensics, 188
Cyber-Katrina, 89
Cyber operations
    armed-attack, 54–55
    distributed denial of service disruption,
        53–54
    ICS, 55–57
    psyber operations, 57
Cyber planning, 46

Cyber power, 185–186
Cyber Security Operations Centre (CSOC), 146
Cyber-security plan, U.S., 1
Cyberterrorism
    assessment (*see* Assessment)
    beam-focusing antenna, 133
    carbon fibers, 133
    CII (*see* Critical information
        infrastructure (CII))
    constructivist research, 37
    contestability, reasons, 26
    Conway's view, 28, 29
    cooperation with criminal organizations,
        134–135
    criminal sanction, 155
    critical infrastructure systems, 130, 134
    cyber attack, 123
    cyber-crime, 2
    cyber espionage, 2, 129
    cyberspace, 135
    cyberwarfare, 123
    DDoS attack, 27
    definition, 123
    Devost's argument, 29
    ECS, 132
    EMP, 132
    extremists and terrorists, 132, 134
    Four Waves of Modern Terrorism
        (Rapoport), 31
    Gordon and Ford's discussion, 28
    ICS-CERT (*see* Industrial Control Systems
        Cyber Emergency Response Team
        (ICS-CERT))
    industrial microwave models, 132–133
    inter-state cyber-attacks, 2
    intertextuality, 36
    legal definition, 199
    media coverage and publicity, 33
    "munitions" category, 132
    nature of terrorism, 35
    observations and open issues, 202–203
    'old terrorism' and 'new terrorism', 31
    online terrorist activity, 157
    powers and procedures, police officer,
        156–157
    pre-charge detention, 157
    problems, 2
    responding to threat, 201–202
        (*see also* Adaptive responses)
    terrorism and state terrorism, 34
    'terrorism matrix', 156
    terrorism precursor offences, 161–170
    and terrorism, relationship
        behaviours, 157–158
        definitions, 158

terrorists' online preparatory acts, 159–160
themes on, 30–31
threat assessment, 200–201
threats, 27
tools and high-level technical skills, 134
TPIMs notice, 157
violence, criterion, 32
by Western nations, 132
Yannakogeorgos's contribution , 199
zero-day exploits and code, 131
Cyber threats mitigation
CISOs and CERTs, 181
critical infrastructure, 181–182
domain names, 181
Cyber war
attacks, country, 98
behaviors and assumptions, 85–86
cyber espionage, 95
and cyber terrorism
computer network, 88
concept, 87
definitions, 87
digital technology, 88–89
electronic Pearl Harbor, 89
government press, 89
netwar, 87
non-violent activities, 87–88
DDOS, 92
Estonian authorities, 91
intelligence agencies, 86
Iraq Net, 91
media, 90
military strategy, 93
NSA, 94
nuclear regime, 86
political and military power, 86
Red October, 92
Spectrum of State Responsibility, 96
superpowers and international terrorism, 85
surrogate terrorism, 97
terrorism, assertions, 91

D
DCS. *See* Distributed control systems (DCS)
DDoS. *See* Distributed Denial of Service (DDoS)
Dean, J., 91
De Goede, M., 144
Deibert, R., 97
Denning, D., 28, 32, 88, 105, 106
Derian, J.D., 197
Desouza, K.C., 25
Destructive Scale, 67

Deterrence, cyberspace
anonymity and attribution, 189
capabilities, 189–190
terrorist risks, 189
Devost, M.G., 28, 29
Discretionary decision-making
inevitability
absolute/unfettered discretion, 168
constitutionalism, 167
dangers, 167–168
legal system, 167
prosecutorial discretion
Australian offence, 168
CPS, 169–170
illegal activities, 168–169
information collection, 168
inherently innocent, 169
Distributed control systems (DCS), 124
Distributed Denial of Service (DDoS), 2, 27,
53–54, 92, 106, 184
Domain name system (DNS), 50–51

E
Eco-system, 191–192
Einstein, Albert, 177
Embar-Seddon, A., 30
Enhanced Cybersecurity Services
program (ECS)
Ewing, K., 167
Extension, hyperconnection and
hyperspatialised terror
GNSS signal, 79
'hyperspace' and 'hypercrime', 77
ICT, 76–77
location-tags, 78
Machine to Machine (M2M)
connectivity, 79
Machine to Machine to Human (M2M2H)
connectivity, 79
RFID tagging, 79
'technological organs', 76

F
Ford, R., 28, 156

G
GCHQ. *See* Government Communications
Headquarters (GCHQ)
Giacomello, G., 93, 110, 137
Giles, J., 98
Globalisation, 25, 31

Gordon, S., 28, 156
Government Communications Headquarters
        (GCHQ), 147, 148
Grounded theory methodology, 178
Guitton, C., 94, 96

H
Hacktivism, 2, 12, 29, 106, 177, 179, 186
Hacktivists, 2, 6, 12, 69
Hardy, K., 1–22, 26, 32, 158, 198, 201
Harm principle, 161
Harvey, M., 140
Hawkins, K., 168
Hayden, M., 140
Healey, J., 96, 98
Heidegger, M., 65, 137
Hensgen, T., 25
HMI. *See* Human-machine interface (HMI)
Hollis, D., 97
Holt, T.J., 157–158
Hood, C., 142
Hülsse, R., 35
Human-machine interface (HMI), 56, 124

I
IAD. *See* Information Assurance Directorate
        (IAD)
ICS. *See* Industrial control systems (ICS)
Inchoate offences, 161–163
Indoctrination, 49
Industrial Control Systems Cyber Emergency
        Response Team (ICS-CERT)
    cyberattacks against U.S. infrastructure
        systems, 127–128
    cyber mercenaries, 129
    "IceFog," 129
    sophisticated cyberattacks, 128
    unauthorized access, 128
Industrial control systems (ICS)
    ICS-CERT, 127–128
    SCADA, 124–125
Information Assurance Directorate (IAD), 94
Information Communication Technology
        (ICT), 63, 72–73, 76–77
Intention requirement, 5
Internet Corporation for Assigned Names and
        Numbers (ICANN), 51
Internet radicalization, phases
    alternate domain name systems, 50–51
    indoctrination, 49
    Internet misuse, 47

    pre-radicalization, 48
    self-identification, 48–49
    two pyramid model, 48
    violent extremism, 49–50
Intertextuality, 36
Iraq Net, 91
IT and cyberspace, 175

J
Jackson, R., 31, 36
Jarvis, L., 25–38, 176
Joint Committee on Human Rights, 166

K
Kostopoulos, G., 29
Kurtz, P., 90

L
Ladder climbing, 187
Landler, M., 91
Laqueur, W., 33
Law, technology/agency/intent
    Anti-Terrorism, Crime and Security Act,
        2001, 69
    Bill on Involuntary Homicide, 71
    UK Computer Misuse Act, 71
    UK CPS guidelines, 70
    USA PATRIOT Act, 2001, 69–70
Legal definitions, terrorism
    Australia, 9–14
    Canada, 14–17
    New Zealand, 17–20
    United Kingdom, 4–9
Legrand, T., 137–152, 201
Lester, A., 166
Lewis, J.A., 96
Lynn, W.J., 140

M
Macdonald, S., 7, 155–171
Markoff, J., 91
Maurer, T., 191
May, T., 141, 143, 144, 149
McGuire, M.R., 63–80, 200
McLuhan, M., 76
Meisels, T., 34
Morris worm (virus), 64
Motive requirement, 5, 10
Move Zero, 58

N

National Cyber Security Programme
(NCSP), 146
National Information Assurance Strategy
(NIAS), 145, 146
National Security Agency (NSA)
and IAD, 94–95
and SID, 94
NCSP. *See* National Cyber Security
Programme (NCSP)
New Zealand, definition of terrorism
basic structure, 17–18
cyber-attacks, 19
jurisdictions, 19
Section 5 of the Terrorism Suppression
Act 2002 (TSA), 17
sub-section (3)(d), 20
vs. UK, Australian and Canadian
definitions, 18–19
NIAS. *See* National Information Assurance
Strategy (NIAS)
Nissenbuam, H., 92
Nouri, L., 25–38, 176, 199
NSA. *See* National Security Agency (NSA)

O

O'Connell, M.E., 98
Office of Cyber Security and Information
Assurance (OCSIA), 146
Operational execution, 46

P

Phase Zero, 58
PLC. *See* Programmable logic controllers (PLC)
Political protest exemption, 1, 11, 12
Pollitt, M., 29, 106
Pragmatism, 177–178
Pre-charge detention, 157
Preparatory offences, 7, 19
Pre-radicalization, 48
Probability Risk Assessment (PRA), 68
Programmable logic controllers (PLC),
54, 56, 124, 176
Psyber operations, 57

R

Rapoport, D., 31
Real time cyber command, control
and communications, 52
Responses, aligning. *See also* Adaptive
responses
cyber security policy, 179–180

radicalization, 179
time span, 179
types of responses, 179–180
Ronfeldt, D., 87
Rule of law, 157, 167

S

Sanger, D.E., 92
SCADA system. *See* Supervisory control and
data acquisition (SCADA) system
SDSR. *See* Strategic Defence and Security
Review (SDSR)
Secret preparatory communications, 51–52
Self-identification, 48–49
Signals Intelligence Directorate (SID), 94
Simester, A.P., 163, 167–170
Smith, C, 141
Smith, G.C., 91
SNMP overloads, 54
Soo Hoo, K., 26
Spatio-temporal Scale, 67
Spencer, A., 35
Stark, R., 88
Statutory definition of terrorism, 3, 156
Stevens, T., 93
Stohl, M., 85–98, 157, 200
Strategic cyber terrorism, 58–59
Strategic Defence and Security Review
(SDSR), 146
Supervisory control and data acquisition
(SCADA) system, 56, 124–126,
128, 148, 176, 186, 192
Sutherland, M., 150

T

Technical classifications
cyber forensics, 188
information and communication
technologies, 188
monitoring, 188
types, 187
Technological crime
Marx' views on technology, 65
Morris worm, 64
telegraph network, 66
Technological risk
agency and intent in law, 69–71
causation and cyberterrorism
enablement, 74–75
ICT, 72–73
phlogiston, 73
crime, 64–66
destructive scale, 67

Technological risk (*cont.*)
    extension, hyperconnection and
        hyperspatialised terror, 76–80
    ICT, 63
    PRA, 68
    spatio-temporal scale, 67
Terrorism Act 2000 (TA2000)
    elements, 5
    harm requirement, 5
    intention requirement, 5
    motive requirement, 5
    preparatory offences, 7
Terrorism Act 2006 (TA2006), 7
Terrorism precursor offences
    and discretionary decision-making,
        166–170
    full and inchoate offences, 161–162
    normative involvement principle
        actions, 163
        collecting information, 163–164
        encouragement, 165
        Joint Committee on Human Rights, 166
        mental elements, 164
        non-endorsement defence, 165–166
        online preparatory acts, 162–163
        section 58 of Terrorism Act 2000, 164
Terrorism Prevention and Investigation
        Measures (TPIMs), 8, 13, 157
Terrorism Suppression Act 2002 (TSA), 17–18
Terrorists' online preparatory acts
    communication, 160
    fund-raising, 160
    planning, 159–160
    propaganda, 159
    recruitment, 159
    training, 160
The Australian Security Intelligence
        Organisation Act 1979, 13
The Onion Router (TOR), 51
Thomas, T.L., 89
Timlin, K., 96
Toffler, A., 175
Tomkins, A., 168
Toolkit, 176
TPIMs. *See* Terrorism Prevention and
        Investigation Measures (TPIMs)
Trojan Horse, 28
Turpin, C., 168

U
UK, definition of terrorism
    anti-terror laws, 8
    factors, 6–7

    Section 1(2)(e) of Terrorism Act, 8–9
    TA2000, 4–6
    TA2006, 7
    Terrorist Asset-Freezing Act 2010, 8
UK, state strategies
    challenges, 148
    critical infrastructure, 141–143
    against cyber foes, 145–148
    cyberspace, 138
    cyberterrorism, 137–138, 143–145
    cyber-terror terminology, 137
    cyber threats, 139, 141–143
    digital landscape, 140–141
    government policy, 138
    internet-based economy, 139
    public domain, 138
    risk and information-sharing
        challenges, 152
    security strategy, 1–2
    Stuxnet virus, 138
    threats
        cyberterrorism and critical
            infrastructure, 149–151
        private sector, 149
    virtual and physical dimensions, 137
    voluntary compliance, 151–152

V
Vehicle-Borne Improvised Explosive Devices
        (VBIED)
    car bombing, 108
    civilian casualties from suicide (Iraq),
        108–109
    complexity factor, 110–112
    cost factor, 109–110
    cyber *vs.* traditional methods, 108
    destruction factor, 112–114
    media impact factor
        media's mission, 114
        performance violence, 114–115
        terrorist acts, 115–116
Violent extremism, 49–50
Virtual environments, 192–193
Von Hirsch, A., 163

W
Warner, M., 93
Weapon of mass disruption (WMD), 184–185
Webster, S.C., 94
Weimann, G., 29
White, C.K.C., 87
Whiting, A., 25–38, 176, 199

Williams, G., 1–22, 26, 158, 198, 201
Wilson, C., 123–135, 200
WMD. *See* Weapon of mass disruption (WMD)

Y
Yannakogeorgos, P.A., 43–60, 199

Z
Zanini, M., 87
ZDEs. *See* Zero-day exploits (ZDEs)
Zedner, L., 161
Zero-day exploits (ZDEs), 131, 132
Zero day vulnerabilities, 54
Zombie virus, 124

Printed in the United States
By Bookmasters